The Law of Freedom

The Law of Freedom

Justice and Mercy in the Practice of Law

Daniel L. Rentfro Jr.

FOREWORD BY
Eric Stoddart

CASCADE Books • Eugene, Oregon

THE LAW OF FREEDOM
Justice and Mercy in the Practice of Law

Copyright © 2019 Daniel L. Rentfro Jr. All rights reserved. Except for brief quotations in critical publications or reviews, no part of this book may be reproduced in any manner without prior written permission from the publisher. Write: Permissions, Wipf and Stock Publishers, 199 W. 8th Ave., Suite 3, Eugene, OR 97401.

Cascade Books
An Imprint of Wipf and Stock Publishers
199 W. 8th Ave., Suite 3
Eugene, OR 97401

www.wipfandstock.com

PAPERBACK ISBN: 978-1-5326-5100-7
HARDCOVER ISBN: 978-1-5326-5101-4
EBOOK ISBN: 978-1-5326-5102-1

Cataloguing-in-Publication data:

Names: Rentfro, Daniel L., Jr., author. | Stoddart, Eric, 1960–, foreword.

Title: The law of freedom : justice and mercy in the practice of law / by Daniel L. Rentfro Jr. ; foreword by Eric Stoddart.

Description: Eugene, OR : Cascade Books, 2019 | Includes bibliographical references and index.

Identifiers: ISBN 978-1-5326-5100-7 (paperback) | ISBN 978-1-5326-5101-4 (hardcover) | ISBN 978-1-5326-5102-1 (ebook)

Subjects: LCSH: Christianity and justice—United States. | Criminal justice, Administration of—Religious aspects—Christianity. | Mercy.

Classification: BL65.J87 R46 2019 (print) | BL65.J87 R46 (ebook)

Scripture quotations are from New Revised Standard Version Bible, copyright ©1989 National Council of the Churches of Christ in the United States of America. Used by permission. All rights reserved worldwide.

Manufactured in the U.S.A. 10/24/19

To Anne, in gratitude, and
For Ryan, in thanksgiving.

Speak and act as those who are going to be judged by the law that gives freedom, because judgment without mercy will be shown to anyone who has not been merciful. Mercy triumphs over judgment.

—Jas 2:12–13

Contents

Foreword by Eric Stoddart | ix
Preface | xi
Acknowledgments | xv
List of Abbreviations | xvii

1. Jacob's Lawyer | 1
2. The Lawyer's Dilemma | 9
3. How Our Legal System Creates the Lawyer's Dilemma | 19
4. The Dilemma in the Bible: The Book of Micah | 32
5. A Brief History of (Legal) Equity | 39
6. The Theology of Equity: Thomas Aquinas and John Calvin | 49
7. The Theology of Equity (Continued): Equity English Style | 62
8. Clients vs. Courts: The Dilemma in History and Theology | 73
9. Humility: Virtue or Vice? | 94
10. Jacob's Lawyer (Part Two): Equity in Action | 105
11. *Orley Farm*: Trollope's Case Study in Equity | 123
12. Conclusion: The Decadence of Equity? | 136
    Afterword: Equality versus Equity | 148

Further Reading | 155
Bibliography | 157
Index of Persons | 163
Index of Words, Phrases, and Titles | 167
Index of Scriptural References | 171

Foreword

Populism as a political strategy offers simple solutions to complex problems. To be a successful populist requires identifying and then exploiting grievances. There is always an Other who is the target of populist hatred. It is convenient when long-standing but ill-founded suspicions can be reactivated. The demagogue artfully arraigns the justice system as biased towards bad minorities at the expense of the good people of the majority. "Law and order" becomes a dog-whistle appeal for common-sense judicial decisions. Experts arrive with nuances that are designed to muddy the waters in favor of minorities.

With such manipulations and falsehoods ethno-nationalist, right-wing politicians are lionized by sectors of the mainstream and social media across the United States, England, and parts of continental Europe. Minorities face harassment, disenfranchisement, and physical violence. In this vortex of rabble-rousing, victims of discrimination hope that law and order will be maintained. But their dream is of law that is ordered by justice.

Equity, the subject of this book, is what is at stake in addressing and resisting populism. The law, shorn of equity, might be rightly feared as a mere cover for restoring privilege. The law imbued with equity might be welcomed by those whose circumstances fall into the law's grey areas but are viewed with deep suspicion by those who see flexibility as irredeemably unreliable.

This is a timely study because the myth of a perfect law requires it to be laid to rest lest it continue to be a rallying point for populist politicians. In acknowledging that when equity is practiced a few may be advanced but others may be diminished, a small step might be made to defuse the armaments of grievance so adeptly deployed by populist politicians. An examination of the roots of equity is needed in order that not only lawyers

FOREWORD

and judges, but intelligent social commentators appreciate that is not free-floating. Equity is, as Daniel Rentfro's books argues, anchored in traditions of moral reasoning, including theology. I commend this thoughtful exploration as an important contribution to the moral and spiritual formation of those committed to justice and mercy in society.

Eric Stoddart, BD, PhD.
Associate Director of the Centre for
the Study of Religion and Politics
St Mary's College
University of St Andrews
Scotland

Preface

This book is about "equity," a word that means different things to different people. A banker thinks of equity as the value of property in excess of the liens against it. To a stockbroker, equity means the shareholder investment in a corporation. To a legal historian, the term represents the system of law that originated in English chancery. In the Hebrew Bible, and in much general modern usage, it connotes something like "fair" or "forthright"; the roots of the biblical word come from the word for "straight" and "level." Present-day trial lawyers use the word to refer to forms of nonmonetary relief (such as injunctions) that modern law offers as a limited alternative to the recovery of damages.

Rather than those definitions, I have two different and distinct things in mind, both of which have theological connotations. First, equity refers to the discretionary departure from strict enforcement of existing law. This usage goes all the way back to both Greek philosophy (especially Aristotle) and Hebrew law. As far as we can tell, the concept arose independently in each. In this sense, it carries forward from Aristotle to Thomas Aquinas, particularly in Aquinas's discussion of laws in *Summa Theologiae*. Second, and similar to but not exactly the same as the biblical sense of "fairness," equity came to carry the religious meaning of "mildness" or "compassion," a willingness to go above and beyond the strict requirements of the law. This second sense sees equity as a personal rather than a legal quality, but one that, ideally, surfaces in legal situations. This sense of the word has strong Christian associations, tied to the "Golden Rule" in Matthew 7:12 (although Aristotle also alludes to it). Equity in this sense plays a strong role in John Calvin's view of society.

Unfortunately, equity (in both of these senses) has become a pale shell of what it once was. In part because of its theological heritage, equity has been tossed aside in the secularization of our jurisprudence. That was, sadly, unnecessary, because the principle of equity (again, in both senses) plays a part in Aristotelean ethics, and so has its own non-theological basis. More than unnecessary, it was devastating. Civilizations have recognized for more than two and a half millennia the inherent imperfections in the application of general law; unusual or unanticipated facts in individual cases make it impossible to justly decide all cases by general rules. The genius of the common law, it was said, was the authority of judges to flex the joints of general rules to judge individual cases justly. Now, not so much. To a large extent, we threw this capacity out because of a new, but misguided, notion that law and morality had nothing to do with each other, thereby ignoring our legal system's foundation in received notions of morality.

The title of this book comes from that most Jewish of all the New Testament writings, the Epistle of James. The letter, which was written by Jesus' brother (the head of the Jerusalem church), recognizes the reality of judgment under Mosaic law while holding out the hope for a merciful judgment by way of the gospel news. James, of all people, would never have claimed that Jesus abolished the law; he perfected it, making the law a source of freedom from sin rather than simply a vehicle for condemnation.[1] My goal is to show that equity is the lawyer's law of freedom. It does not abrogate judgment; it ameliorates and perfects it, allowing lawyers to both seek justice and promote mercy.

Although I have both law and theology degrees, I am a practicing lawyer, not an academic. I write about what I know. This book is neither a treatise on law nor a book of academic theology. Equity's decline hurts lawyers by implicating them, sometimes unwillingly, in the injustices that result from that decline. Clients bring lawyers claims that are legally sustainable, even indisputable, but that conflict with the lawyer's own moral beliefs. As a citizen and a Christian, I know that all of us share this problem

---

1. The early church regarded the letter to be written by James, Jesus' brother and the head of the Jerusalem church. That belief has been challenged, and at times virtually abandoned, over the centuries. My sense is that current scholarship moves back towards the view that Jesus' brother in fact wrote the letter, or that at least we have no firm evidence for disagreeing with the ancient tradition. See, e.g., Wright, "Royal Law."

in our own lives and careers. The final chapter especially addresses how society itself suffers from this development.

"Mercy triumphs over judgment," James tells us.[2] The hope of this book is to show a way in which, perhaps, judgment and mercy walk together.

---

2. Jas 2:13.

Acknowledgments

This book started out as my dissertation in the "Bible and the Contemporary World" program at the University of St Andrews. John Perry was my dissertation advisor, and the dissertation, and hence this book, would not have happened without him. Not only did he give me prompt and insightful comments on every mediocre draft I sent him (and there were many), he put me onto Hooker's *Laws of Ecclesiastical Polity*, which then steered me toward Hooker's Puritan contemporary William Perkins. (John also stuck by me even when, in the midst of the project, my Northwestern Wildcats astonishingly beat his Fighting Irish at Notre Dame Stadium one November Saturday—for which I believe he still owes me a pint.) Eric Stoddart, the program's director, has helped me throughout the program and after, by helping me see how to turn a dissertation into a book (how well that succeeded the reader will judge) and by giving me invaluable comments on the first draft. Steven Holmes's module on public theology helped change the way I look at public and social issues, helping me see that a purely secular view of fundamental questions of public right is simply impossible. Steve, as head of school, and Eric were instrumental in securing my appointment as an honorary research assistant at St Andrews, which gave me access to the scholarly resources I needed to finish the book.

I owe a special debt also to the staff of the Styberg Library at Garrett-Evangelical Theological Seminary in Evanston, Illinois, for affording me working space, borrowing privileges and cheerful and responsive help during two month-long research breaks from my day job; to my partners and staff in my law firm, for keeping the ship afloat while I took that break; to the Adult Christian Formation group at the Episcopal Church of the Advent in Brownsville, Texas, which acted as a sounding board for many of the ideas in this book; to colleagues Chester Gonzalez, Mark McQuality, and William

ACKNOWLEDGMENTS

Chriss, who took the time to read and comment on portions of this book; and the the staff at Wipf and Stock, especially editor Charlie Collier, copy editor Caleb Shupe, and typesetter Calvin Jaffarian, for holding a new author's hand through the publication process. I am more thankful than I can express to my family—Mark, Amanda, Ryan, Elizabeth, and especially Anne—without whom I would be a different, lesser person, and this book would not have been written. And, finally, it is only appropriate that, having practiced law under the gentle guidance of my father Daniel Rentfro Sr. for twenty-three years, I put down my pen on this, the feast of Saint Joseph.

DANIEL RENTFRO JR.
March 19, 2019

Abbreviations

Institutes Calvin, John. *Institutes of the Christian Religion.*
Laws *The Laws of Ecclesiastical Polity.*
MR American Bar Association, Model Rules of Professional Conduct.
ST Thomas Aquinas, *Summa Theologiae.*

1

Jacob's Lawyer

One Friday morning, a well-turned-out middle-aged gentleman, Jack, comes into your law office, asking for a few minutes of your time. He apologizes for the lack of an appointment, politely telling your receptionist that there is some urgency. Skipping the usual pleasantries about the weather or the pennant race, Jack gets right to his story. He is the younger of twin brothers. He knows that under the ancient property laws of your state, the eldest son gets a double share (the "birthright") of the family wealth. He contends, however, that he, not his brother, holds the birthright, because Harold (whom they always called "Red"), his brother, sold it to him many years ago. Years later, their father gave Jack a ritual paternal blessing, reaffirming (in Jack's mind, at least) his entitlement to the birthright. For a long time, Jack, fearing for his safety, has avoided Harold. That he can do no longer. Their father nears death, and Jack wants to reconcile with his brother—while saving his inheritance. Jack also tells you that he has acquired substantial wealth on his own, and he wants your help in hiding as much of it as possible from his brother: what lawyers tactfully call "asset protection." Finally, he wants you as his intermediary with Harold, who has something of a temper and was, at one point, planning revenge.

In re Isaac's Estate, the case that just walked into your office, teems with ethical complications. On the one hand, Jack (your prospective client) has authentic legal arguments for a double portion of the estate. Harold, his older brother, surrendered the birthright voluntarily. On the other hand, when you press Jack about the incident, he reluctantly tells you that all he really gave up was a hot lunch after a hard morning's work.

What's more, the transfer frustrated their father's wishes. Harold was always his father's chosen, Jack the favorite of their mother Becky. (Jack never told Isaac about the transfer of the birthright.) Harold was usually away from the house, working in the family business, while Jack hung around the house all day with his mother.

You press Jack a bit on the blessing story, and, after an uncomfortable pause, Jack tells you that Isaac did ceremonially bless him, but he may have been confused. Confused? you ask. Yes, he may have thought he was blessing Harold. (Here, your spider-sense kicks in big time.) Well, actually, Jack happened to be trying on some of Harold's clothes that day. Then he mumbles something about it all being his mother's idea. (*Undue influence*, you're thinking now.) You ask Jack if he knows of any reason why his mother would have preferred him over his older brother; only, he says, that his mother disliked Harold's wife, who was from another clan.

Something in all of this reminds you of a story that had circulated around the courthouse, about a man named Laban, and a squabble with a nephew over rights to the livestock. The nephew, a clever lad, culled the herd, took the good head for himself, and then left in the middle of the night. You ask Jack about it, and he freely, even proudly, admits that was him. Yes, he did pull one over on Laban, but he had worked hard for Laban for over twenty years, and the ploy was only payback for a swindle Laban had pulled on him, tricking Jack to marry his older daughter Leah rather than his beloved Rachel.

You've learned by now that cases that read like novels have two things in common: they can be easier to get into than out of, and there's always one little fact that your client fails to tell you. Prudence dictates that you do your own investigation before you accept Jack's case. You wonder how many lawyers he's brought this case to before you; if he lawyer-shops, there are only a few in town that Jack might have talked to. You'd also hope to know if Isaac, Becky, or Harold have lawyers already. They might be a source for that odd fact that you suspect Jack hasn't shared with you yet.

So, you tell Jack that you have to excuse yourself, as you've got another project with a 5:00 pm deadline, and ask him to return next week. Too late, he says; he may run into his brother in the next few days, and his father may die at any time. He needs help today. (These cases always seem to walk in on Friday.)

If you must answer right now, you lean towards "no." In part, your reluctance comes from your initial impressions of Jack. He appears to have spent his life playing tricks on people, and you cannot but wonder if you're the current target. Certainly, lawyers are asked all the time to represent people that are not moral paragons, and, as most lawyers, you've become astute—the hard way—at figuring out when someone is trying to play you. You're bothered at least as much, however, by the basic unfairness of Jack's claim. What did he give up for the birthright? A bowl of stew. If that were a legitimate deal, why did Becky feel it necessary to trick old Isaac into blessing Jack?

If Jack is playing you, and his history suggests that he is, the truth of his situation may be far worse than what you've been told. What you keep coming back to is the gnawing feeling that, ethically, you're being asked to take the wrong side of the case. Jack still won't take no for an answer. First, he argues with you: Harold voluntarily sold out. He was a big boy. A deal's a deal. Then he reasons with you: Whatever the circumstances, Isaac transferred his paternal benediction to Jack, and such things should be taken seriously. Then he cajoles you: He tells you how everyone says you're the lawyer that can help him. He tells you that he can pay you. Then he pleads with you: he seems genuinely afraid of Harold. When none of those work, he goes silent for a moment, and then asks you the hardest question of all: What do *you* think he should do?

Meanwhile, you think: *Why should Harold get a double share just because he happened to emerge from the womb first?* Most jurisdictions have completely abandoned any remnant of primogeniture (the rights of the eldest son). Is Harold's claim to the birthright, based on being fifteen minutes older than Jack, any more rational than Jack's, based on a hot lunch? *Not really*, you think; the only justification is, because the law is the law.

The Lawyer's Dilemma

In re Isaac's Estate exemplifies what I will call the Lawyer's Dilemma. The essence of the Lawyer's Dilemma is this: a client or prospective client has legitimate legal rights, the assertion of which trouble the lawyer personally for non-legal, especially moral, reasons. In layperson's terms, the client stands on the right side of the *law*, but on the wrong side of *justice*.

The Model Rules of Professional Conduct obligate a lawyer to take a case he can competently handle if he has the time and the client can pay his fee, unless "the client or the cause is so repugnant to the lawyer as to be likely to impair the client-lawyer relationship or the lawyer's ability to represent the client."[1] Perhaps—not everyone would agree—this gives a lawyer the right to turn down any case that doesn't suit the lawyer's fancy.

---

1. *MR*, 6.2.

In a big city, someone such as Jack would easily find someone to take his case. In a small town, however, that's unlikely. More to the point, "repugnant" is a powerful word. Here, as Jack and his sons point out, Harold sold his birthright voluntarily. Jack lived up to his end of the bargain, and Harold shouldn't get to renegotiate. Most of us have argued more dubious cases (successfully) in the past.

Lawyers have internal conflicts over prospective cases for many reasons. A lawyer may be asked to use her legal skills to achieve a result that seems legal, even admirable, but also imprudent or risky. Or she may be asked to clean up the mess made by behavior that the lawyer finds personally or socially unsuitable, albeit legal. Consider, for example, the environmental lawyer, asked to help a client achieve minimal technical compliance with environmental protection laws, or shift financial responsibility for a catastrophic event such as an oil spill. Or a lawyer may be asked to represent someone he finds personally offensive—a reputed gangster, for instance—in a routine matter such as a home purchase.

All of these are worrying. I am most concerned, though, with legitimate legal claims that produce results harsh, or punitive, or severe. The client, the legal system itself, and the public at large have genuine expectations that the law will be enforced according to its terms. Demands of compassion or notions of fairness often counsel otherwise.

There are practical reasons why lawyers feel the conflict. Often, perhaps even usually, claims that are legitimate but unjust are held by people with money. Lawyers too scrupulous in the preference of personal morality over professional opportunity may find themselves with nothing to do. Also, young lawyers often have little influence over which cases their firms take. Those matters no doubt complicate the lawyer's decision-making. The Lawyer's Dilemma, however, exceeds the realm of the practical, even legal concerns. Instead, the Lawyer's Dilemma involves a particularly acute form of an essentially theological problem.

Why This Is a Theological Dilemma

For the Jews, the distinction between law and religion made no sense. Torah, the Hebrew word for the first five books of the Hebrew Bible (the Christian "Old Testament"), means "law." Law, it was believed, came from YHWH, and so true law could never oppose divine will. Several of the real-life cases we'll consider in these pages involve Deuteronomic law, either from the Ten

Commandments themselves (coveting being a prime example) or other Mosaic law, such as caring for widows, orphans, or aliens.

Christianity has been more ambivalent about the relationship between divine will and human law. On the one hand, Christian theologians over the centuries have found human law's roots, in some form or fashion, in divine reason and will. Thus, Jesus himself says that he came not to abolish the law but to fulfill it. On the other hand, we have the centuries-old debate about Pauline attitudes towards the law and gospel, especially in Luther's two-kingdoms theology at the start of the Protestant Reformation. For the moment, it suffices to say that Christians reject the modern "positivist" view that the law and morality trains run on separate tracks, a view we shall examine in chapter 3. Furthermore, many elements of our law, both criminal and civil, have religious foundations, many from the Hebrew Bible (again, especially the book of Deuteronomy). Ignoring those foundations leads to incoherent thinking about the law. Law serves a purpose, and we find ourselves in the midst of an attempt to retrofit a millennium of law to some new, ill-defined purpose.

Second, the Lawyer's Dilemma involves a problem of agency, responsibility, and will. Lawyers act as agents for their clients. The principal, not the agent, always determines the goal of an endeavor. Christians, on the other hand, regard themselves as agents of God, literally members of Christ's body, his hands and feet in the world.[2] Yet Jesus himself tells us that we cannot serve two masters.[3] Can a lawyer be loyal to both his client and his maker? We hear the issue debated politically all the time; the presidential candidacies of John Kennedy and Mitt Romney spring to mind immediately, and personal (including religious) views on social issues are a frequent topic in judicial confirmation hearings. The same sort of conflict arises in law practice every day. Dual agency, I believe, lies at the heart of Thomas Shaffer's question, "Can a Christian be a lawyer?" Chapter 10 talks extensively about Shaffer's work.

Two Types of Equity

This problem has, literally, been with us from the beginning. Hence our point of departure, the story of Jacob and Esau. Jacob gets to keep Esau's

---

2. See, for example, 1 Cor 12:27. Except where noted, all Scripture references are to NRSV.

3. Matt 6:24; Luke 16:13.

birthright, despite having essentially swindled him out of it. Yet, Esau extends the olive branch to Jacob, while Jacob plots to either buy his peace or hide his wealth (Gen 32:1–21). I take Esau's desire to reconcile as sincere. We're told that Esau came with four hundred men to meet Jacob. If Esau wanted to kill Jacob, he could have done so right then and there. He doesn't need to draw Jacob on to Seir, Esau's home. It seems clear, though, that Jacob doubts Esau's sincerity, and so reneges on his promise to follow Esau to Seir. We would do well to regard their failure to fully reconcile as the ripple effect of the trick Rebekah and Jacob played on Isaac.

In this book, we will consider equity in two senses. Jacob's behavior in alternately offering Esau a share of his questionable bounty and trying to preserve it raises "meaning one" equity questions: Does Jacob have a "just" claim to his wealth?[4] The text lacks clues about Jacob's motivations, but we easily imagine that he acted both out of remorse for what his mother and he had done, and fear for his own well-being. An added complication is that the law itself, on which both Esau's original and Jacob's derivative claim are based, is archaic, and some would say unfair. Why should either of them get a double share? Wouldn't the right—the truly just—thing to do be to give them each half? Yet, as long as both of them insists on his rights, that seems to be the one result that the law precludes.

Esau's gesture of reconciliation manifests equity in the second, personal sense. Esau says that he has all he needs and doesn't covet Jacob's wealth.[5] He has a colorable legal claim to recover the birthright, and he certainly appears to have the strength to take it back forcefully. Yet he doesn't. Again, we don't have any clue to Esau's motivations either.

Equity functions as a lens through which to interpret disputes. Law concerns the relationship between persons, and equity shapes both our view of the other person in the relationship and the rights and responsibilities flowing from that relationship. Lawyers, unfortunately, get out of their comfort zones when they start talking in those terms, rather than sticking to the letter of the law and the four corners of the contract. Our capacities to judge others, and to judge when to depart from existing rules, are both limited—limited by our role as agent of the client and officer of the court, and by our own human frailties. So, whether we act out of loyalty to law or

---

4. Like all analogies, this one eventually breaks down. Jacob does not appear to take possession of the land Isaac promised him until after the meeting with Esau. So, Jacob was really trying to protect the wealth he took from Laban (and his own neck) by placating Esau.

5. Gen 33:9.

conscience, whether we formulate our own plans or judge those of others, we must do so with caution, with what Scripture calls "humility," a topic to which we turn in chapter 9.

Jacob's life, when it has run its course, shows us why we need some humility stirred into our judgment pot. Undeniably, Jacob was far from perfect. Approached to be his lawyer, it would be easy to give ourselves a pat on the back for our moral discernment, say something mildly condescending, and turn him down as a client, sure that he stands on the wrong side of this small bit of history. We would have been mistaken, both about the significance of the story and Jacob's role in it. Events turned out astonishingly different from what we might have expected.[6] Jacob, now Israel, starts out, apparently, on the wrong foot when he replicates Rebekah's partiality for a younger son (Joseph) over older ones.[7] This seemingly ends dreadfully, as the brothers vengefully sell Joseph into slavery and lie to their father that a beast killed Joseph. But, as it is wont to do, providence intervenes. Joseph becomes the regent of the nation of Egypt, just in time to sustain the Egyptians in the approaching famine. Reunited with his family, Joseph saves them from starvation. Israel's family, ensconced in Egypt, grows into the great people, God's chosen people, that God promised to Jacob's grandfather Abraham, and confirmed to Isaac and Jacob himself. These same Israelites, now enslaved, are liberated from Egypt by God through Moses, and become "a covenant to the people, a light to the nations" (Isa 42:6). Christians believe, of course, that providence goes much farther than that. Jacob becomes the patriarch of both Israel and Judah, out of which comes Jesus, the savior and redeemer of the world.[8]

This unexpected turn of events should remind us why we need be humble about our own opinions and judgments. Every lawyer, indeed every person, has experienced this. The case we have lost, or the advice that didn't get followed, yields results that we never could have anticipated. We

---

6. Rebekah seems to be the only person in the story that knew that special things were in store for Jacob, and she had the benefit of divine revelation. YHWH tells her during her pregnancy, "Two nations are in your womb, and two peoples born of you shall be divided; the one shall be stronger than the other, the elder shall serve the younger." But even she does not seem to be able to let things take their course.

7. The preference for younger over older brothers, a common theme in the Old Testament, gets more attention in chapter 11.

8. Islam has a comparable "surprise beginning." Jacob's uncle Ishmael, banished along with Ishmael's mother Hagar, turns out to be the ancestor of Mohammed and the patriarch of Islam.

have all had the experience of seeing a fired employee move to accomplishments beyond her, or our, wildest imagination. Criminal convictions do, on occasion, lead to reformation, while repeated slaps on the wrist can lead to tragedy. No doubt, we should condemn bad or vindictive behavior. In doing so, however, we'd do well by a bit of caution about too much confidence in human law or human judgment.

When the law pretends to have perfect judgment, it reduces the potential for surprise endings. Equity makes the system admit that it makes mistakes, that people are individuals, that we cannot lump them into broad categories such as illegal alien or malingerer, and that the system needs the ability to step back and look at itself. And, in fact, Jacob's own story both commends some humility to us and shows us how dangerous these dilemmas can be. As Jacob prepared to meet Esau, alone in the wilderness, he spends a sleepless night wrestling with a stranger, ending up with a lame hip, but with the courage to meet his brother. Wrestling with God can be dangerous. It can leave us injured. It can change our identity, as it literally did for Jacob.

With that in mind, let us consider some specific examples of the dilemma.

2

The Lawyer's Dilemma

Throughout the book the reader will find examples of ethical dilemmas that lawyers face regularly. To start off, here are two genuine instances taken from my own practice, with details changed for privacy's sake:

A young lawyer, whom we'll call Ms. Morales, is an assistant city attorney for a medium-sized community. Her duties include the legal affairs for the city's public housing department. Getting to work early on a typical Monday morning, she finds two memos on her desk:

1. The first memo concerns Brennan C., a long-time (and generally satisfactory) maintenance supervisor. Brennan injured himself on the job Friday afternoon. In routine post-accident drug screening, Brennan tested positive for cocaine. The city had no prior evidence that Brennan used illegal drugs. Like many public employers, the city has a non-discretionary "one strike and you're out" policy for illegal drug use. In other words, Brennan's firing is imminent, automatic and non-appealable. The case, however, has a sad twist. Brennan plans to retire on his fifty-fifth birthday, which is three months away, fifty-five being the earliest retirement age. The city's plan will pay Brennan a guaranteed monthly amount for the rest of his life and his spouse's life when he "retires." Retirement is the crucial word. If Brennan loses his job for "cause" (such as violating the drug policy) he forfeits his pension. (This type of forfeiture, commonly referred to as a "bad boy clause," is legal in governmental plans, although not in private ones governed by ERISA.[1]) The personnel director, the author of the memo, recognizes the hardship this causes Brennan. In fact, he knows

---

1. The Employee Retirement Income Security Act of 1974, 88 Stat. 829, generally codified at 29 U.S.C. chapter 18.

that Brennan plans to sell his home and move to California to be near his grandchildren. The personnel director also says, however, that the zero-tolerance policy, mandated by the city's worker's compensation carrier, has been consistently applied. (Ms. Morales knows differently, as there are two cases in federal court right now, charging the city with discriminatory application of employee discipline rules.) The personnel director raises a concern about the precedent that retaining Brennan will set. The memo concludes by asking if there are any legal impediments to firing Brennan.

2. The leasing manager sends instructions to evict Deidre J., a chronically delinquent tenant. Deidre seldom pays the rent until she gets a notice to vacate and is now three months behind. Moreover, the neighbors complain about Deidre's brother Doyle, who appears to be living in the unit and, rumor has it, sells drugs on the street corner across from the community center. Deidre, a single mother, raises three children, two of whom attend the city's "Head Start" preschool program, which gives preference to public housing residents. There are five hundred families on the waiting list for apartments like Diedre's. The leasing manager says that she feels for, and even likes, Deidre, whom she considers, all in all, a caring mother. She also says, however, that the regional Housing and Urban Development auditor visits next week and will look at the delinquency rate and interview residents about their satisfaction with the agency. She concludes by saying that, as much as she regrets it, she can't wait any longer, and wants the eviction filed this week.

An ancient conflict between strict law (including rigorous enforcement of contract rights) and common compassion lies behind these examples. The friction goes beyond legal philosophy, showing up in history, politics, and even in literature. It lies at the heart of two of Shakespeare's plays, *The Merchant of Venice*[2] and *Measure for Measure*.[3]

The accounts of Samuel Johnson's long friendship with James Boswell contain not one but two discussions of this conflict. Boswell wrote two books about Johnson. The more famous of Boswell's two books, his *Life of Johnson*, still stands as the greatest biography of all time. The other (published first), *The Journal of a Tour to the Hebrides with Samuel Johnson*,

---

2. Carpi, "Law, Discretion, Equity."
3. Dickinson, "Renaissance Equity"; Dunkel, "Law and Equity."

LL.D,[4] told the story of a 1773 trip to the Western Isles.[5] Most readers are doubtless familiar with Johnson's career as the author of the dictionary, the greatest literary critic, and finally the great practical moralist of his day. Less well-known is that Boswell was not just a writer; he was a lawyer from a family of lawyers. His father, Alexander Boswell (Lord Auchinleck), was a justice on the Court of Session, the supreme civil court of Scotland.

The first-in-time anecdote, from the *Life of Johnson*, occurs soon after Boswell becomes a lawyer. Boswell asks Johnson a question that all new lawyers ask sooner or later: "What do you think of supporting a cause which you know to be bad?" Johnson gives what today would still be the conventional answer:

> Sir, you do not know it to be good or bad till the Judge determines it. I have said that you are to state facts fairly; so that your thinking, or what you call knowing, a cause to be bad, must be from reasoning, must be from your supposing your arguments to be weak and inconclusive. But, Sir, that is not enough. An argument which does not convince yourself, may convince the Judge to whom you urge it; and if it does convince him, why, then, Sir, you are wrong, and he is right. It is his business to judge; and you are not to be confident in your own opinion that a cause is bad, but to say all you can for your client, and then hear the Judge's opinion.[6]

By "bad," Boswell means "dubious" or "legally uncertain," in the same way that trial lawyers today refer to having a good case or a bad case. Johnson's reply reminds Boswell of the roles the participants play in litigation. Advocates advocate, he says, and judges judge. Every law student hears this at some point in his or her first year of school.

The *Tour to the Hebrides* tells of a second interchange that occurred roughly five years later. Sir William Forbes, a friend of Boswell's, suggests that "an honest lawyer should never undertake a cause which he was satisfied was not a *just* one." Johnson replies:

> A lawyer has no business with the justice or injustice of the cause which he undertakes, unless his client asks his opinion, and then

---

4. The degree was honorary. Johnson, unlike Boswell, was neither trained as or engaged in the practice of law.

5. Johnson published his own account of the trip, *A Journey to the Western Islands of Scotland*. Both books are classic reads. It's commonly said, however, that Johnson's book is about Scotland, Boswell's about Johnson.

6. Boswell, *Life of Johnson*, 388.

> he is bound to give it honestly. The justice or injustice of the cause is to be decided by the judge. Consider, sir; what is the purpose of courts of justice? It is, that every man may have his cause fairly tried, by men appointed to try causes . . . If lawyers were to undertake no causes till they were sure they were just, a man might be precluded altogether from a trial of his claim, though, were it judicially examined, it might be found a very just claim.

Boswell calls this "sound practical doctrine," which "rationally repressed a too refined scrupulosity of conscience."[7] (One doubts "a too refined scrupulosity of conscience" tops many lists of client grievances against lawyers today.)

At first glance, the second story seems simply a rerun of the first. Indeed, law school professors use them interchangeably. In truth, Johnson makes two distinguishable points, because Boswell and Forbes had different concerns. Boswell's worry was the appropriateness of arguing a dubious *legal* point. Legal ethics deal with that concern extensively. Lawyers are perfectly free to argue a case that, to all appearances, has the law against it. We do this in several ways. We distinguish our facts from precedent that seems on point. We argue that a statute doesn't apply, or that another statute contradicts the first, or (in a contract case) that the document is ambiguous. In a pinch, we contend that unfavorable precedent should be overruled, or a statute declared invalid. Johnson's advice to the fledgling lawyer that the court, not the advocate, determines the legal sufficiency of a claim is spot on.

Forbes, however, raises a different topic: the morality of bringing an action that could yield an *unfair*, *harsh*, or *inequitable* result—one, in other words, that violates *primary* justice. Johnson, immensely intelligent, would have perceived the distinction, and his response shows it. It would have made no sense to say that a lawyer should keep to himself his opinion about the *legal* viability of a claim. What is legal advice if not that? Rather, Johnson tells Forbes that the lawyer may form an opinion about the decency, we might call it, of the client's case, but that he should only offer it if asked. I disagree. Lawyers should tell their clients what they think about a claim's justness. I call that the lawyer's "prophetic" role, and we shall talk about that in chapter 10.

Johnson also tells Forbes that the lawyer should bring the claim regardless of its intrinsic morality. That proposition is what this book is

---

7. Boswell, *Tour to the Hebrides*, 9–10.

about. Do the ethics of a proposed action, an action legally supportable, cast dishonor on the lawyer, or even the legal system itself?

For the moment, though, let's think about the underlying assumptions behind Johnson's statement. Johnson would vest the judge with the power, indeed the obligation, to address both the legal validity and the justness of a claim. At his time, Johnson's view was the orthodox one. For most of Western history, in fact, courts have passed on the justness of a claim as well as its legal soundness. This practice was based in part on the received wisdom that certain moral truths were objectively true, and any law that violated those truths was invalid or, at a minimum, worthy of neglect by the judge when the application of the law led to a result that violated these fundamental truths.

By the end of the eighteenth century, however, legal scholars and philosophers began to question the court's right to pass moral judgment on a legal claim. By the twentieth century, these doubts were substantially more serious. Both philosophy and jurisprudence contributed to this transformation. We'll explore this more thoroughly in the next chapter. For the moment, let us briefly note two things. First, several legal movements, most notably utilitarianism and legal positivism, promoted the idea that law and morality had nothing to do with each other. Second, and related to the first, both politicians and the public (at least in the United States) have become increasingly suspicious of what lawyers call "judicial discretion" (and certain politicians, for political gain, call "abusive" or "runaway") in favor of legislative dominance in law-making.

The conflict between strict enforcement and compassion vexes Christian lawyers even more, because of mercy's centrality to Christianity.[8] The conversation between Johnson and Lord Forbes about the morality of a lawyer ignoring the justness of a claim would have had decided Christian overtones. Forbes, one of Boswell's literary executors, was said by Boswell to be "at once both a good companion and a good Christian." Boswell, who was raised a Presbyterian, seriously attracted to Catholicism, and ultimately confirmed as an Anglican, was perennially in fear for his soul, confessed his sexual indiscretions to friends (other than Johnson) almost compulsively, and would have realized that acting unjustly had soteriological implications.[9] Johnson himself was profoundly religious. Even more than Boswell, he had periods

---

8. Undoubtedly much the same could be said of other theistic religions. Indeed, the text that I use to frame the dilemma, the book of the prophet Micah, comes from the Hebrew Scripture. In no way do I deny the existence of a similar dilemma for lawyers from other faith traditions. I'm simply not qualified to speak intelligently about those.

9. See Zaretsky, *Boswell's Enlightenment*, 103.

of deep depression, seeing himself as the most abominable of sinners surely fated for damnation. Moreover, Johnson, poor most of his life, was deeply concerned with the welfare of the downtrodden. It was Johnson, we recall, who said "a decent provision for the poor is the true test of civilization."[10]

The conflict between law and morality troubles the Christian lawyer in at least three ways. First, many Christians subscribe to the "divine command" theory of ethics. Morality consists in following God's commands, no more and no less. There have been centuries of debate about whether moral rules are good because God orders them, or whether God orders them because they are independently good. (This is the famous "Euthyphro" dilemma, from the Socratic dialogue of the same name.) Christian theories of God call this dilemma false, because not even an omnipotent God could order something contrary to his wholly good ("omnibenevolent" is the technical, tongue-twisting term) nature. God being essentially good, his commands can no more be evil than a triangle can have four sides. A corollary of divine command theory is the fear of divine punishment. Obeying or disobeying God leads to either temporal or eternal rewards and punishments.

The second might be called the divine imitation model. Christianity being unique in having an embodied divinity, divine imitation is a specifically christological model. It looks beyond the teachings to the life of Jesus as a moral exemplar. Thomas à Kempis's *The Imitation of Christ*, one of the great manuals of Christian devotion, has been beloved by Christians for seven hundred years. However, à Kempis's book concerns itself primarily with Christ's interior life, rather than outward activity. Many of our most famous saints, notably Saint Francis, adopted the life goal of physically imitating Christ. More recently, notably in Richard Burridge's *Imitating Jesus*, theologians pay attention to Jesus's activities, and make ethical deductions from what the Gospels report Jesus doing. Burridge contends that we must read the Gospels as biography, and view Jesus as as much a moral paradigm as a moral teacher. Christ was humble and merciful, and therefore so should we be. Jesus was holy, and we should imitate his holiness. Most importantly, for Burridge, Jesus was "radically inclusive," forgiving sinners and even inviting them into his company. So, the argument goes, should we.

A third, completely different, collision between the problem and Christian belief comes out of the "natural law" theory. John Carnes defines natural law so: "A natural law theory holds that the fundamental principles

---

10. Boswell, *Life of Johnson*, 446.

of morality and legality, and hence of society, are rooted in the nature of the universe, and more specifically, in the nature of man himself, that they are 'rational,' and that they are universal and eternal."[11] Natural law theory is not exclusively Christian, although many Christian theologians, including Aquinas, have believed in natural law. Hugo Grotius, sometimes called the "father of natural law," believed that natural law was consistent with Christianity, and in fact was based in Christian truth, which, as he saw it, was the source of all truth about the world. According to Grotius, however, "the law of nature is a dictate of right reason, which points out that an act, according as it is or is not in conformity with rational nature, has in it a quality of moral baseness or moral necessity; and that, in consequence, such an act is either forbidden or enjoined by the author of nature, God."[12] In other words, natural law, based on right human reason, would be true for and available to anyone, even non-theists. As a result, Protestants have frequently objected to natural law theories, which hold that natural law is available to all, because that seems to place Scripture in an inferior position behind nature (and reason) as a source of divine truth. Natural law, as a strictly legal theory, no longer holds much sway in the age of legal positivism, because it cannot be "verified"; unlike statutes, for instance, which have a stamp of legislative approval on them, there is no way to objectively verify the bona fides of a natural law proposition (such as that lying is wrong.)

Nevertheless, natural law theories do enjoy something of a revival among theologians and philosophers, notably through the work of theologians John Finnis,[13] Germaine Grisez, and Jean Porter,[14] and political philosopher J. Budziszewski.[15] We might regard this revival as more of an interest in natural law as a moral rather than as a purely legal theory, and there is something intuitively appealing to the idea that certain moral propositions, such as that torture is wrong, are true for reasons other than because everyone accepts them. Why would this matter to a Christian lawyer? Because natural law, in holding that there exists a law higher than positive law, obligates a lawyer (whose professional duties are bound up in human positive law) to choose. If natural law emanates from God's reason, a lawyer that chooses statutory over natural law violates divine reason.

11. Carnes, "Christian Ethics and Natural Law," 303.
12. Neff, *On the Law of War and Peace*, 28–29.
13. See, e.g., Finnis, *Natural Law and Natural Rights*.
14. See, e.g., Porter, *Ministers of the Law*.
15. See, e.g., Budziszewski, *Written on the Heart*.

Nevertheless, Johnson tells Forbes that a lawyer should keep his moral opinions to himself, and to ignore them when deciding whether to take a case. It reminds us of J. P. Morgan's famous line: "I don't know as I want a lawyer to tell me what I cannot do. I hire him to tell how to do what I want to do." Except, in this case, we worry about "should not" rather than "cannot" do. Does this mean faithful Christians cannot be good lawyers? No; a "solution" to this seemingly irresolvable dilemma exists, one with a long theological history but one that has been forgotten of late. The theory of *equity*, an old-fashioned legal concept, finds its roots deep in theological soil. Johnson's confidence that the court would concern itself with the justness of the claim rested in the historically strong commitment to equity in the English legal system.[16]

"Equity" in the law carries philosophical, substantive, and procedural connotations. It also has a theological meaning. When I use "equity" as a legal term, I borrow Blackstone's definition, which he borrowed from Hugo Grotius: "the correction of that wherein the law (by reason of its universality) is deficient."[17] When I use it as a theological term, I refer to a personal quality that values the moral over the legal.

I've chosen four theologians—Thomas Aquinas, John Calvin, Richard Hooker, and William Perkins—to illustrate why the legal concept of equity in the Anglo-American system, its roots in theology, remains indispensable even in the post-Christian age. Hooker and Perkins lived and wrote in the great English "age of equity."[18] Aquinas and Calvin, respectively, were their theological ancestors.

I then move to two modern writers: American scholar of law and religion Harold Berman and English moral theologian Oliver O'Donovan, comparing Berman's historical approach to the role of higher justice in the legal system with O'Donovan's theological examination of the same question. I will examine changes over time in legal theories of contract law, and the theological implications of those changes. I suggest several developments in modern legal philosophy that aggravate the problem, including

---

16. "Every just law is dictated by reason; and . . . the practice of every legal court is regulated by equity." Boswell, *Life*, 496.

17. Blackstone, *Commentaries*.

18. I am mindful of the presence of equity in other legal systems, such as Germany, where Oldendorp in particular found the need for equity compelling. Berman, *Law and Revolution II*, 91–92. Space requirements (not to mention the large gap in my knowledge of civil law) force me to concentrate on the Anglo-American legal system.

the elevation of legislation over common law as the basis of legal norms, and the development of legal positivism.

There is no doubt an Anglican tint to this. Writers from other denominations have written perceptively about these issues. This book touches on two of them: Nicholas Wolterstorff's work on justice and rights, and John Witte Jr.'s several books on the relation between law and religion. (Witte was a student of Harold Berman.) But, just as easily, I could have included other Anglican theologians, such as Rowan Williams, who, throughout his scholarly career, before, during, or after his tenure at Lambeth, wrote about the intersection between public policy and theology.

In fact, several reasons support the Anglo-centrism of the book. No doubt, a similar book could have been written about the impact of the Lutheran Reformation on German law, with a special concentration on the German legal scholar Johann Oldendorp. In fact, Oldendorp's highly developed theory of equity has real similarities with what I propose for a modern view of equity in the last chapter. However, John Witte Jr. has already written a very fine book (*Law and Protestantism: The Legal Teachings of the Lutheran Reformation*) that has a lengthy discussion of Oldendorp's work. That discussion would make this a much longer and completely different book.

Moreover, this book is intended primarily for American practicing lawyers. It seems to me that it makes most sense to examine the rise, pinnacle, and decline of equity in the Anglo-American legal system under the light of Anglican theology. After all, the basis for equity practice in American law came from rules and principles established in the English court of chancery.

Third, the Anglican Communion has both by history and theology focused on issues of political theology, including the relation between church and state and the balance between positive and higher law. Indeed, Stephen Langton, Thomas á Becket's successor as archbishop of Canterbury, was instrumental in solidifying the recognition and endurance of the Magna Carta and may have been one of its authors. Three hundred and fifty years later, the Elizabethan settlement, the foundation for what we now know as the Church of England, was itself a compromise between competing visions of church governance and political power. Those circumstances also produced an Anglican confession that bears allegiance both to Aquinas and to Calvin in a way no other denomination does, so that its social theology draws on both Aquinas's view of equity as perfection of the law and Calvin's as equity being a personal quality that rises above the law. The theological reason comes from an emphasis on a concern for theology of, for, and in society that goes back all the way to Anselm of Canterbury.[19]

One must stop somewhere, and the line between Anglicanism and Lutheranism is where this book stops. Before reaching the end, however, I will make a slight detour, and devote a chapter to Trollope's *Orley Farm*, which tells the story of a twenty-year battle over a codicil to a will in a way that shows a handful of lawyers dealing with the conflict between law and morality, duty and loyalty, at every point along the spectrum from positivism to unbridled equity. What, one might ask, does a nineteenth-century novel have to do with law and religion and the twenty-first century? There are two answers. As Mark Fortier shows us, equity is a cultural phenomenon that manifests itself in many ways, including literary. Second, lawyers tell stories to make a point. Jesus did the same thing; we call them parables. Think of *Orley Farm* as a parable about the close of the age of equity.

Mercy, although fundamental, is not the only value that demands our moral allegiance. Christianity strongly emphasizes the importance of law, including the enforcement of promises and the punishment of wrongdoing. Equity, which sees itself threatened by several elements of modern legal theory and practice, serves to promote a balance between strict justice and compassion, which in turn diminishes the intensity of ethical challenges for lawyers.[20] Less equity, less true justice, and more ethical problems for lawyers and judges. And, despite T. S. Eliot's warning that Dr. Johnson is "a dangerous person to disagree with,"[21] I hope to show that the only way a Christian lawyer can confront the Dilemma is by making the justice or injustice of the client's cause the lawyer's business also, regardless of whether the client asks.

First, however, we examine how modern jurisprudence and legal education help the dilemma flourish.

---

19. Dackson, "Anglicanism and Social Theology," 619. Dackson argues that as far back as Anselm, we can find the roots of Anglican social theology. For Anselm, it was a concern for restitutive justice, the notion that Jesus's sacrifice was not punishment on mankind, but rather restitution to God of what was rightfully God's: absolute human obedience.

20. Judges face a similar dilemma, often a more acute one, because of the evangelical admonition to "judge not." The theological and jurisprudential issues that the two vocations face are different enough that in a book of this size I can only address the one.

21. Eliot, "Metaphysical Poets," 383.

3

How Our Legal System Creates the Lawyer's Dilemma

Before we start our discussion of equity, let's first examine how legal theory, legal training, and rules of professional conduct in the United States all create ethical dilemmas for lawyers.

The turn of the nineteenth century saw the rise of a philosophical movement, along with a substantially related legal theory. The philosophy was utilitarianism; legal positivism was the legal theory. Utilitarianism is the best-known of a group of moral philosophies under the heading "consequentialism." Consequentialist theories judge actions solely by the good they cause or the evil they avoid. "The ends justify the means" is a serviceable, albeit a bit cheeky, *precis* of consequentialism. The theory considered the great antithesis of consequentialism is "deontological," or rule-based, morality. Deontological theories break down further into "duty-based" and "rights-based" theories. Deontological models judge actions not by their consequences, but by whether they accord with agreed-upon rules of conduct, fulfill duties the actor owes others, or honor the basic rights of other persons.

To illustrate: A father and his teenage son are gravely injured in an auto accident and rushed to the hospital. The father asks the emergency room doctor how his son is doing. The doctor knows that the son has died. What does he tell the father? A rules-based moralist might say that lying is always wrong, and that, as painful as it may be, the doctor must tell his patient the truth. A consequentialist, on the other hand, would look at it and say that no good, and some harm, may come from telling the father (he may react emotionally and lose the determination to live himself) so the doctor should lie, or at least avoid answering.[1]

---

[1]. These situations are enormously complex. The doctor practices under a set of rules, one of which is "do no harm." Therefore, the doctor might be deontologically barred

A third category, "virtue-based" theories, judge actions according to broad standards of virtue (such as honesty or bravery). Something is ethical if it is the type of thing that an ethical person would do. Virtue-based ethics are more subtle than deontological, because they recognize unavoidable conflicts between moral rules. In our example from the last paragraph, telling the truth involves a substantial cruelty to the father. Therefore, virtue ethics would ask the question "what would a truly virtuous person do in this situation?" Virtue ethics are said to be founded on what the Greeks called *phronesis*—practical wisdom.[2]

Utilitarianism judges both actions and beliefs by how—i.e., to what extent—they promote good states of being, such as happiness, and eliminate bad states, notably suffering: hence, by their *utility*. Utilitarianism qualifies as an ethical system, in the common-sense meaning, because it is impartial; everyone's well-being counts the same. Hedonism, on the other hand, the philosophy of the ancient Epicureans, recognized only the relevance of what promoted pleasure and inhibited pain for one's self, and so we don't typically think of hedonism as an ethical option (although all of us practice it all the time.)

Utilitarianism was not strictly a legal theory, but it did have legal reform as one of its goals. A utilitarian view of the law does not *exactly* disclaim any connection between law and morality. It instead claims that the only true morality is one that leads to the most happiness, irrespective of rules, customs, traditions, or even binding commands from authorities to the contrary. This means two things. First, it calls into question whether there is a moral obligation to follow the law if doing so causes pain. Second, it suggests that the laws should be appraised by how useful they are. Jeremy Bentham, one of utilitarianism's early exponents, puts it colorfully when he called the concept of preexistent natural rights "nonsense upon stilts." He thought the same of theories of natural or transcendent law, based on moral or religious principles. Bentham believed the relevant question to be whether a law was useful to society, not whether it was moral. That the application of a rule might trigger a harsh or painful result in an individual case was irrelevant if it generally led to the greater overall

---

from telling the father the truth about his son. However, telling the father "I can't answer that question" probably tells the father all he needs to know.

2. *Phronesis* has also been identified as the quality that enables an equitable approach to the law. See Scharffs, "Role of Humility."

good, by increasing the excess of happiness versus sorrow; in fact, such individual pain was to be expected.

At more or less the same time that utilitarianism emerged as a philosophy, legal positivism, which was specifically jurisprudential, also served to diminish the significance of moral norms for the legal system. Legal positivism is a descendant of utilitarianism; Bentham's student John Austin deserves as much as anyone to be considered the "founder" of legal positivism. Austin's initial claim was rather modest. Aquinas, and others, had argued that an immoral law—laws that violated divine law, basic human reason, or common morality—was no law at all and could be regarded as a nullity. Austin said they were wrong. A law's *morality* was irrelevant to the question of its *validity*. "Law" was neither more or less than the command of the "sovereign."[3] Austin wrote, "The existence of law is one thing; its merits or demerits are another thing. Whether a law be, is one inquiry; whether it *ought* to be, or whether it agree with a given or assumed test, is another and a distinct inquiry."[4] Austin admitted that a moral evaluation of a law was appropriate.[5] He simply thought that the narrow question of a law's validity was a political question rather than a moral one.

I suspect that most lawyers today would accept this view, sometimes called "soft positivism." In the United States, the highest criterion for evaluating the validity of a law is itself another body of law: the United States Constitution. A valid law cannot violate a provision of the Constitution. So, for instance, a state statute that allowed a suspected terrorist to be tried a second time for the same act, if the first trial resulted in an acquittal, would clearly violate the Fifth Amendment. That would be the case even if everyone, except for the twelve jurors, agreed that the first trial had been a gross miscarriage of justice, and even if everyone thought that the world would be safer with the terrorist in prison.

On the other hand, few of us would say that the second trial was prohibited by the rule against punishing the innocent, found in the twenty-third

---

3. There has been great debate over the years about what makes an entity the "sovereign" but for our purposes let's think about it as being the "government."

4. Austin, *Province of Jurisprudence Determined*, 278.

5. Austin, *Province of Jurisprudence Determined*, 41. We should note that Austin appears to have come around to a utilitarian view of morality, at least as a gap-filler for divine law: "The commands which God has revealed we must gather from the terms wherein they are promulg[ate]d. The command which he has not revealed, we must construe by the principle of utility." Austin, *Lectures on Jurisprudence*, 52. By utility, he meant something like the common good.

chapter of Exodus (although we might conclude on that basis that the second trial was immoral).[6] This is why judicial decisions concerning the conflict of state or federal statutes with personal rights must always find recognition of those rights, either express or implicit, in the Constitution itself. Our law requires more than the allegation that a law—say a state law prohibiting same-sex marriage—violates the inherent autonomy of every person. Rather, we must say that either the law deprives same-sex couples of a right derived from the Constitution (such as the right of privacy, or association) or that, in violation of the constitutional guarantees of due process or equal protection of the laws, it illegally discriminates against a class of persons without sufficient legal justification for doing so.[7]

Later varieties of legal positivism progressed beyond Austin's premise that a law's *validity* does not depend on its ethics, to the more aggressive claim that, ethics being a private affair, ethical questions are irrelevant to the *prudence* or *wisdom* of a law. The privatization of morality had been a philosophical debate for a couple of centuries; Thomas Hobbes and David Hume (who strenuously argued that "is" should be distinguished from "ought") were central participants. It was only in the nineteenth and into the twentieth century, however, that such theories began to have significant practical impacts on the way lawmakers (and judges) look at law.

The most famous American example we have is Oliver Wendell Holmes. Thirty years a United States Supreme Court Justice (preceded by twenty years on the Massachusetts Supreme Court), Holmes is routinely christened the "greatest judge in American history." Holmes also wrote two of the most influential texts in the history of American legal theory. First, there was *The Common Law* (1881), which contains his famous line "the

---

6. Alfonse Bartkus was acquitted by a federal court in Illinois of robbing a federally insured bank. The State of Illinois then prosecuted Bartkus for the same crime and obtained a conviction. The United States Supreme Court held that this did not violate the double jeopardy clause of the Fifth Amendment, because of the "dual sovereignty" doctrine, even though the factual basis of the two prosecutions was essentially identical; Bartkus's actions violated both federal law and Illinois law. The United States Supreme Court upheld the Illinois conviction. *Bartkus v. Illinois,* 359 U.S. 121. Many people thought this was unfair, even if legal, and the Illinois legislature passed a law prohibiting state prosecution after a federal acquittal on the same facts. This still didn't free Mr. Bartkus, whose sentence was eventually commuted by the governor.

7. Scholars discuss whether the Declaration of Independence is a source of fundamental rights, so that a court could invalidate a statute by finding, for instance, that it violated the principle that all persons are created equal. For now, at least, the answer appears to be "no," even though it is included, along with the Constitution, in the United States Code as "Organic Laws."

life of the law has not been logic; it has been experience." Sixteen years later came "The Path of the Law," which formulated his famous "prediction theory": from a client's perspective, the question of whether an act is illegal is whether, given all the circumstances, he will be punished if he commits it. From the Holmesian view, the speed limit is whatever traffic police will enforce, so that in vast stretches of the American West at certain times of the day there is no illegal speed. Later in the century this idea took hold under the name "legal realism."

Holmes, ironically, is regarded as a great defender of social welfare legislation such as wage and hour laws. One of his most famous opinions was his dissent in *Lochner v. New York*[8] in which he defended a state statute limiting daily and weekly work hours against the argument that such limits violated a constitutional "freedom of contract." In fact, Holmes had no truck for the view of law as morality and defended the New York statute because he thought the legislature had the right to pass it, not because he agreed with it.[9] The morality of a law was none of a judge's business. The relation (if any) between act and moral obligation, he said, was a question for philosophy, not law.[10]

This side of Holmes was legal positivism par excellence. The content of the legislation, and the philosophy behind it, offended Holmes, who was a thoroughgoing social Darwinist.[11] Nevertheless, Holmes defended the right of the legislature to pass the law, pointing out that it was no different than Sunday closing laws, or even prohibitions against usury. In other areas, Holmes defended legislation that strikes us as highly reactionary, because (again) he felt the legislature was the proper venue for social welfare decisions. When we call Holmes America's greatest jurist, we choose to forget *Buck v. Bell*,[12] which sustained the state of Virginia's right to forcibly sterilize intellectually disabled persons. No wonder, then, that H. L. Mencken once said that Holmes was much more interested in the rights of lawmakers than the rights of man.[13]

---

8. 198 U.S. 45 (1905), dissenting opinion.

9. Alschuler, *Law Without Values*, 86.

10. Holmes, *Common Law*, 219.

11. We recall that his Lochner dissent has the famous line "The Fourteenth Amendment does not enact Mr. Herbert Spencer's *Social Statics*." One almost detects the word "sadly" lined out of the draft opinion.

12. 274 U.S. 200 (1927).

13. Mencken, "Mr. Justice Holmes," 122–23.

No one seriously disputes that courts owe legislatures substantial deference. What we have seen in the last century, especially in the last fifty years, however, is legislative encroachment into areas long considered common-law matters. Tort law was the province of the courts to develop; strict products liability, for instance, was entirely judge-made. Today, we look first to the statute books for applicable law. The view that law-making is the sole prerogative of the legislature is now so engrained that we forget that it is itself simply one among many models, and a recent one at that. This realignment of roles runs across all areas of the law: strict sentencing guidelines versus discretionary sentencing in criminal cases;[14] statutory validation of boilerplate language waiving basic legal rights; legislative support for foreclosures on valuable real property at a fraction of its true market value; and legislation that promotes or even requires arbitration rather than litigation of claims.

In the process, judges' ability to make discretionary substantive rulings dribbles away.[15] While Dr. Johnson assumed that a judge had the authority to rule on the morality of a case, as law divorced itself from morality, a judge's ability to rule on the fairness of an action diminished also. One cannot help noting that, in each of the examples in the previous paragraph, the trial judge's lack of ability to intervene harms the less powerful side of the transaction: the criminal defendant, the borrower, the consumer.

More recently, the "law and economics" model (sometimes referred to as the "Chicago School," because many of its founders were associated with the University of Chicago) revives utilitarianism under another name, by attempting to quantify the merits and flaws of all social policies according to predictions of economic cost versus benefit.[16] The law and economics theory in its more modest form applied the criteria of economic efficiency to certain discrete bodies of law, notably antitrust. So far so good. Antitrust laws govern economic activity, and so it makes sense that economic effects

---

14. See, e.g., *Rummel v. Estelle*, 445 U.S. 263 (1980), upholding a mandatory life sentence for a third felony conviction, even though the three offenses involved a total of less than $250 in stolen goods or services.

15. Trial court judges still largely control trial procedure.

16. To be sure, the post-Austinian form of legal positivism, which sought to eliminate the moral dimensions of the law, are not universally endorsed today. Notably, Ronald Dworkin has tried to reintroduce modern notions of morality—specifically fairness and equality—into the process of adjudication, through his theory of "interpretevism." See, e.g., *Law's Empire*. But Dworkin's work, for all its sophistication, seems to me to falter precisely when it attempts to justify the basis for his conception of morality.

should be the standard by which one evaluates them. The Chicago School goes much farther, however, and contends that all of the common law can, and even should, be evaluated according to its tendency to promote overall wealth.[17] Like legal positivism, the law and economics efficiency model takes moral equations out of the picture and replaces them with wealth as the sole criteria for evaluation. Since wealth maximization, shocking as this may seem, is occasionally amoral, the potential for conflict between a lawyer's legal duties and moral choices increases.

Legal positivism and law and economics theory are only two manifestations of an even larger phenomenon. The twentieth century witnessed the growth of the "instrumental" view of the law, something that has been called the "ordinary religion of the law school classroom."[18] The instrumental view turns law from a way of *being* to a method of *doing*. Utilitarianism and law and economic theories are instrumentalist. Rather than either reflecting who we are as a society, or defining who we are, they see law as a way of achieving some other social policy.

Much high-visibility litigation is exceedingly instrumental. We seem to care much more about the social implications of the result than its impact on the actual litigants. Take *Gideon v. Wainwright*.[19] Until 1963, a state had to provide a lawyer for an indigent criminal defendant only in two instances: in capital cases, or if, out of due process concerns, "special circumstances" (such as the defendant's mental capacity) demanded it in a non-capital case. Neither applied to Clarence Gideon; his charge was breaking and entering, and there was no question about his competence. Nevertheless, the Supreme Court, which had been waiting for the opportunity to overrule the prior line of cases, held that, under the Sixth Amendment, all indigent criminal defendants have a fundamental right to appointed and paid-for defense counsel in a case punishable by imprisonment. The Court's decision had nothing to do with the guilt or innocence of Mr. Gideon. The right Gideon asserted, and the court recognized, was the right to a fair trial. Mr. Gideon's case was the vehicle through which the Supreme Court got rid of the old line of cases.

---

17. "All" is scarcely an overbroad claim. We have, for instance, books and articles on the economic arguments for a more lenient euthanasia policy. See, e.g., Posner, "Euthanasia and Health Care."

18. Cramton, "Ordinary Religion," 250.

19. 372 U.S. 355 (1963).

We rarely think to ask what happened when Florida tried Clarence Gideon the second time, or if he even was tried again. Abe Fortas, lead counsel in the *Gideon* case (later to be appointed by Lyndon Johnson to the United States Supreme Court), reportedly didn't even want to meet Mr. Gideon.[20] As it happened, the jury acquitted him when he was retried (with a lawyer) after the case returned to Florida. The point is that Mr. Gideon was an instrument used to reform the criminal justice system; his guilt or innocence was essentially irrelevant, even though having a lawyer turned out to be a genuine, not just a technical, right.

Lawyers that represent public interest groups or practice public interest class action litigation seldom have an identifiable person as the effective client.[21] There may be discrete groups of persons, such as immigrants that suffer individual injuries through broad brush executive orders. The work of representing those individuals is grubby, underpaid, and largely invisible. The publicized litigation, such as class action, tends to look more like legislation than dispute resolution.

That is a topic for another time. I have something else in mind. The instrumental view that I am concerned with, which creates the moral dilemmas that are the subject of the book, concerns the use of the law as a tool—that is, an instrument—to get a client what the client wants. It values law only as a means to an end. This type of instrumental view attaches long before an actual client with an individual problem walks through the door. A new lawyer learns, and then in his professional oath swears, to become an instrument for achieving his client's goals. In the process, the lawyer sublimates his own goals, desires, and—most significantly for our purposes—his beliefs, to his client's.

No doubt, lawyering inherently contains this instrumentalist aspect. A lawyer has fiduciary duties towards her client, obligating her to put her client's interests above, not merely equal to, her own.[22] Attorney-client is

---

20. Fortas did request a written history from him to use in writing his brief. *Gideon's Trumpet*, by Anthony Lewis, which tells the story of the Gideon case, is worth a read for any lawyer.

21. Cramton calls these the "hired gun" and "social engineer" models of professional behavior. In each instance, the lawyer's relationship to the end is the same, although the end itself may be for the benefit of an individual or a larger group. Cramton, "Ordinary Religion," 251.

22. Fiduciary relationships were one of the earliest developments in the law of equity. One way to view the Lawyer's Dilemma would be as a conflict between the equitable obligations *to* the client and inequitable demands made *by* the client.

not the only fiduciary relationship. Trustor/trustee/beneficiary is the classic one. The relationship between corporate directors and stockholders is another. Those relationships all require the fiduciary's subordination of personal business or financial interests to those of his principal.[23] Lawyers, however, owe clients more than their financial loyalty, because clients have more than financial goals, and even achieving financial goals can have extra-financial impacts on third parties. All of that brings ethical baggage along. Therefore, a lawyer seemingly must ignore his own moral views of how others should be treated in favor of his client's interests.

That alone would be enough of a challenge. In fact, however, the modern rules create a tripartite relationship by focusing on the lawyer's role as an "officer of the court" as well as her relationship with her client. The lawyer's power to act for her clients comes from the state, so, the way the state sees it, the state can reasonably demand that the power be used to advance the goals of the legal system, indeed the larger interests of the state.

The rules of professional conduct aim to resolve the conflict between the client and the legal system, by saying that there are some things a lawyer can refuse to do in service of his client. Some of the restrictions are self-evident; a lawyer can neither lie to the court nor make use of perjured testimony.[24] Some are common sense; with limited exceptions, a trial lawyer cannot be a witness in the same case, out of fear that the line between testimony and argument disappear entirely. Some are less obvious; for instance, despite the adversarial nature of our judicial process, a lawyer is obligated to inform the court of legal authority contrary to her client's position, even if her adversary overlooks it. Still others go to a lawyer's basic rights; for instance, a lawyer loses some of her full First Amendment rights to comment about pending cases, or (in court) to express her opinion that her client tells the truth, or the opposing party fabricates.

---

23. The fiduciary obligation for a lawyer goes beyond mere financial considerations. Admittedly, once a lawyer takes a case, he is not to prefer that moderately lucrative assignment in favor of a potentially well-paying one. He is also not to consider that the work will diminish the lawyer's standing in the community or among his friends; or that the demands of the case will interfere with weekend barbecue plans or children's dance recitals. Those are all things to think about before taking a file—indeed, before becoming a lawyer. Once the lawyer finds herself in the fray, however, it is too late to back out. That is why many if not most lawyers, sooner or later, feel as if they have made a Faustian bargain.

24. Lawyers often testify in court, either on attorney's fees or about some procedural matter. Until recently (and in some places still) lawyers were not sworn in before testifying, because they were considered to always be "under oath" in court, whether speaking as a witness or an advocate.

The rules recognize that an adversarial system depends on effective and vigorous representation of all viewpoints within the bounds of the law.[25] Various reasons are advanced for the advocacy system. At certain times and places, it has been thought a civilized alternative to gunfights or swordplay. Alternatively, we have heard a "marketplace of ideas" defense of advocacy-based litigation.[26] In any event, truth is the goal.[27] Truth, that is, as defined by the state. By that, I mean that the state sets the parameters of the inquiry, by defining what is or is not a contract, or good cause, or unconscionable. Caught between that obligation and the duty to pursue the right, as defined by the client's wishes, there is little room for the good, as defined by the lawyer's morals. Thus, lawyers find themselves obligated to do that which both law and Scripture tell them they cannot—serve two masters, the client and the law.

Lawyers will appreciate the irony in this. Even though agency law seriously discourages, and often disallows, dual agency, the Model Rules actually promote this conflict, apparently without note of the problem. "A lawyer, as a member of the legal profession, is a representative of clients, an officer of the legal system and a public citizen having special responsibility for the quality of justice,"[28] the Rules start out, ignoring the inevitable conflicts between the client's interests, the state's, and the public's.

Recall that the law we speak of, in the age of positivism, cares nothing about moral complications. Clients regularly have legitimate legal rights, the enforcement of which will cause real, perhaps irreparable, harm to someone else. There are tort causes of action for interference with contract and so forth, but they invariably exclude claims based on the enforcement of a legitimate legal right. I can collect a debt, even if it deprives the debtor of the funds he set aside to pay college tuition for his daughter or to buy medicine for his mother. I am entitled to enforce a non-compete agreement against

---

25. "(W)hen an opposing party is well represented, a lawyer can be a zealous advocate on behalf of a client and at the same time assume that justice is being done." *MR*, Section 8.

26. John Milton in *Aeropagetica*, and two centuries later John Stuart Mill in *On Liberty*, each advance the idea that the best way to arrive at the truth was a "free market" of ideas, analogous to the economic theory that competition drives out inferior goods (or in this case, ideas).

27. Berman claims that as early as the twelfth century there developed a view of law as scientific, in which the advocate played a (partisan) role in a system intended to achieve objective truth. Berman, *Law and Revolution*, 157.

28. *MR*, Preamble, 1.

an ex-employee, even if the employee's working for another company causes me no damage at all. (A judge will likely ask about potential damages before issuing an injunction but, practically speaking, sending the new employer a copy of the agreement will stop the hiring in its tracks.)

The morality of pursuing a small claim that is financially trivial to a wealthy creditor but would devastate an indigent debtor is a different matter, one for which theories of the majesty of the law or the dignity of contract provide little solace. Once again, the Rules are of little help. They do provide that a lawyer may withdraw from representation if "the client insists upon taking action that the lawyer considers repugnant or with which the lawyer has a fundamental disagreement."[29] But if the client is in the right legally, then a feeling of repugnance suggests a fundamental disagreement, not with the client, but with the law itself.

All lawyers feel that conflict. The Christian lawyer,[30] however, has an additional burden. The ethical conflict is more than a straightforward conflict between personal mores and legal expectations, serious though those are. Christianity calls its followers to act as God's agents in the world.[31] The Christian lawyer, then, finds himself involved in a *triple* agency: the state, the client, and the gospel. Some have wondered whether one can even be a Christian and a lawyer. Professor Joseph Allegretti said that was an open question, and that at best one is a Christian first, and a lawyer second.[32]

When duties of religion and law conflict, the obligations of religious conscience come first. But how do we know when they really conflict? A lawyer *could* conclude that our legal system is simply a tool for the rich and powerful, or for the state itself, and that the Dilemma is unavoidable and irreconcilable. That lawyer needs a career change: perhaps a practice dedicated solely to cases and clients that align with the lawyer's morals: representing the underprivileged or indigent in a free legal services NGO, for example, or working for environmental protection. There are economic restraints on all lawyers, however, and often the decision to take a file or keep a client lies not with the associate doing the heavy lifting on the file (trying to make partner) but with someone else—partner or partnership committee. Moreover, taking this attitude would abandon the field to non-theists, something unpleasant to contemplate.

29. *MR*, 1.16(b)(4).
30. As well as lawyers from other faith traditions. See chapter 2, footnote 8.
31. "Now you are the body of Christ, and each of you is a member of it" (1 Cor 12:27).
32. Allegretti, "Can Legal Ethics Be Christian?," 463.

Alternatively, a lawyer could also conclude that there is simply no place for religious ethics in legal ethics, the two being separate fields of concern. Joseph Allegretti analyzes this position at length, and finds it wanting.[33] He says that "Christian lawyers want not only to obey their profession's codes of conduct, but to live in harmony with their own deepest values."[34] Allegretti writes:

> Consider a divorce case. A "good lawyer" is expected to fight vigorously for her client's right to custody of the children. But what if the client is a bad or an abusive parent? The Christian lawyer cannot ignore the wishes and well-being of the children whose interests are at stake. Or consider a corporation that is engaged in an activity that is legal but harmful to society. The "good lawyer" is free to devote herself unreservedly to her client's interests, but the Christian lawyer must also consider the injury being done to the common good.[35]

Indeed. Those examples, unfortunately, do more to highlight than to resolve the problem. The divorce case may be the "exception that proves the rule." The court is mandated to look out for the best interests of the children. That is contrary to the normal case, where the court's job is to be the neutral referee. The divorce lawyer can have some confidence in the court to reach the right result. In the second case, the "amoral corporation," on the other hand, positivism tells us that the law itself defines the public good. The lawyer that refuses to defend the corporation because of a differing opinion about the public good neglects his obligation to his client and to the law. The conflict there is not between law and morals, but between different conceptions of what is moral. We are all familiar with failures of this kind: the nineteenth-century slave trade, or twentieth-century apartheid. The only proper course for the Christian lawyer asked to defend those abominations was to withdraw. Most cases, however, are more ambiguous. How about representing tobacco companies or gun manufacturers? The government could—for guns, many think should—ban smoking and assault rifles. But it has not. There are libertarian (for smoking) and constitutional (for

---

33. Allegretti, "Can Legal Ethics Be Christian?," 463.

34. Allegretti, "Can Legal Ethics Be Christian?," 459. Ronald Dworkin, admittedly writing from a non-theist position, describes this as the choice between having a good life and living well, between success, financial comfort, fame, and so forth, to which morality is peripheral, and a full life, to which morality is central. Dworkin, *Justice for Hedgehogs*, 202.

35. Allegretti, "Can Legal Ethics Be Christian?," 463.

gun-owning) arguments against government intervention in each case, arguments that, even if you disagree with them, you must confess that serious people take seriously.

Most lawyers have some belief that the law is a social good (whether because they see it, on religious grounds, as a gift from God, as an expression of fundamental human rights, or as simply the way in which society is properly ordered.) The real question is how to handle the cases that challenge that belief, or that invoke a higher good. For lawyers that stay in practice, this dilemma will sooner or later be insoluble, unless the system both promotes respect for the law and recognizes values outside of law. Because the lawyer's obligations to his client come subject to his duties to the court, his fiduciary act of subordination, his "humbling" himself, is to a system with the potential for the application of a higher law. Moreover, it constitutes an act of trust by the lawyer: trust in the court to make a just decision.

With that in mind, let's discuss why the Lawyer's Dilemma is peculiarly a religious one.

4

The Dilemma in the Bible: The Book of Micah

The Hebrew prophet Micah relates perhaps the most familiar version of a surprisingly common, albeit a bit peculiar, set piece in the Old Testament. Scholars call it a *riv*: a lawsuit between God and his people Israel. (*Riv* literally means "indictment," or "controversy".) God charges Israel with failing to honor the covenant it made when God rescued the Israelites from Egypt. God orders Israel to do three things as restitution for its breach of the covenant. But God's demand has a puzzling, indeed dismaying, contradiction in it. That contradiction lies at the heart of the ethical challenge for lawyers and forms the basis for my theory that equity remains vital to a functional legal system.

We find the *riv* trope throughout the Hebrew Bible: first in Deuteronomy, and then in 2 Samuel, 2 Chronicles, Isaiah, Jeremiah, Ezekiel, and Hosea, as well as in Micah. Hosea's formulation is typical:

> Hear the word of the Lord, O people of Israel; for the Lord has an indictment against the inhabitants of the land. There is no faithfulness or loyalty, and no knowledge of God in the land. Swearing, lying, and murder, and stealing and adultery break out; bloodshed follows bloodshed. Therefore the land mourns, and all who live in it languish; together with the wild animals and the birds of the air, even the fish of the sea are perishing.[1]

The *riv* form comes out of what scholars call the "vassal treaty" tradition. Early twentieth-century archaeologists uncovered evidence of Hittite treaties, and later (in the 1950s) Assyrian treaties from the reign of Esarhaddon, who ruled Assyria and various tributary states in the seventh

---

1. Hos 4:1–3.

century BCE. The forms of the Hittite and Assyrian treaties vary somewhat, but share basic elements: a dominant ruler (the "suzerain") reminds the subjected peoples of the benefits that the suzerain has conferred on the subject peoples, and the continued benefits of remaining loyal (with corresponding penalties for disloyalty.) Biblical scholars examining the treaties noticed intriguing parallels with covenant language in the Hebrew Bible. The hypothesis was that the *riv*, essentially a suit for breach of promise, used the vassal treaty tradition as a model. Just as a suzerain would warn a vassal kingdom of the consequences of disobeying a treaty, in the Hebrew Bible the prophets, acting as "prosecutors," sent what amounts to an oral "demand letter" to Israel, reminding the people of their obligations under the covenant with Yahweh, followed by formal charges brought by YHWH for failure to heed the warning, with appropriate penalties.

Micah's career dates from the end of the eighth century BCE.[2] Micah was a near-contemporary of Isaiah of Jerusalem and of the prophet Amos. He prophesied at the time of the Assyrian conquest of the northern kingdom, although his prophecies may not have been collected as a book for another hundred years or so.[3] Micah's era was much like ours: tremendous political instability, and great disparity in wealth between the well-to-do and the poor. The Assyrian threat, which ended in the destruction of Samaria and the siege of Jerusalem, lay imminent.

The three Judean kings mentioned in chapter 1, which help us date the book, had mixed careers on the throne. The first, Jotham, "did what was right in the eyes of the Lord" (2 Chr 27:2), but "the people still followed corrupt practices." Jotham's successor, his son Ahaz, was one of Judah's worst kings. He chased after both foreign allies and their gods. Ahaz was succeeded by Hezekiah, portrayed in 2 Kings, 2 Chronicles, and Isaiah as one of Judah's greatest kings, both restoring covenant worship and saving Jerusalem from the Assyrians.[4] Salvation, however, came at a price. Hezekiah's resistance to Assyria, which had made Judah something close to a vassal state when Hezekiah assumed the throne, imposed heavy financial burdens

---

2. We know this because he tells us that he prophesied during the Judean kingships of Jotham, Ahaz, and Hezekiah, which stretched from 759 to 687 BCE.

3. Dempster, *Micah*, 18–19. There is internal evidence that some of the book was written after the Babylonian exile, and scholars differ about which portions were original to Micah, which were compiled from Micah's writings after the fact, and which are new. See generally Williamson, "Micah."

4. Whether he did so by armed resistance or by paying tribute is not clear. 2 Kings portrays the story both ways.

on the people of Judah. This economic suffering forms the backdrop for Micah's prophecy.

Micah, like Amos, is a social critic. Micah's "indictment" charges primarily financial crimes, specifically tied to the Israelites' forfeiture of their inherited properties.[5] The wealthy "covet fields and seize them, and houses, and take them. They defraud people of their homes, they rob them of their inheritance."[6] Some of the behavior Micah condemns—covetousness and theft—violates the Decalogue. Other alleged crimes, notably fraud, come from Mosaic law, but not from the Decalogue.[7] Micah also denounces instances of greed that, strictly speaking, are legal: exercise of foreclosure rights or simply sharp business dealing.[8] Indeed, if the heavy taxes were levied to fight off the Assyrian threat, a political realist would argue that this was sound statecraft. (Notice, again, the parallels to our own day.)

Micah sees all of these as a failure of *mispat*, "justice," which Koch calls "the preservation and promotion of institutional ordinances which are vitally necessary to the community."[9] The financial burdens under Hezekiah's generally sound rule result from his father Ahaz's unfaithfulness to YHWH and his flirtation with foreign powers. Therefore, restoring *mispat* requires not only that financial equity be reestablished, but that the wrongdoers be punished. (Again, some things never change. One thinks of the lingering resentment over President Obama's decision to forego prosecution of individual culprits in the wake of the 2007 financial crisis.) Micah, when he talks about "justice," condemns this kind of behavior.

Micah's "indictment" of Israel alleges more than discrete violations of divine *mispat*. Micah "indicts the organization," as it were. YHWH made a deal with Israel and respected the bargain. Israel did not. In modern parlance, Micah calls Israel a RICO organization. It is in effect the reverse of a class action suit; the class here is unnamed defendants, not plaintiffs. When Micah calls Israel to answer, everyone is implicated, and consequently the earth itself must serve as the jury:

> Hear what the Lord says: Rise, plead your case before the mountains, and let the hills hear your voice. Hear, you mountains, the controversy of the Lord, and you enduring foundations of the

---

5. Koch, *Prophets*, 94.
6. Mic 2:2.
7. Deut 25:13–16 prohibits false weights and measures.
8. Dempster, *Micah*, 95.
9. Koch, *Prophets*, 94.

earth; for the Lord has a controversy with his people, and he will contend with Israel. "O my people, what have I done to you? In what have I wearied you? Answer me! For I brought you up from the land of Egypt and redeemed you from the house of slavery; and I sent before you Moses, Aaron, and Miriam. O my people, remember now what King Balak of Moab devised, what Balaam son of Beor answered him, and what happened from Shittim to Gilgal, that you may know the saving acts of the Lord."[10]

Israel doesn't deny the charges; it proposes restitution, a set of ascending "settlement offers," containing as they escalate more than a hint of cheekiness:

"With what shall I come before the Lord, and bow myself before God on high? Shall I come before him with burnt offerings, with calves a year old? Will the Lord be pleased with thousands of rams, with ten thousands of rivers of oil? Shall I give my firstborn for my transgression, the fruit of my body for the sin of my soul?"[11]

Micah the prophet/prosecutor interrupts, with lines we all know by heart: "He has told you, O mortal, what is good; and what does the Lord require of you but to do justice, and to love mercy, and to walk humbly with your God?"[12]

This verse is exceedingly familiar to us, in contexts from the sublime to the ordinary. It's part of the Episcopal catechism, as a summary of what God requires from his people. Dr. Martin Luther King Jr. frequently used it in his sermons.[13] A Google search for "do justice love mercy" yields forty-three million hits. There are Micah 6:8 T-shirts on Amazon, baseball caps in graduation gift stores, and bumper stickers in card shops. Steven Curtis Chapman made it a verse in his song "The Walk."

But familiarity breeds, if not contempt, at least indifference. We miss how bewildering this command is. How are we to be both just and merciful? Justice, here, means legal justice.[14] The context—a courtroom—proves that.

10. Mic 6:1–5.

11. Mic 6:6–7.

12. This is my own translation, to reflect the current catchphrase. There is more on the translation question in note 16, below.

13. See, e.g., Martin Luther King's "Last Christmas Sermon." In his most famous speech, the "I Have a Dream" address to the March on Washington, he invokes the prayer in chapter 5 of the book of Amos, often a companion piece to Micah 6:8: "we will not be satisfied 'until justice rolls down like waters, and righteousness like a mighty stream.'"

14. The meaning of "biblical justice" or "Old Testament justice" is a continuing debate.

There will be judgment. The "prosecutor" tells us what the crimes are: covetousness (2:2), oppression (2:2), cheating (6:9), deception (6:11), violence (6:12), lying (6:12), covenant unfaithfulness (6:16), bribery (7:3).[15]

Micah, however, goes on. We can hope that God's justice will be tempered with God's mercy:

> Who is a God like you, pardoning iniquity and passing over the transgression of the remnant of your possession? He does not

---

Micah 6:8 often finds itself as a focal point of that debate. Oliver O'Donovan claims that "justice" in the Old Testament refers almost always to *juridical* justice—justice as handed down by courts. O'Donovan, *Desire of the Nations*, 39. On the other hand, Nicholas Wolterstorff argues that "justice" refers in Micah to *primary*, rather than "retributive," justice. Wolterstorff, *Justice: Rights and Wrongs*, 39. But even Wolterstorff takes the position that love does not supersede justice but is part of justice. Stephen Dempster takes something of a middle view. He argues that justice here, and elsewhere in the prophetic books, refers to justice as carried out by rulers: justice enacted, pronounced, and administered. He also argues that justice in this context refers to social justice, the protection of the poor and powerless against the wealthy and powerful. That theme is prominent in the law of Israel, going all the way back to Deuteronomy. We know all too well, however, that modern law does not always, even often, line up behind the underserved. Dempster, *Micah*, 207–12. Thus, reading justice here to mean "primary justice" may make the passage less perplexing, but if anything it enhances the ethical dilemmas for lawyers, by establishing a fundamental dichotomy between judicial and "real" justice. In any event, this book will not adjudicate that dispute.

I also acknowledge that I am deliberately avoiding another scholarly debate, concerning the correct translation of this passage. Both sides of the admonitory phrase are translation in slightly different ways. The RSV and NRSV have "do justice" and "love *kindness*." The New International Version has "*act justly*" and "love mercy." The KJV has "*do justly*" and "love mercy." Modern Jewish scholarship offers a third choice: "goodness." *The Jewish Study Bible (Tanakh Translation)*, 1203n. I leave it to competent textual scholars, which I am not, to decide the best translation. "Mercy" has been traditional for hundreds of years, and is the word commonly thought of in connection with this passage; it will serve for our purposes. I do believe, however, that it is important to capture both the idea of justice in the sense of judgment and mercy in the sense of forgiveness from judgment, because I think they are embedded in the book of Micah and are important to the issues discussed in this book.

15. I have a very sad, personal example of why "justice" necessarily includes legal justice. In 1993, a close friend's son Joey was brutally murdered when a senior in high school, by the mother of Joey's former girlfriend. She was convicted and sentenced to life in prison, but the conviction was overturned on appeal because of a technical defect in the jury charge. For two years, she walked free, but eventually was charged in federal court with using interstate or foreign commerce facilities to arrange the murder. She was convicted again and sentenced to life in a federal penitentiary. During the time she walked free, bumper stickers all over the state called for "Justice for Joey." The people displaying those bumper stickers wanted only one thing. They wanted the culprit convicted and punished. It would be a very odd notion of justice that didn't allow for that.

retain his anger forever, because he delights in showing clemency. He will again have compassion upon us; he will tread our iniquities under foot.[16]

But how do humans accomplish both justice and mercy? This conflict lies at the heart of a paradox central to Christian life in society. Berman, who spent a lifetime writing about the intersection of law and religion, says that "Christianity inherited from Judaism the belief in a God at once both a loving father and a righteous judge—a paradoxical God, who combines both mercy and justice."[17] Much of Berman's work investigates the ways in which Western legal systems have tried to solve this last paradox, and, forgetting the source of the paradox, now find themselves in crisis.

Micah helps us answer the question with which we ended the last chapter: Why does this paradox particularly trouble *Christian* lawyers? As we saw in chapter 2, there are several answers to that question, centering around the theories of "divine command," "divine (or christological) imitation," and "natural law." Divine command theory holds that we are ordered to be both just and merciful. Divine imitation requires that we imitate Jesus, who is both just and merciful. Finally, we operate under a theory of natural, fundamental law that demands both strict justice and mercy.

Micah illustrates all of those. The *riv* trope inherently includes a divine command. When God entered into the Deuteronomic treaty with Moses, God commanded Israel to be both a just and a merciful people, a responsibility that Israel accepted, but then breached. Micah shows us what happens when Israel fails to heed that command. In a more subtle way, Micah also has a divine imitation note. Micah's name is a variation of *mikaya*, meaning "who is like Yah?" That is, who is like God? The final chapter echoes that question: "Who is a God like you?" "No one" is the short answer to that question. But, the Christian obligation to imitate Jesus and the Jewish obligation to imitate YHWH, the heart of divine imitation theology, suggest "everyone, to the extent they can be." Micah's indictment of Israel alleges that Israel failed to follow YHWH's lead in honoring the covenant: YHWH was faithful to his promises to Israel, which answered with unfaithfulness. Finally, Micah also suggests that Israel's failures violate natural law, indeed the nature of reality. Nature itself sits to judge Israel. As it emerges, the punishment God imposes on Israel exquisitely fits the crime, by frustrating the offensive behavior itself: "You shall eat, but not

16. Mic 7:18–19.
17. Berman, *Law and Revolution*, 166.

be satisfied, and there shall be a gnawing hunger within you; you shall put away, but not save, and what you save, I will hand over to the sword. You shall sow, but not reap; you shall tread olives, but not anoint yourselves with oil; you shall tread grapes, but not drink wine."[18] Nature has retaliated against the Israelites, who are now hoist on their own petard.

All three of these have the inherent paradox. If natural laws are foundational, how can two parts of the foundation contradict each other? How can we obey someone that issues contradictory commands, or imitate someone that perfectly embodies two contradictory qualities? We will come back to those questions time and again in this book. The answer Micah gives is that YHWH wants us to rededicate our lives, not offer up ritual sacrifices.[19] In response to an offer of sacrifice, God commands a change in attitude. Israel, which has drifted away from its covenant, offers a cultic form of worship: false worship, because it starts out with material goods and ends up with an abomination (human sacrifice). YHWH asks instead for a different form of sacrifice: self-sacrifice. Israel needs to reform its heart. It needs to humble itself.

But the law expects lawyers to dedicate their professional lives to justice as defined by the law. How do we escape that dilemma? Now it is time to turn to equity.

---

18. Mic 6:14–15.
19. Mays, *Micah*, 142.

5

A Brief History of (Legal) Equity

> Equity is a roguish thing. For Law we have a measure, know what to trust to; Equity is according to the conscience of him that is Chancellor, and as that is larger or narrower, so is Equity. 'T is all one as if they should make the standard for the measure we call a "foot" a Chancellor's foot; what an uncertain measure would this be! One Chancellor has a long foot, another a short foot, a third an indifferent foot. 'T is the same thing in the Chancellor's conscience.
>
> —John Selden, *Table Talk*, 1689

In this chapter, we will discuss equity as a legal concept, before turning in the next chapter to the theological idea of equity. Possessing a Zelig-like ability to show up in different places under different guises, equity has never been solely one or the other. Mark Fortier describes a "culture of equity" that pervaded English religion, law, and politics from the beginning of the sixteenth through the early nineteenth centuries.

Over that time, equity found itself used to support quite different ideas. In the Elizabethan and Jacobean period, the equitable principle of "salus populi suprema lex" ("the common good is the greatest law"), from Cicero's *De Legibus*, justified a strong monarchy, specifically the monarch's discretion to render decisions that bypassed the harshest impacts of common law. By way of contrast, in the turbulent period leading up to the Civil War and during the parliamentary period, the exact same principle was used to limit, not enhance, the authority of the monarch. Thus, John Milton wrote "Parliament is by all equity and right, above a King, and may judge him, whose reasons and pretentions to hold of God only, as his immediate Viceregent, we know how far-fetched they are, and insufficient."[1]

---

1. Milton, *Eikonoclastes*, quoted in Fortier, *Culture of Equity in Restoration*, 167.

Later, in the Restoration period, the tide turned again, and royalists used equity polemically to promote "moderate" and "reasonable" adherence to tradition, as opposed to "radical revolutionary" tendencies which, they said, culminated in regicide.[2]

For the moment, let's concern ourselves with the strictly legal aspect of equity. For as long as there have been laws—long before, in fact, there existed anything that could be called a legal *system*—jurists and philosophers have felt the need for an escape valve, we might call it, from strict enforcement of law in exceptional cases.[3] Time and again, legal systems develop this characteristic in stages. First comes the felt need for promulgated rules of conduct—laws, as it were—rather than social control based solely on adjudication. Eventually, those in authority realize that universal rules of conduct lead to unintended consequences. Given the almost infinite complexities of life, some conflicts stress the logic of a general rule, grating against non-legal notions of fairness or appropriateness. The law attempts to minimize those hard cases the only way it can, through additional rules, either gradations of culpability, such as distinctions between murder, manslaughter, negligent homicide, and mere accidental death, or exceptions to the general rule, such as requirements of mental capacity. No matter how many subcategories we create, however, some cases don't fit well into any of them. Therefore, societies develop ways to counterbalance strict enforcement of the law. One of those ways has come to be called "equity."

Famous though English courts of equity may be, this is neither original nor unique to England. As Fortier says, "equity is not indigenous to England; it wanders there from many places: from Athens, from Rome, from the Holy Land, from Wittenberg and Geneva."[4] Judaism called the principle *lifnim meshurat hadim*, "beyond the strict line of the law."[5] Rabbinic tradition locates this concept in Torah itself, specifically Deuteronomy 6:18: "Do what is right and good in the sight of the Lord."[6] Torah (especially the book of Deuteronomy) being the source of Jewish law, all other laws had to be read in a manner consistent with it, and no specific law could be read or enforced in such a way as to conflict with it. This

2. Fortier, *Culture of Equity in Restoration*, 25.
3. Berman, *Law and Revolution*, 49.
4. Fortier, *Culture of Equity in Early Modern England*, 3.
5. Diamond, "Talmudic Jurisprudence," 616.
6. Ramban (Nachamanides), *Commentary on the Torah—Leviticus,* quoted in Diamond, "Talmudic Jurisprudence," 617.

principle coming from divine law, it even influenced Jewish understandings of YHWH's nature. The Talmud relates a story in which a rabbi asks of YHWH: "[May] Thy mercy . . . prevail over Thy other attributes, so that Thou mayest deal with Thy children according to the attribute of mercy and mayest on their behalf, stop short of the limit of strict justice!" YHWH, the story goes, nodded in agreement.[7]

From Jerusalem we move to Athens. Aristotle wrote about *epiekieia*, the bending of a general rule to fit the exigencies of a special case. Aristotle defined "justice" as "equality"—"treating like things alike." An ambiguity in this famous expression troubles civilization to this day: What makes two things (or persons) "like"? How much, if at all, should we consider the different abilities and circumstances between individuals, rather than treating all persons precisely the same, regardless of contingencies? Aristotle distinguished between "distributive" justice, which takes into account individual differences in handing out rewards and burdens, and "commutative" justice, which acts in a strict proportionality. Distributive justice for the Greeks was not an ancient leveling device; it was primarily concerned with socially or politically administered rewards, which were to be handed out according to *merit*, not need. *Commutative* (or *corrective*) justice governed the affairs between individuals.

Aristotelean equity, part of commutative justice, allowed departure from what Aristotle calls strict "legal justice," as the exigencies of a case required. Here are some examples: a person holds for safekeeping someone else's sword. Athenian law made it a crime to refuse to return bailed property on demand. Must the bailee return the sword if the bailee knows that the bailor intends to use the sword to murder someone? Aristotle says no; it would be unjust to hold the bailee guilty of violating the statute. Another example: the law enhances the severity of a conviction for assault if the assailant uses a metal object in the assault. How about, Aristotle asks, a defendant who slaps someone while wearing a ring on his finger? Once again, the statute doesn't apply. In each case, Aristotle focused on the legislator's intent: the facts present a case that the legislator never thought of and would have made exception for had he thought of it. Equity requires the judge to rule as the legislator would have if confronted with these facts.

We get our word "equity" from Roman law's concept of *aequitas*, meaning "justice" or "fairness." Rome, in fact, personified equity as a deity, "Aequitas Augusti." We see her depicted similarly to Justitia, the goddess

---

7. Diamond, "Talmudic Jurisprudence," 620.

of justice, which has become the "Lady Justice" familiar to us today. Both hold scales, but where Justitia holds a sword, representing the power of the emperor to punish, Aequitas holds a cornucopia, representing the abundance that comes from equitable society. The early Roman legal system, seeking to fit judgment to the particulars of the case, created something like a "minister of equity," the *praetor peregrinus* (also known at times as the *praetor urbanus*).[8] Originally the official in charge of suits involving non-Romans, the *praetor peregrinus* eventually became a sort of overseer of the judicial process, representing the interests of fairness, natural law, and equity (the "*ius gentium*").

In Germany, legal scholarship based on Lutheran theology developed its own theory of equity. Philip Melanchthon, Luther's great protégé, took a conventional Aristotelean view of equity as necessary to resolve the unusual case not contemplated by general law. Johann Oldendorp, a generation later, elevated the discussion to a view of equity as the spirit of the law, calling on judges in every case to apply law according to a "judgment of the soul"—that is, according to conscience as well as strict law.[9]

Finally, equity was an important principle of *canon* law, the laws and regulations adopted by the Roman Catholic church. For centuries in Western Europe, canon law governed not only the internal operation of the church, but also many things that today we would consider purely secular, including marriage, contracts, and inheritance. For a variety of reasons, England never adopted canon law as its own legal system, as some European countries effectively did. However, prior to the Reformation, English jurists were learned in both common and canon law, and canon law principles, notably equity, found their way into both the content and the interpretation of medieval English law, either directly or through the influence of continental legal scholarship, which looked back to Roman law.[10]

Therefore, prominent as "courts of equity" and "chancery" are in English history and literature, England cannot take credit for inventing the legal concept of equity. Once equity got to England, however, it took root. Over time, it went from being a method of interpreting common law, available to all courts, to the establishment of a separate equity jurisdiction, intended to

---

8. Re, "Roman Contribution," 481; Taylor, "Fusion of Law and Equity," 21–22.

9. Space does allow giving Oldendorp the attention he deserves. See John Witte's *Law and Protestantism*, especially 154–68, for a full discussion of Oldendorp's contribution to German legal theory.

10. See, generally, "Medieval English Equity" in Berman, *Faith and Order*.

answer when strict pleading and procedural rules paralyzed other courts. Equity powers were vested in the Lord Chancellor, initially an ecclesiastic and then (beginning with Thomas More) a lawyer. Then, in the nineteenth century, equity jurisdiction was reintegrated into common law courts.

One of the traditional defenses of equity is that it promotes the common good. There were also those, however, that thought that the law itself represented the common good. John Selden, he of the famous "Chancellor's foot" quote, argued just this. Law representing a compact between persons for the common good, abandoning law would always serve private, never public, interests.[11]

Equity was, however, almost from the beginning a controversial part of English law. Berman calls it "probably the most mysterious character in the detective story of English legal history."[12] There were those that thought that equity was the perfection of the law, or, alternately, that it was the higher law that came in to rescue positive law from committing injustice. On the other hand, there were those that didn't care for equity at all. They thought that it was "roguish," an excuse to avoid law rather than perfect it.

The English lawyer and writer Christopher St. Germain, in the 1530s, generally gets credit for starting the theoretical study of equity in England. His book *Doctor and Student* takes the form of a dialogue between a Doctor of Divinity and a law student about the nature, foundation, and object of law. Equity, the doctor tells the student (in Aristotelean fashion), follows the intent rather than the letter of the law, when the generality of a rule leads to a result that would offend either the law of God or the law of reason.[13] Equity has a "right wiseness" that tempers judgment with the "sweetness of mercy."[14] If, St. Germain writes, any law excluded such exceptions, it would be "manifestly unreasonable," and persons would be excused from following it by the "law of reason."[15] St. Germain may have been the first, but he was far from the last, commentator on the subject. Some were responses to St. Germain, attacking the whole Chancery system. Some were rejoinders to the rejoinders, including a rebuttal by St. Germain himself. Some were more theoretical ruminations on the interplay of law and equity, or law and religion.

11. Selden, *Table Talk*, 47–48.
12. Berman, *Faith and Order*, 55.
13. St. Germain, *Doctor and Student*, 45.
14. St. Germain, *Doctor and Student*, 44.
15. St. Germain, *Doctor and Student*, 48.

The theories of English equity, and the conflict between law and equity, were set out in *The Earl of Oxford's Case*, which tested the limits of the rule, long established but frequently ignored, that Chancery lacked jurisdiction of appeals from common law courts. The facts are somewhat complex, but worth examining. Magdalen College (Oxford) owned seven acres of land in Covent Garden that it wished to transfer to Spinola, a Genoese merchant, in satisfaction of a debt. A statute prohibited colleges from transferring land. The master of Magdalen College came up with the idea of conveying the land to the queen, since the statute did not expressly prohibit transfers to the monarch. The queen then transferred the land to Spinola, who in turn sold it to Edward de Vere, Earl of Oxford. The earl built houses on it and leased one of them to a gentleman named Warren. Magdalen College (in what was surely not its most ennobling moment) decided on further reflection that the transfer to the queen (for which the college had been paid) was void after all, claimed title to the land, and leased Warren's house to one "Smith." Smith and Warren got into a lawsuit over possession of the house, and the King's Bench ruled that the transfer to the queen had indeed violated the statute, making the earl's title (and by extension Warren's lease) void. Henry de Vere, the new earl (his father Edward having died) filed a petition in Chancery to enjoin the enforcement of the King's Bench order. Lord Ellesmere, the chancellor, issued the injunction, holding that the law of God,[16] conscience, reason, and fairness all led to the conclusion that the college had received valuable consideration for the land, the earl had paid valuable consideration for the land, and that therefore equity should protect the earl's interests and prevent unjust enrichment of the college. (There seems to have been little doubt that the transfer to the queen was solely intended to circumvent the statute.) There now being two competing final judgments, the case went to the Crown (by this time James I), who held in favor of the chancellor's order, saying:

> (A)s mercy and justice be the true supports of our Royal Throne; and it properly belongeth to our princely office to take care and provide that our subjects have equal and indifferent justice ministered to them; and that when their case deserveth to be relieved in course of equity by suit in our Court of Chancery, they should not be abandoned and exposed to perish under the rigor and

---

16. Specifically Deut 28:30: "He that builds a house ought to dwell in it."

extremity of our laws, we . . . do approve, ratifie[sic] and confirm, as well the practice of our Court of Chancery.[17]

Thus was reaffirmed the supremacy of equity.

However, because of the ambivalence towards a "pure" form of equitable jurisprudence, something unexpected began to happen. Equity, the judicial function that originated in response to the rules-induced legal sclerosis in the common law courts, started forming its own rules. Fortier says that "in the 18th Century equity as exceptional is being replaced by a sense of equity as regular and common; equity as outside of rules and law is being replaced by the organization of equity as rule and law."[18] Some commentators argued that this was an illusion. The only rule in equity court was that a decision had to conform to the law of God (or of reason, depending on the theology of the commentator) and that the new equity "rules" were simply manifestations of that principle. That being the case, equity, which had been concerned with avoiding injustice in specific cases, found itself looking more and more towards the common good rather than the individual. So, Lord Nottingham, Lord Chancellor in the second half of the seventeenth century, was to say that the conscience employed by the chancery court was a general "conscience of the community" rather than the individual conscience of the judge, and that in fact there were certain things beyond the court's power, even if they would shock the "inward and regular conscience." On the other hand, Richard Francis, in his popular *Maxims of Equity*, published in 1728, said that a ruling truly based on conscience by definition could not be arbitrary, because such a ruling would be "determine(d) according to the original and eternal Rules of Justice."[19]

Dissatisfaction with the "unpredictability" of equity continued, however. Jeremy Bentham, who never had a kind thing to say about equity courts, thought that the jurisdictional split was nothing but a historical accident, and an unfortunate one at that. In an early preview of legal positivism, Bentham thought that an overarching set of statutes could replace not only equity procedure but the common law as well.[20] Bentham was not alone in his disgust with the chancery courts. Dickens's *Jarndyce v. Jarndyce* in *Bleak House*, which goes on for generations and then ends as moot when costs have devoured the entire estate, was not unheard of in real-life

17. Cary, *Causes in Chancery*, 181–82.
18. Fortier, *Culture of Equity in Restoration*, 8.
19. Francis, *Maxims of Equity*, 5.
20. Riley, "Jeremy Bentham and Equity," 40.

litigation. In fact, as Fortier shows, equity gradually transformed again from a legal to more of a sociopolitical theory, supporting general progressive social causes, rather than acting as a jurisdiction available to aggrieved or set-upon individuals.[21]

For at least two centuries, common law and equity judges lived in an uneasy truce, with occasional open warfare over the principles of strict enforcement versus judicial discretion.[22] Eventually, the *jurisdictional* separation of equitable and common law courts was abolished.[23] Certain legal relationships (e.g., fiduciary and trusteeship), substantive law (such as promissory estoppel and unconscionability), and legal remedies (e.g., injunction) that originated in equity jurisdiction survived the merger of the two courts, but as rules rather than as powers. The merger of common law and equity jurisdiction gave a single court both the authority to announce principles of law applicable to future cases, and to depart from settled law in the name of true justice, albeit in highly restricted and regular ways rather than ad hoc.

For a long time, despite the pronouncement of King James, debate raged about whether common law or equity won the battle. Section 25 of the Judicature Act says that equity preempts common law rules in the case of conflict. However, this is increasingly done through general rules, rather than on a case-by-case basis. Thus, in the early part of the twentieth century, Dean Roscoe Pound wondered whether equity had decayed to the point of uselessness.[24] Little has happened to allay those concerns. *Law and Contemporary Problems* held an entire symposium on the question in the early 1990s. One contributor (Douglas Laycock) proclaimed that equity had triumphed.[25] Other commentators, however, expressed serious doubts, of the sort expressed in this book. That can only be because, even after

---

21. Fortier, *Culture of Equity in Restoration*, 14–15.

22. In addition to the refinement of legal theory, there were political and theological changes. England moved from a theory of royal law, as expressed by James I, under which the crown had absolute power (being ordained by God) but also the obligation to use that power justly, to a system that invested ever more power in the parliament. Seeing such a move, the crown would have great motivation to build judicial flexibility into the system, both (from a cynical perspective) to preserve the crown's own power, and (theologically) to make the law more a reflection of divine law, and to protect the crown's soul.

23. In England, via the Judicature Act of 1875; in the United States federal courts, via the Conformity Act of 1934 and the Federal Rules of Civil Procedure of 1938.

24. Pound, "Decadence of Equity."

25. Laycock, "Triumph of Equity."

all these years, the participants appear to talk about different things when they speak of equity. No doubt each of them understood what he or she meant, and what the other meant. Professor Laycock was clear, in saying that equity had triumphed, that he meant the remedies and other formal aspects that the English Chancery Courts offered as an alternative to common law pleading. He had little to say, and most of that unflattering, about the ameliorative, discretionary, face of equity. In other words, equity has triumphed even though it has clearly become less—I can think of no better way to say it—*equitable*.

Why? Because without an institutional target such as the court of chancery, the fear of "unbridled" judicial discretion has manifested itself philosophically rather than structurally. The target now is judicial discretion itself, rather than a discretionary court. For example: injunction, one of the hallmarks of equitable power in the Chancery Court, in Texas (my state of practice) gets an entire chapter in the state Civil Practice and Remedies Code, statutory attention in twenty-six other codes (and fourteen times in the uncodified statutes), plus its own section in the Texas Rules of Civil Procedure. I suspect Texas is typical in this regard. Dean Pound was right. If equity has won the war, the legislature has dictated the peace accord.

In fact, the centuries-long balance between strict enforcement and equitable discretion teeters: politically, from resentment (both liberal and conservative) of "activist" judges, governmentally, as legislation more and more takes the place of common law and even equitable precedent,[26] and (most ominously) philosophically, as all of these trends coalesce to cast suspicion on a fundamental value—equitable discretion—that has resided in all bodies of law for two millennia or more.

This shift carries ethical repercussions for the lawyer. Advocates swear to zealous and single-minded pursuit of the client's goals. Frequently, however, the goals of the clients, although legally sanctioned, offend the moral sensibilities of the lawyer. For Christians, those would be sensibilities of mercy, redemption, and forgiveness. As we saw in chapter 2, the eighteenth century assumed that the justness of a claim was part of a judge's concern. In the nineteenth century, the earliest professional oaths required a lawyer to examine the "justness," i.e., the fairness, of a claim, in addition to its legality. With rare exception, that no longer

---

26. Section 65.001 of the Texas injunction statute says that "the principles governing courts of equity govern injunction proceedings if not in conflict with this chapter or other law." What that seems to mean is that equitable relief always requires the historic principles of equity, such as irreparable injury, plus any statutory add-ons.

obtains.[27] Does this require lawyers to abdicate their personal, in favor of legal, ethics, choosing judgment over mercy?

There has been no lack of attention paid to this problem.[28] We rarely recognize, however, the problem's true source. Both the structure and underlying principles of our legal system come from a time that viewed law as divinely inspired, although the substance of laws it carries out is now regarded as entirely secular. In the process, we have forgotten the centrality of equity as a value in all Western legal systems.

As we have seen, philosophers across history have seen the necessity of exceptions to the law in onerous cases. In Western Europe, where laws bore religious significance, legal equity was grounded in theology as well as philosophy. Lately, as jurisprudence becomes secularized, equity comes to be regarded as an artifact of the newly abrogated religious grounding of law—even though equity was a component of Greek and Roman legal philosophy also. Indeed, Cicero said that it was the glue that holds society together.[29] As a result, we find ourselves in a process both incompatible with religious theories of equitable justice and out of touch with a foundational principle of all legal systems. To those foundations we now turn.

---

27. Andrews, "Lawyer's Oath," 24.

28. See, e.g. Moliterno, "Lawyer Creeds and Moral Seismography"; Floyd, "Practice of Law as a Vocation."

29. Cicero, *De Oficcius*, quoted in Haas, *Concept of Equity*, 20.

6

The Theology of Equity: Thomas Aquinas and John Calvin

Mark Fortier, the author of two books on equity in English law, literature, and culture, says, "(Equity) is both a word and a set of ideas, and... this distinction needs to be made and maintained."[1] It is, says Fortier, a "keyword," to use philosopher Raymond Williams' term.[2] Fortier, quoting from W. B. Gallie, calls it "an essentially contested concept," a term with many uses, none of which can be asserted as "correct."[3] As we say, for the Hebrews, it meant something like moral uprightness. For the Romans, it meant fairness, equality, or impartiality.[4] For Aristotle, equity was both a legal concept—exception to positive law as a way of avoiding injustice—and a personal quality, meaning prudence, moderation, and kindness.[5] These are sometimes referred to as the functional and the material aspects of equity.

They both strive towards what Aristotle called absolute or higher justice (higher in comparison to legal justice), but they do so in different ways. Here's a common (if trivial) real-life example. Like many lawyers and other professionals, I have quite a lot of business travel on airplanes. What's more, in the Age of Mobility, most of my immediate family, including a grandson, live 1,500 miles away, so I have regular occasions for happier travel also. Thus, I regularly witness the inevitable battle for overhead luggage space—what I call the "bin wars." Now, the carry-on rules are quite clear: no more than two items, only one in the overhead bin, and nothing that exceeds certain

---

1. Fortier, *Culture of Equity in Restoration*, 2.
2. Williams, *Keywords*.
3. Fortier, *Equity in Early Modern England*, 21.
4. Fortier, *Equity in Early Modern England*, 7.
5. Aristotle, *Nicomachean Ethics*, 98–99.

dimensions. Nonetheless, the ways in which people attempt to work within, bend, or evade the rules pay a rather base tribute to human ingenuity. To wit: If one only has a single bag, may it go up in the bin, even if it would fit under the seat? At what point may one decide that there's enough leftover bin space to safely put a second bag up top? May one put one's bag in front of someone else's without permission? Is permission needed to move someone else's bag (within the same bin) to free up space for an additional item? Am I limited to the bin directly over my seat, or may I put a bag in a bin in the front of the plane and then move to a seat in the back?

Sad to say, I've seen arguments over all these questions. I, ruefully, confess that I've participated in a couple myself. The "bin wars" illustrate both faces of Aristotelean equity (or its absence.) Some skirmishes involve the interpretation of the rule for a specific situation. Am I truly not supposed to put two bags overhead, even if the plane is half-empty and everyone has plenty of room? I would hope not, because the rule's purpose is to allocate a scarce resource; on this flight, there is no scarcity. Other conflicts go to the selfish or selfless motivation for an action. What are the ethics of putting my single bag in the bin, leaving the space in front of me free, so that I have room to stretch out? The rules certainly allow it. But if it means that the family boarding last has to gate-check its diaper bag, what sort of person does that make me? ("Judge not," one whispers to no one in particular, seeing a fellow passenger do this.)

When Christianity developed its own version of "equity," it drew on both of those meanings. Christian theories of law consider equity a part of law; either a counterbalance to strict enforcement of human law (*one* goal of the law), or as ideal justice (*the* goal of the law, reflecting divine law). Christian ethics feature equity in Aristotle's second sense, as a virtue, a personal quality that inhabits and transforms the entire person and, one hopes, the entire community. In that sense, it is an *alternative* to (human) law. The parable of the unforgiving servant is a familiar example.[6] The servant forgiven a ten-thousand-talent debt by his master wouldn't forgive a hundred-denarii debt from another servant.[7] The parable doesn't claim that the servant had no legal claim to his debt. It makes the case for the higher way of mercy over

---

6. Matt 18:21–35.

7. A talent, I am told was six thousand denarii. So, the one debt was six hundred thousand times larger than the other!

justice. (Lawyers will also recognize this early example of the maxim that one must do equity in order to receive it.)[8]

We will examine equity in the first sense through the writings of the Dominican friar Thomas Aquinas (one of the four Latin "doctors of the church"). The second, personal sense finds a full expression in the French theologian and reformer John Calvin, author of *The Institutes of the Christian Religion*. In the next chapter we will follow Aquinas's and Calvin's thoughts on equity in the writings of their English heirs, for Aquinas the English divine Richard Hooker, author of *The Laws of Ecclesiastical Polity*, and for Calvin the Cambridge-educated English cleric William Perkins.

I do not suggest that equity in the first sense is a purely Catholic concept, the second a Reformed one. That would be a major oversimplification. Nevertheless, purely for convenience, I will from time to time refer to equity in the first sense as "Thomistic" and the second as "Calvinist." Both senses have theological bases, and it matters, when we talk about equity, to distinguish whether we use the concept as Aquinas did, or Calvin. Both are relevant, but for different reasons.

Aquinas and the Classical Tradition

Thomas Aquinas, whose writings form a bridge between classical and early modern philosophy, and also between pagan and Christian moral theology, drew heavily on the Aristotelean concept of *epieikeia*.[9] Aquinas was the greatest of the "scholastic" theologians, who emphasized the importance of reason and reasoning as understanding the world and God's relation to it and to man, including the nature and source of law. Scholasticism dominated Western universities—indeed was central to the foundation of those universities—for hundreds of years. The scholastics, including Aquinas, endured claims that they were not truly Christian at all, but pagan philosophers in Christian clothing. Many of the early Protestant reformers particularly detested scholasticism as contrary to the doctrine of "sola scriptura": sole reliance on Scripture for revelation. That criticism is utterly unfair, Aquinas's concept of law being deeply intertwined with his concept of God.

---

8. Snell, *Principles of Equity*, 42–44.

9. Aquinas uses the term *epikeia*, apparently a cognate of the Aristotelian *epieikeia*. For consistency in this book I will stick to the term "equity," even though Aquinas and Calvin meant somewhat different things by the term.

Aquinas, born somewhere between 1224 and 1226 to an aristocratic family in Castle Roccasecca in central Italy, was undoubtedly the greatest medieval theologian, and arguably the most important Roman Catholic theologian of any era. He was also, as even non-theist philosophers now admit, among the most significant philosophers in the entire European canon. Aquinas joined the Dominican order in his late teens, over the objection of his family, who had higher ambitions for him (probably to be the abbot of the great Benedictine monastery of Monte Cassino). Aquinas's family felt so strongly about it that they held Thomas in effective house arrest for the better part of a year before relenting. Once allowed to fulfill his Dominican vocation, he dedicated his life to writing and teaching at Paris, Naples, Orvietto, Rome, then back to Paris and Naples. Aquinas taught first university students, and then fellow Dominican friars. Among his many works, two are most well-known: the *Summa Contra Gentiles*, in which Aquinas attempts to prove the existence of God based on personal observation and philosophical reasoning, and above all the *Summa Theologiae*, a massive work in which Aquinas tried to summarize the whole of Christian theology, from a view that was completely orthodox but decidedly Aristotelean. We don't precisely know why Aquinas wrote the *Summa Theologiae*—that is to say, we are not entirely sure who its intended audience was—but many scholars believe that Aquinas intended it for Dominican novices, rather than advanced students.[10] It is not entirely clear when he began it, although it's generally believed that it was in 1265, in Rome. He worked on it until the end of 1273, a few months before his death in March 1274.

Aquinas grouped the *Summa*, which he never finished, into four parts. The grouping perplexes the new reader a bit. The titles refer to *Prima Pars* (First Part), *Secundae Pars* (Second Part), and *Tertia Pars* (Third Part), but the second part, the longest, is subdivided between the *Prima Secundae Partis* (the First Part of the Second Part), which treats morality in general, and the *Secunda Secundae Partis* (the Second Part of the Second Part), which takes up specific virtues. The First Part is pure theology, the nature of God and God's creation. The Third Part, which Aquinas left unfinished, moves to the person of Christ, and then the Sacraments.[11] The First Part of the Second Part includes an entire section on law, including

---

10. See Davies, *Thomas Aquinas's Summa Theologiae*, especially chapter 1, on which I have drawn for this brief introduction to Aquinas.

11. As if it were not confusing enough, a portion of the Third Part is designated the "Supplement."

the essence of law, various types of law, and the Old (i.e., Hebrew) and New (i.e., gospel) law, that today is referred to informally as Aquinas's *Treatise on Law*.[12]

Why would Aquinas, a theologian, care about law? To answer that question, we must look outside the *Treatise on Law* to Aquinas's views on the nature of God, the nature of man, and the relation between God and man. Aquinas saw that God has reason and will; that God's will causes all things; that God acts reasonably and purposefully in accordance with God's will; that things are alive only insofar as they exist in God; and that the world makes sense only because it stems from God's reason. (This avoids a persistent problem for modern atheist philosophy. Why do the same rules of physics apply everywhere in the universe? In other words, why does the world make sense? Aquinas, deeply aware of the problem, finds the answer in his understanding of God.) Therefore, God's reason forms the basis for all law.

Aquinas grouped "law" into four categories. The highest, what he called "eternal" law, was nothing less than the mind of God—divine wisdom. Eternal law might be considered the logic and order behind creation itself, as understood by God. Aquinas calls the second type of law "divine law." These classifications can be confusing, because both eternal law and divine law come from God. Eternal law is divine reasoning *as perceived by God*. Divine law is divine reasoning *as conveyed to humans*. Think of it, perhaps, as the difference between geometric theorems themselves and as described in a geometry textbook. For Christians, Scripture epitomizes divine law.

Third comes what Aquinas calls "natural law." To the postmodern ear, natural law sounds an awful lot like the laws of nature: gravity and Newton's laws of motion and so forth. Or it might sound like human and animal instincts. Aquinas meant something different. When he spoke of natural law, he meant human participation in the eternal law. Basic moral premises that flowed logically from eternal law are implanted in all humans. It is part of our nature, inherent in the way we view the world more than knowledge we possess. Thus, the political philosopher J. Budziszewski calls his book on natural law *What We Can't Not Know*. The highest of these principles was that we are always to seek the good and avoid the evil. Aquinas posited a human quality, *synderesis*, the ability to know natural law.

---

12. The entire *Summa* is available online at www.newadvent.org/summa. In this book, all references to the *Summa* are to that version. The portions commonly referred to as the "Treatise on Law" start at Question 90 of the "Prima Secundae Partis."

Finally, we get to Aquinas's fourth category, human law, the law that lawyers deal with in court. Law, according to Aquinas's famous definition, is "an ordinance of reason for the common good of a community, promulgated by the person or body responsible for looking after the community."[13] Aquinas, unlike many theologians, saw human law not simply as necessary, but as a good thing. Aquinas did not believe that human societies could be governed directly by divine law, or solely by natural law. Although human law flows from natural law, societies differ, so human law must address differing conditions; there are no "one-size-fits-all" bodies of human law. Instead, human laws are outworkings of natural law, devised by human reason. Humans, being created in the image of God, are to use their reason and will to conform human law to divine and natural law. Statutory law, then, must be consistent with natural law, and it has to be reasonable.

Aquinas said that human beings are created to be happy. Ultimate happiness lies in obtaining a vision of the divine essence, but earthly things, including peace, orderliness, safety, and basic necessities, are essential to ultimate happiness, and therefore all form part of what Aquinas called the common good. Human law's purpose is promoting the common good.[14] Some laws are inherently opposed to the common good, by being aimed at the glorification of the sovereign only. Other laws may be hypothetically aimed at the common good but in the process treat certain persons unfairly or impose burdens unequally in the name of the common good.[15] Any law that fails to promote the common good fails in its essential purposes. Such laws, Aquinas rather remarkably said, simply were not binding on a person's conscience.

Aquinas, like Aristotle, thought that human laws should be enacted legislatively rather than made through case-by-case judgement.[16] He wrote: "it is better that all things be regulated by law, than left to be decided by judges," because (1) "it is easier to find a few wise men competent to frame right laws, than to find the many who would be necessary to judge aright of each single case"; (2) because legislators have the luxury of reflection, whereas judges have to make on-the-spot decisions; and (3) because legislators "judge in the abstract and of future events" and

---

13. Aquinas, *ST* I-II, question 90, article 4.
14. Aquinas, *ST* I-II, question 90, article 2.
15. Aquinas, *ST* I-II, question 96, article 4.
16. Aquinas, *ST* I-II, question 95, article 1. See also Chroust, "Common Good and the Problem of Equity," 114.

are therefore less likely swayed by emotion or prejudice.[17] Aquinas never claimed, however, that general law could achieve specific justice.[18] Human law will always be imperfect, because no human creation achieves perfection. Humans, after all, see darkly, as looking in a glass.[19] That said, Aquinas also saw that the diversity of the human condition made it impossible to craft a law that would fairly decide every case.[20] Sometimes, the application of general law frustrates its purpose. Therefore, Aquinas proposed the concept of *epikeia* or equity, which flows from "the dictates of justice and the common good" rather than the strict imposition of human law.[21] Because the possibility of human actions are "innumerable in their diversity," it "was not possible to lay down rules of law that would apply in every single case. Legislators in framing laws attend to what commonly happens: although if the law be applied to certain cases it will frustrate the equality of justice and be injurious to the common good, which the law has in view."[22] Aquinas then gives Aristotle's example of the murderous bailee who wants to redeem his sword. The flaw lies not in the law, and equity does not pass judgment on the law. Rather, equity fulfills the underlying intent of the law to effect justice.

Because all law stems from reason, "human intellectual participation in God's eternal law"[23] in Aquinas's terms, inequitable laws and inequitable application of law, in failing to meet their purpose, offend God.[24] This makes the pursuit of equity mandatory rather than aspirational, and makes following the letter of the law to an unjust result sinful.[25] Justice, for Aquinas, was both a philosophical principle ("rendering to each one his right") and a virtue (the habit of doing so).[26] Equity, not an alternative to the law, or even a commentary on the law, epitomizes a higher form of

---

17. Aquinas, *ST* I-II, question 95, article 1.

18. We shall see that legislatures deciding particular cases troubles O'Donovan theologically, and complicates the ethical dilemma for lawyers.

19. 1 Cor 13:12.

20. Aquinas, *ST* II-II, question 120, article 1.

21. Aquinas, *ST* II-II, question 120, article 1.

22. Aquinas, *ST* II-II, question 120, article 1.

23. Porter, *Ministers of the Law*, 89.

24. Aquinas, *ST* I-II, question 90, article 1.

25. Aquinas, *ST* II-II, question 120, Article 1, reply to objection 3.

26. Aquinas, *ST* II-II, question 58, article 1.

"legal justice" that remains a part of overall justice.[27] Moreover, Aquinas, five-hundred-plus years before Austin and Bentham, saw equity as a kind of modesty embedded in the law itself,[28] defeating overly ambitious claims for the letter of the law.[29] One way to understand the problems caused by the abandonment of common-law powers, with their element of judicial discretion, in favor of strict statutory law, would be to see it as a rejection of Aquinas's admonition that the law remain modest. The absence of that modesty—or to put it another way, blind confidence in the powers of the law—constitutes a sort of idolatry; it expects the legislature to do something—cure every specific problem with a general solution—that lies beyond the power of even the wisest humans.

Aquinas includes the discussion of equity, indeed the entire discussion of justice, in his section on virtues, rather than the section on law. But he makes clear that "equity" is not a personal virtue that competes with the requirements of justice, but a philosophical "virtue," comparable to what consistency would be for logic. It is the higher form of justice, a necessary element to a sound legal system. It is not, in the way he uses it, a moral virtue. "Clemency" and "meekness" are personal ones, opposed to the vices of anger and cruelty. They form the attitude with which we approach justice, such as by denying us pleasure in seeing another punished, but they are not part of Aquinas's theory of justice.[30]

To sum up: Aquinas found equity to be essential to the true purpose of the law, the common good. Equity operates within the law, not as an alternative to it. Equity comes from "reason," the human connection to God's eternal law. Therefore, humans are obligated to pursue equity. Finally, in Aquinas's view, equity implements the highest form of justice, which pure "legal" justice cannot promise for all cases.

---

27. Aquinas, *ST* II-II, question 120, Article 2, reply to objection 3.
28. Aquinas, *ST* II-II, question 120, Article 2, reply to objection 3.
29. Aquinas, *ST* II-II, question 120, Article 2, objection 3 and reply to objection 3.
30. Aquinas, *ST* II-II, question 157.

Calvin and The Reformed Tradition

John Calvin (1509–64) was the most significant figure (save Luther himself) in the Protestant Revolution, and at least Luther's equal as a theologian. Calvin's *Institutes of the Christian Religion* could be regarded as the Protestant version of Aquinas's *Summa Theologiae*: a summing-up of the entire Christian religion, in this case from the Reformed perspective.

Calvin began his studies at the University of Paris with an eye towards the priesthood, then at the age of nineteen switched to the study of law, first at Orleans and then at Bourges. Shifting gears again, he returned to Paris and the humanists, learning Greek and studying Plato and Aristotle, in preparation for a career as a humanist-style close reader of and commentator on Scripture. Over time, however, Calvin became more and more convinced of the justice of Luther's criticism of the Catholic Church, and at some point he "converted" to Protestantism. (Calvin says little about his conversion, so we don't know whether this was a gradual process or more of a Damascus-type incident.) Calvin spent several years on the run because of religious persecution, from Paris to Basel to Geneva to Strasbourg and then back to Geneva. On return to Geneva, the city acquiesced in Calvin's vision of a theocratic form of government, and he remained there for the balance of his life.

Calvin's first scholarly project, a sign of things to come, was a commentary on Seneca's *De Clementia* (*On Mercy*).[31] Like Aquinas, in those early days Calvin saw equity as a part of and perfection of the law. In his *Commentaries on Seneca*, he writes of "what equity and right are, in contrast to the letter or rigor of the law. For while law demands complete and unwavering rectitude, equity [*aequitas*] remits something of the law."[32] Seneca, he says, recognizes that perfect justice stands well neigh impossible, so that the judge should always err on the side of clemency rather than cruelty.

Calvin's early immersion in classical authors stood him in good stead even as his interests turned towards theology. His view of equity was multifarious, and incorporated much of the Aristotelean view, carried forward by Aquinas, of equity as a departure from strict law in the interest of mercy and fairness. Calvin, however, also emphasized equity as a personal quality, similar to Aristotle's second concept of the term. Calvin's view of equity, as Aquinas's, comes from his theology of God. Where Aquinas's equity was

---

31. Haas, *Concept of Equity*, 10.
32. Calvin, *Commentary on Seneca's De Clementia*, 181.

tied to God as reason, Calvin's stems from God's standing as a judge both merciful and just towards hopelessly sinful humans. If God were perfectly but solely just, none of us would escape divine punishment. (One remembers Hamlet's admonition to Polonius to treat the players much better than they deserve, for "use every man after his desert, and who should 'scape whipping").[33] It follows, then, that humans, created in the image of God, should likewise temper their justice with mercy.

Calvin eventually came to see equity and justice as inseparable rather than opposed.[34] Equity leads to *true* justice (in many translations *righteousness*)—granting each person his rightful due.[35] Mutual respect for each other's rights stems from a justice rooted in love,[36] without distinction between love for those close to us and love for everyone else. Charity, love for one's neighbor, takes priority over enforcement of one's rights. Insisting on strict justice, i.e., recovering one's due or rights, doesn't always lead to fair and just results. There will be cases when legitimate rights conflict, or when one person has rights and the other has none, but the enforcement of the legitimate right would clearly result in injustice for the one with no rights. True justice, therefore, requires equity, which takes note of legal rights but deals with them according to the Golden Rule.[37]

Although Calvin, a lawyer by training, concerned himself with law, including the role of equity in law,[38] his broader theology highlighted this: equity's *personal* function. Calvin saw equity as a virtue, a reformation of the individual, a striving towards righteousness. The Golden Rule,[39] which obliges a Christian to value her own interests no greater than anyone else's, underlies his concept of equity.

---

33. Shakespeare, *Hamlet*, 2:2
34. Haas, *Concept of Equity*, 51.
35. Calvin, *Institutes* III, chapter 7, paragraph 3 (quoting from Titus 2:11–14). Unless otherwise noted, all quotations from the *Institutes* are to the Beveridge translation.
36. Calvin, *Institutes* III, chapter 7, paragraph 3, as quoted in Haas, *Concept of Equity*, 51. Beveridge, here and elsewhere, refers to "righteousness" rather than "justice."
37. Haas, *Concept of Equity*, 51.
38. He went so far as to call it "the basic principle of natural law." See Haas, *Concept of Equity*, 71.
39. Matt 7:12.

THE THEOLOGY OF EQUITY: THOMAS AQUINAS AND JOHN CALVIN

Equity makes up part of what Berman calls Calvinism's "communitarian" ethos. Calvin's theology had an essentially social view of human beings. Based on divine covenant theory, Calvinism saw Christian society as fundamentally corporate, requiring a devotion to values of public responsibility, community service, and mutual trust,"[40] rather than as an aggregation of individual interests. Thus, for example, joint stock corporations were organized to promote some public good rather than simply for private profit.[41] This interest in community benefit took Calvin's thought to some surprising places. For instance, Calvin deviated from Torah-based law by approving usury (with strict limits), but only if the transaction served some common good, or if the charging of interest promoted equity.[42] In a letter (probably to the banker Claude de Sachinus), Calvin set out his views on lending and equity which included these rules: (1) lending should not be a business; (2) the poor should not be charged interest; (3) one should not lend so much that he has no funds for charitable works; (4) lending should comport with "natural justice"; (5) the borrower should profit as much or more from the loan as the lender; and (6) the loan should serve the common good, not simply private interests.[43]

This communitarian ethos, flowing out of the Golden Rule, meant that both the enforcement and the foregoing of legal rights in commercial transactions have their place. Keeping contractual promises was important, but so was an awareness of common social interests that could condemn the enforcement of otherwise legitimate rights. The individual may justifiably go to court to redress grievances, especially when his "necessities" are at stake.[44] Equity, however, remains the *spirit* in which he goes; he should not insist too strictly on a rigorous enforcement of his rights. Thus: "So Christ, to prevent hatred and quarrels and contests and all kinds of injuries, restrains the persistence that is the root of these evils, and tells his people to be inclined

---

40. Berman, *Law and Revolution II*, 10. See chapter 8.
41. Berman, *Law and Revolution II*, 10.
42. Hass, *Concept of Equity*, 117–21.
43. Quoted in Stückelberger, "No Interest from the Poor," 62–63.
44. Calvin, *Commentary on the Epistle to the Corinthians*, 6:7.

towards moderation and equity, not forcing their rights all the way, but winning an amicable settlement on such a basis of equity."[45]

As part of this communitarian instinct, concern for the poor dominated Calvin's social theology. As he saw it, our obligations extended beyond a negative obligation—"harm not the poor"—to a positive responsibility to assist the destitute.[46] Calvin writes "indeed this is the dictate of common sense, that the hungry are deprived of their just right, if their hunger is not relieved."[47] (A millennium earlier, Basil the Great, one of the "Cappadocian Fathers," wrote that those who have two coats in their closet steal one from the neighbor who has none.) Calvin never claimed that caring for the poor was a solely Christian obligation; as part of the natural law, it was an obligation that everyone, Christian or not, could understand, and that bound everyone. Calvin did, however, also have specifically Christian reasons for his thinking about the poor: an eschatological basis, relief of the poor being a necessary precondition to the coming of Christ's kingdom, and a theological one, related to his doctrine of God, specifically human obligations to imitate Christ.

Calvin's equity, however, requires more than kindness for the poor. It requires each of us to do what we can to contribute to the common good throughout our daily lives. Specifically, we must *work*, if we can; living without working steals from the community. Paul, in his Second Letter to the Thessalonians, says, "Anyone unwilling to work should not eat. For we hear that some of you are living in idleness, mere busybodies, not doing any work. Now such persons we command and exhort in the Lord Jesus Christ to do their work quietly and to earn their own living."[48] Calvin comments, "This is the first law of equity, that no one make use of what belongs to another but only use what he can properly call his own. The second is that no one swallow up, like some abyss, what belongs to him, but that he be beneficent to his neighbors, and that he may relieve their

---

45. "Commentary on Matthew 5:25," quoted in Haas, *Concept of Equity*, 52. Haas refers to three different translations of Calvin's commentaries, and he does not make clear which he quotes here. Some translations use "justice" in place of "equity." Calvin's original reads "*en se monstrans ainsi traitables*," suggesting an internal quality of "tractability" consistent with Calvin's view of equity as a personal virtue. O'Donovan notes that "moderation" became something of a synonym for "equity" in the Reformation. O'Donovan, *Ways of Judgment*, 98.

46. Tuininga, "Good News for the Poor," 227.

47. Calvin, *Commentary on Isaiah*, 58:7.

48. 2 Thess 3:10–12.

indigence by his abundance."⁴⁹ Calvin's target here is not the "idle poor," but the "idle rich," who lived not off their own efforts, but the labor of others, or of accumulated capital.

Because the law operates as an instrument of Christian community, the magistrate must also judge equitably. The power of the magistrate comes directly from God.⁵⁰ Judging equitably means impartially; the magistrate shall carry out her duties without regard either to personal considerations or the identities of the litigants.⁵¹ Indeed, *true* humility (or modesty) is the antidote to tyranny.⁵²

To summarize: Calvin viewed equity as a legal principle, adjusting strict law in hard cases. In his early years, he saw equity as an alternative to law, but came to view it as an integral part of law. So far, Calvin's view aligns with Aquinas's. More important, however, Calvin conceived of equity as a virtue, an attitude with which to approach one's neighbors in society, especially when resolving disputes.

We have, then, two great theologians, each writing about man, law, and society, each (looking all the way back to Aristotle for support) proposing that equity is a central part of a just society, but in distinctly different ways. If our legal system has forgotten, or forsaken, this heritage, it's no wonder that, as Berman says, we are in a crisis.

In the next chapter, we'll look at how this tradition is specifically part of English theology of law, through the work of two of England's great Reformation theologians, Richard Hooker and William Perkins.

---

49. Calvin, *Commentary on Second Thessalonians*, 3:12.
50. Calvin, *Institutes* IV, chapter 20, paragraph 9.
51. Haas, *Concept of Equity*, 111.
52. Stevenson, "Calvin and Political Issues," 183.

7

The Theology of Equity (Continued): Equity English Style

From equity's classical and Reformed roots, we move to the theological bases for equity in England, examining the writings of Richard Hooker and William Perkins.

Richard Hooker and *The Laws of Ecclesiastical Polity*

Richard Hooker's career coincided almost exactly with the height of the English Reformation, and with the intensification of the battle between the common-law and chancery courts. Scholars debate whether Hooker should be classified as the "first Anglican" or firmly within the Reformed tradition.[1] The answer to that question, it seems to me, depends at least in part on whether we are talking about Hooker's theology or his ecclesiology. Hooker's great work, *The Laws of Ecclesiastical Polity*, rejected Puritan theories of church organization and government, and defended the "Elizabethan settlement."[2] Hooker's theology, on the other hand, was much closer to Reformed positions; Ian Breward says that Hooker "intended to

---

1. See, e.g., Joyce, *Richard Hooker and Anglican Moral Theology*, versus Littlejohn, *Richard Hooker: A Companion*.

2. The "Elizabethan Settlement" was an attempt by the government of Elizabeth I to steer a middle course in English church establishment after the turbulence of Henry VIII's reign, followed by the Protestant monarch Edward VI and the Roman Catholic Mary Tudor. The Elizabethan Settlement included the "Act of Supremacy," which proclaimed Elizabeth the head of the English church, and the "Act of Uniformity," which reinstated the 1552 *Book of Common Prayer* (with revisions). An attempt to bring some semblance of peace between the Catholics and the Reformers, the Settlement reinstated something similar to traditional Catholic practice, but under the authority of the monarch rather than the Pope.

THE THEOLOGY OF EQUITY (CONTINUED): EQUITY ENGLISH STYLE

correct and complement, rather than to replace, continental scholarship."[3] Hooker even took pains to praise John Calvin.[4] Therefore, we should not be surprised to find that Hooker's views on equity contain elements of both Thomism and Calvinism.

Hooker was born in 1553 or perhaps early in 1554 (the records are not clear) near the cathedral city of Exeter, in Devonshire. At the age of fourteen or fifteen, he entered Corpus Christi College, Oxford, which in the day was distinctly Calvinist.[5] While there, however, he would have read widely among many of the fathers and doctors of the church, including Aquinas, in addition to Calvin. In 1577, Hooker earned his master's degree and was named a fellow of Corpus Christi College. In 1585, he was elected master of the Temple Church in London. Built in the twelfth century by the Knights Templar, by Hooker's day Temple Church served the Inner and Middle Temple, two of the "Inns of Court" that were at once educational institutions, professional associations, and accommodations for London lawyers.

Temple Church was at the center of the battle for control of the church in England. Indeed, Hooker found a competitor within the very walls of the church. The Puritan Walter Travers, deputy master of the Temple and the other finalist for Hooker's position, had "lecturer" privileges at the church (even though he was not ordained by the Church of England), giving him the right to preach daily. The competing sermons from Hooker (in the morning) and Travers (in the afternoon) made Anglican and Puritan arguments for all manner of theological issues, as well as church government; it was said that "the pulpit spoke pure Canterbury in the morning and Geneva in the afternoon."[6] Travers had already set out a plan for a change from an episcopal to a presbyterian church organization in England. The "Battle of the Pulpit" continued for the better part of a year, until John Whitgrift, Archbishop of Canterbury (and Hooker's ally), banned Travers from preaching in the temple.

---

3. Breward, "Significance of William Perkins," 116.

4. Hooker called Calvin "incomparably the wisest man that ever the French Church did enjoy, since the hour it enjoyed him." *Laws*, 1:3. Throughout this book, I have taken the liberty of modernizing Hooker's spelling. Admittedly, this passage is at the focal point of the "Anglican versus Reformed debate." Some think Hooker is disingenuous here. Compare, for instance, Thompson, "Philosopher of the Politic Society," 14–15, with Grislis, "Hermeneutical Problem in Richard Hooker," 173. Joyce and Littlejohn continue the debate in their recent books.

5. Secor, *Richard Hooker*, 48.

6. Secor, *Richard Hooker*, 181.

In 1591, Hooker left the Temple Church for a living in Wiltshire. While there, he wrote *The Laws of Ecclesiastical Polity*. Written as a response to Puritan attacks on the Elizabethan Settlement, the *Laws* sets out Hooker's theories of ecclesiology and the relation between church and state. In the *Laws*, Hooker emphasizes the "Scripture, reason, and tradition" understanding of church authority that came to be (and still is) called the "Anglican tradition." It has been pointed out that, ironically, Hooker, a divine, wrote a lawbook, in contrast to Calvin's *Institutes*, a theological tract written by a lawyer.

Ostensibly, Hooker wrote solely about church law and church organization. Those topics may have provided the impetus for the book, but the *Laws* has long since been considered a masterwork of political theology. Egil Grislis writes that "Although it was written in a polemical setting, [the *Laws*] is basically an inquiry into the first principles which sustain the structure of the church and inform the system of his Christian theology. Such major areas of inquiry as the problem of subjectivity, the interpretation of Scripture, the nature and activity of God, the created world, the nature of man, the meaning of sin . . . are all worked out not only with careful attention to detail, but also in a genuine systematic coherence."[7] It is that inquiry into "first principles" in the context of political conflict that makes Hooker relevant to our topic. After all, the nature of man, man's sinfulness, and the subjectivity of judgment regarding those topics sum up the problems of law in a fallen world.

Hooker's starting point, a recognition of Scripture as absolute authority for the regulation of human conduct, would have been non-controversial even in Puritan circles. Nevertheless, we must admit, he noted, that sometimes Scripture is silent or ambiguous. Then, Hooker said, we must consult not only the tradition of the church (which would have been the standard Roman Catholic answer) but also human reason. Neither Scripture nor natural law, as we learned from Aquinas, can solve all instances of human conflict. Hence, the need for human law.

Hooker had an elaborate hierarchy of laws that reflects his Thomistic influences. The "first law eternal" is that law by which God himself is governed. The "second law eternal" combines the "law of reason" and Scripture

---

7. Grislis, "Hermeneutical Problem in Hooker," 167.

(which Hooker called "divine law"). By the "law of reason," Hooker means something like "natural law."[8] As such it is available to all humans. The "second law eternal" includes "human law," but only insofar as it bases itself on reason or Scripture.[9] That law, Hooker says, is rooted in both reason and political reality. On the one hand, human reason can access eternal law, so, for Hooker, as for Aquinas, human law, to be legitimate, must always be reasonable. In fact, "God is law," he wrote.[10] On the other hand, human law is necessarily *local*; the particulars of a society's laws vary according to the needs of the day and time (although not so much as to violate fundamental law).[11] The structure of Genevan society is appropriate to Geneva, perhaps, but that does not necessarily make it appropriate to England.

By "reason," Hooker does not mean its modern sense of an individual capacity, the distinctive conclusions of a specific person. Reason is "the receptacle of divine truth, not a scrutinizing, critical faculty of the mind," allowing us to discover truth more than formulate it.[12] Reason is communal—the opinion of wise persons.[13] Informed "common sense," we might call it. What's more, reason in Hooker's sense of the word, like Aquinas's, implies an element of humility. Thus, Hooker admits that sometimes even the wisest persons judge imperfectly. "Companies of learned men be they never so great and reverend," are to yield unto reason, no matter "the simplicity of his person which doth allege it."[14]

Equity comes from the law of reason. Equity is both contained in and reflected by the law, but it is not exclusive to the law. God always acts reasonably, although God's reason might be only partially and intermittently available to humans. Equity extends the divine reasonableness of the law to cases that escape the flawed general human law. For Hooker, "general laws" were like "general rules of phisick" (i.e., medicine):[15] fine for the ordinary case but

8. Joyce, *Richard Hooker*, 138.
9. Thompson, "Philosopher of the Politic," 25.
10. *Laws*, 1:59.
11. Berman, *Law and Revolution II*, 234.
12. Booty, "Hooker and Anglicanism," 233.
13. Medieval chancery practice also used "conscience" in a communal rather than an individual sense. Klinck, *Conscience, Equity, and the Court of Chancery,*" 17. Klinck observes that "conscience" was used as something of a synonym for "justice," "reason" or "truth." Once again, we find Hooker balanced between the Roman and the Reform tradition.
14. *Laws*, 1:181–82.
15. *Laws*, 2:44. We shall return to this metaphor.

positively harmful in the unusual instance.[16] "Not without singular wisdom therefore it has been provided, that as the ordinary course of common affairs is disposed of by general laws, so likewise men's rarer incident necessities and utilities should be with special equity considered."[17] As for Aquinas, equity is not simply unbridled mercy, because equity does not call for avoidance of the law. Equity does not "turn the edge of justice" but gives law its "right meaning." (It's hard to miss the Aristotelean touch here.) Therefore, equity perfects, rather than abrogates, human law. Law being the product of reason, reason compels equity.[18]

Yet, no sooner do we settle into a comfortable view of Hooker as the English Aquinas than we find this, an appeal to a Calvinist internal sense of equity. Hooker continues:

> We see in contracts and other dealings which daily pass between man and man, that, to the utter undoing of some, many things by strictness of law may be done, which equity and honest meaning forbids. Not that the law is unjust, but unperfect; nor equity against, but above the law; *binding men's consciences in things which law cannot reach unto.*[19]

Here, he says that equity stands "above the law." Hooker is not contradicting himself. He has not forgotten what he just wrote. Rather, he expands what he means by "equity." Used this way, equity recognizes that there are things that law simply cannot do, but depend on character itself. The idea of a conscientious equity lying in the hearts of men, above the strict requirements of the law, echoes Calvin's vision of social equity.

Here we have just what Fortier described: equity as a set of ideas. These two quotes, one characteristically Thomistic, the second Calvinist, come from the same section of the *Laws*. (No wonder that both Reformers and Anglicans claim Hooker as their own.) Balanced against the hierarchy of laws is Hooker's view that government itself comes out of man's sociality.[20] Humans are not able on their own to supply those things necessary for

---

16. Recall Aquinas says that strictly applying general law in the wrong case could be positively injurious. Aquinas, *ST* II-II, question 120, article 1.

17. *Laws*, 2:44.

18. Porter, "Hooker, The Tudor Constitution," 110.

19. *Laws*, 2:44, emphasis added. Here, and elsewhere, I have modernized Hooker's spelling.

20. *Laws*, 1:96.

THE THEOLOGY OF EQUITY (CONTINUED): EQUITY ENGLISH STYLE

"a life fit for the dignity of man."[21] Therefore, law allows humans to bind together in community for the common good. Any law that interferes with that goal is by its very nature unreasonable.

In summary: Hooker's view of equity places him, as with many things, with one foot in Anglican and the other in Reformed thought. His views of law have strong ties to the canon law tradition; Hooker sees a need for moral consistency in the law, in accord with conscience, making equity a part of law. Law for Hooker, like canon law, was not simply rules, but more of a "dialectical process of adapting rules to new situations."[22] At the same time, however, other parts of Hooker's legacy have strong Reformed roots.

William Perkins: The Reformed Casuist

A. J. Joyce points out interesting parallels between Hooker's views on equity and the development of Chancery practice, which happened more or less simultaneously.[23] Hooker, as Master of Temple Church for six years, would have breathed the same air as the Chancery lawyers. Sadly, if Hooker gave practical ethics advice to his lawyer parishioners, little if any of it survives. Hooker's near contemporary William Perkins, by contrast, spoke and wrote frequently and directly to lawyers.[24] Perkins was both a Cambridge don and an acclaimed preacher. Born in 1558, four years after Hooker, Perkins earned both a BA and an MA from, and then became a fellow of, Christ's Church, Cambridge. Although strongly influenced by John Calvin in his theology, Perkins was essentially loyal to the Church of England and was relatively successful in staying out of the most virulent of the battles among Puritans, the Roman Catholic Church, and the Church of England.

Perkins (1558–1602) was no less a scholar than Hooker. Christ's College, in Perkins's day, was a center of Aristotelianism.[25] It helps us to avoid too-neat categorization to remember that Hooker, the "Anglican," came

---

21. *Laws*, 1:96.
22. Berman, *Law and Revolution*, 253–54.
23. Joyce, *Richard Hooker*, 207.
24. Perkins's early ministry was also in and about the law, although a different aspect: he had a ministry to prisoners in the Cambridge jail.
25. Breward, "Introduction," 4–5.

from the "Calvinist" Corpus Christi College, Perkins from the "Aristotelian" Christ's College. Nevertheless, we can fairly say that where Hooker crafted a scholarly blend of the scholastic and Reformed view of equity, Perkins, certainly highly educated himself, took a more practical tone.[26] Ian Breward, the scholar most responsible for reviving interest in Perkins, writes that Perkins had both "an ability to clarify and expound complex theological issues which aroused the respect of fellow scholars and a gift for relating seemingly abstruse theological teaching to the spiritual aspirations of ordinary Christians."[27] We will focus on two of Perkins's shorter treatises. "Epieikeia," with its distinction between public and private equity, explicitly concerns the Reformed view of equity, and will be the focus in this chapter. We will take up "A Treatise on the Vocations or Callings of Men" in chapter 10.

Perkins wrote on an enormous breadth of topics. His first major work, *The Golden Chaine*, written in 1590 and translated into English in 1591, concerned salvation. *A Discourse of Conscience,* published in 1596, took the topic of conscience in a different direction from the traditional Roman Catholic; it was followed in 1606, four years after Perkins's death, by *The Whole Treatise of the Cases of Conscience*, a larger treatment of the same topic. Perkins in fact has been called "the father of Reformed casuistry." *A Reformed Catholike* (1597) was his major defense of the Church of England against claims that it had rejected the fundamental doctrines of the Roman Catholic Church. One could almost imagine Hooker and Perkins standing back to back, defending the Church of England against attacks from the left and right.[28]

Perkins, a close follower of Calvin, profoundly believed in the importance of the community over individualist needs.[29] Like Hooker, however, Perkins also unites the Thomistic view of equity as based in rationality with the Reformed view of equity as a communal value. Thus, the theme of taking care of the less fortunate hangs over his discussion of equity. Perkins was deeply interested in the qualities of a just society, including specifically its treatment of and provision for the poor. The Elizabethan Era was full of serious social and economic problems, not unlike Micah's era. Real wages were falling, prices were rising, unemployment was high, and there were serial famines. England was in and out of war with France, Spain, and the

---

26. Hence Louis Wright subtitled his article on Perkins "Elizabethan Apostle of 'Practical Divinity.'"

27. Breward, "Significance of William Perkins," 113.

28. See Patterson, "Richard Hooker and William Perkins," 71.

29. Patterson, *William Perkins*, 163.

THE THEOLOGY OF EQUITY (CONTINUED): EQUITY ENGLISH STYLE

Netherlands. As a result, the era saw great disparities in economic status between rich and poor.

Hooker was not a "Leveler." He never said that justice required absolute economic equality. He did believe, though, that all persons were entitled to sufficient material goods for life's essential needs (assuming they were willing and able to work for it), and he believed that society should provide for those that were unable to earn their living. (He had no use for vagrants and beggars.) In this regard he followed Calvin, who, as we recall, said that equity called on us to work if we could, for the benefit of all, and not take more than our needs required. In fact, Perkins believed that the use of one's wealth to support the poor came second only to the obligation to support one's own family. Although he did not regard the accumulation of wealth as sin in and of itself, he did believe that wealth had to be acquired justly, and that excess wealth was entrusted to the wealthy as stewards, to use that wealth for God's purposes.[30]

Perkins offers two bases for mitigating the "extremity of the law." The first has to do with the person of the offender. A young boy steals to avoid starving. Do either his age or his extreme poverty justify an exception to the general rule (which Perkins endorses) that theft merits execution? Yes they do: "[t]he equity or moderation, I say, in this case is not to inflict death, for that were extremity, but to determine a punishment less than death: yet such a one as shall be sufficient to reform the party from his sin, to punish the fault, to terrify others and to satisfy the law."[31] Like Calvin, Perkins rejects the enforcement of even a legitimate law if enforcement would cause injustice for the person with no rights.[32] Like Aquinas, Perkins asks whether enforcement of the law would meet the intentions of the lawmaker. What purposes are served by punishment? Perkins lists reformation of the wrongdoer, retribution, protection of society and satisfaction of moral standards (sometimes called denunciation.) These are the classic justifications for punishment.[33] Yet Perkins says that, for the starving urchin, these are best achieved *not* by

---

30. Patterson, *William Perkins*, 135–49.

31. Perkins, "Epieikeia," 487.

32. Haas, *Concept of Equity*, 51.

33. O'Donovan discusses the justifications for punishment in *Ways of Judgment*, 102–7.

strict justice but by mitigation. The possibility of mitigation in the odd case legitimates strict justice in the typical one.

In other words, Perkins the Calvinist adopts the classic Thomistic basis of equity, the inability of positive law to decide every individual case. "No lawmakers, being men, can foresee or set down all cases that may fall out. Therefore when the case altereth, so must the discretion of the lawmaker show itself and do that which the law cannot do."[34] Here, the two forms of equity intersect; the special circumstances that the law fails to provide for involve the person of the offender more than the nature of the offense. The starving boy is, to use Hooker's analogy, the wrong patient for the medicine (acknowledging, of course, that few of us today would see making theft a capital crime "good medicine" in any case).

Thomism versus Calvinism is not the only duality in Perkins's theory of equity. Perkins identifies two *types* of personal equity, "public" and "private." *Public* equity applies not only to government officers and official deeds; it governs "all the public actions of a man's life, so that by the rule and direction of this equity, thus described, men may know how to guide themselves in suing bonds and taking forfeitures."[35] A private dispute, once brought into court, involves public equity. *Private* equity, on the other hand, carries with it "four degrees or principal duties. First, to bear with natural infirmities. Secondly, to interpret doubtful things in the better part. Thirdly, to depart from our own right sometimes. Fourthly, to forgive private and personal wrongs."[36]

By this definition, then, a lawyer spends his professional life in both the private and the public realms. The counseling he gives his client ought to include considerations of private equity and will be woefully thin if he doesn't. There may be times when the lawyer thinks true justice would be best served by the client "departing from (the client's) own right." The client may put the worst possible interpretation on the adversary's behavior, and equity suggests playing the devil's advocate. The lawyer, in short, confronts whether an otherwise private dispute should go to court, at which point

---

34. Perkins, "Epieikeia," 485.

35. Perkins, "Epieikeia," 489–90. As with Hooker, I have modernized Perkins's spelling.

36. Perkins, "Epieikeia," 492–93.

THE THEOLOGY OF EQUITY (CONTINUED): EQUITY ENGLISH STYLE

it becomes a public matter calling for public equity. The dilemma for the lawyer arises when the client's sense of private equity falls short, calling on the lawyer, as his agent, to act out that inequity in public.

Just as Perkins refused to say that all accumulation of wealth was sinful, he declined to say that Christians should never take their disputes to court. They should remember, however, that the law is precious, indeed a gift from God. Being a gift from God, "God's ordinance," it may be used to resolve civil disputes. So, he tells us that

> [I]t is a devilish opinion in the world that a man cannot go to law and be in charity. We must know that a man may go to law and yet be in charity, for to forgive the malice and to sue for recompense are things indifferent. It is not so much charity to forbear the recompense, as it is to forgive the malice. If therefore a man forgive not the malice, he is out of charity; but he may sue for satisfaction and be in charity. . . . Law is not evil, though contentious men and unconscionable lawyers have vilely abused it: but it is God's ordinance and may lawfully be used, so it be on this manner.[37]

Like all gifts from God, it must not be wasted, "(used) for every trifle, every trespass, every ill word." In such cases we are both to forgive the malice *and* the damage. "For the law is abused in being executed upon trifles, and those lawyers shame themselves and dishonor their profession, who are willing that every trespass of sixpence damages be an action in the law."[38]

In fact, law's status as a gift from God makes lawyering a dual civil/religious vocation. Perkins writes:

> [T]he laws of men are policy, but equity is Christianity. . . . Divines must take lawyers' advice concerning extremity and the letter of the law: good reason then that lawyers take divines' advice touching the equity which is the intent of the law. Moreover, their law is but the ministry of equity, but our law, the word of God, is the fountain of equity.[39]

Equity, a higher law coming from divine law, comments and corrects human law and legal systems. Law being subject to divine equity, lawyering then turns out to be a "ministry of equity."

---

37. Perkins, "Epieikeia," 499.
38. Perkins, "Epieikeia," 499.
39. Perkins, "Epieikeia," 491.

For Perkins, our obligation to act equitably stems from a divine imitation view; we are obligated to model God's infinite forgiveness.[40] All persons, not just the lawyer, are so obligated. As we are not God, but made in God's image, we will never fulfill the obligation flawlessly, but try we must. In this lies the dilemma; the lawyer's act of subordination to his client threatens a loss of control of his capacity to forgive.

Perkins takes his epigraph to "Epieikeia" from Philippians 4:5: "Let your moderation of mind be known to all men: The Lord is at hand." This is theological deductive reasoning; we are to display our moderation precisely *because* the Lord is at hand.[41] Here, from Perkins, the "Practical Divine," comes *practical* wisdom for a lawyer challenged by an inequitable client. Philippians 4:5, like Micah 6:8, acts as a touchstone for proper lawyer-client relations. Perkins says, "Nay, civil society and common dealing betwixt man and man cannot continue unless one man yield to another."[42] This "yielding to another," whether called moderation, humility, subordination, or equity, lies at the heart of Perkins's view of the law.

As with Aquinas and Calvin, so with Hooker and Perkins. In Elizabethan England, during the great flourishing of equity practice, two of the leading theologians of the day promote equity as a specifically Christian value, drawing from Aristotelean values, but different ones. The difference here is that while Aquinas and Calvin lived three hundred years apart, Hooker and Perkins, born less than five years apart, could have been brothers.

Next, we will turn to two modern writers, the historian Harold Berman and moral theologian Oliver O'Donovan, to assess how the decline of equity impacts society today.

---

40. Perkins, "Epieikeia," 506.
41. O'Donovan, *Ways of Judgment*, 98.
42. Perkins, "Epieikeia," 482.

8

Clients vs. Courts: The Dilemma in History and Theology

In this chapter we will examine the work of two modern writers, Harold Berman and Oliver O'Donovan. First, however, let us review where we have gone so far.

By both training and oath, a lawyer sublimates her own goals, desires, and beliefs to her client's. A lawyer has *fiduciary* duties towards her client, obligating her to put her client's interests *in front of*, not merely equal to, her own. Moreover, codes of professional conduct oblige the lawyer to zealously represent her client to the exclusion of other concerns.

A lawyer also serves as an "officer of the court."[1] Her power to act for her clients comes from the state, which expects the lawyer to exercise that power in pursuit of legal justice. The advocacy process, like the "marketplace of ideas" theory of politics, assumes that vigorous debate best determines the truth.[2] The lawyer's duties as an officer of the court restrict what she can do in representing her client.

Thus, lawyers serve two masters: the client and the law. Conflicts are bound to arise. If that were not enough, the lawyer's duties to client and court conflict with the lawyer's own religious or moral values. Clients regularly have legitimate legal rights, the enforcement of which will cause real, perhaps irreparable, harm to someone else. Although it is not *legally* wrongful to enforce one's rights even at the cost of devastating another life, ethics, especially Christian ethics, counsel otherwise.

---

1. At least in the United States. It appears that in England solicitors are considered officers of the court, but barristers representing private parties are not.

2. Berman claims that as early as the twelfth century there developed a view of law as scientific, in which the advocate played a (partisan) role in a system intended to achieve objective truth. Berman, *Law and Revolution*, 157.

Most lawyers, no doubt, believe that the "law" represents a social good (whether because they see it, on religious grounds, as a gift from God, as an expression of fundamental human rights, or as simply the way in which society properly ordered itself). On the other hand, most lawyers would agree with Aquinas and Hooker that no law is perfect for all situations. Lest private-practice lawyers always be plagued by this dilemma, and because the lawyer's obligations to his client come subject to his duties to the system—in other words, because he has to play within the rules—the system owes him an obligation in return: to step outside of itself occasionally, and do the right, rather than the legal, thing. Society asks the lawyer to trust the system to achieve justice. The system ought to earn that trust.

The lawyer's dual responsibilities to client and court require a vigorous equity in both Calvin's and in Aquinas's sense. The lawyer's role as counselor requires Calvin's type of equity, which aims at transforming the self as well as the system. On the other hand, Thomistic equity takes over once the lawyer finds himself in front of a judge or jury. If the law flows from practical reason, we should expect that the court will evaluate the justness of a case rather than simply its strict legal merits. Thomistic equity allows the lawyer both to argue against an overly strict interpretation of the law, when that serves his client's interest, and to argue for strict enforcement in other cases, trusting that the court will not apply the law so harshly as to achieve an unjust result. Paradoxically, the Christian lawyer must trust that the court will sometimes tell him "no."

These two concepts of equity, seemingly distinct, share two important qualities. First, each seeks to promote the common good, whether through a law-ordered society or through attitudes of mutual regard. Second, each promotes a vision of humility towards the law, and towards the self. Aquinas saw the common good as the basis for law itself. Hooker, when he speaks of "wisdom," means *community* wisdom, not just individual reason. Equity in this sense involves intellectual humility, subordinating one's judgment to a higher good and a common understanding. Calvin calls for *social* humility—a recognition that one's interests do not always trump the neighbor's. Calvin worries less about perfection of law than about misuse of admittedly imperfect law. Calvin's view accords best with Christian ethics. There is nothing "unchristian" about the enforcement of law, and mercy does not overrule or supersede law.[3] The common good requires both, because not enforcing law

---

3. This is the topic of *Justice in Love*, Wolterstorff's follow-up to *Justice: Rights and Wrongs*.

against wrongdoers endorses wrongdoing, and ultimately normalizes immoral behavior. On the other hand, the law cannot pretend to perfection, and regarding the law as perfect idolizes the law.

Berman explores these themes as a legal historian, O'Donovan as a moral and political theologian. In each case, we find that a system without equity fails to balance Micah's twin charges of justice and mercy. Whether we call this cognitive dissonance or a moral dilemma, it both leads to disrespect for law and lawyers, and jeopardizes the moral health of the lawyers who inhabit it.

The Historic Basis for the Dilemma: Harold Berman

Harold Berman lived a life straight out of a novel. Born in Connecticut near the end of World War I, he studied at Yale and Dartmouth, and then joined the army as a cryptographer. Stationed in Europe during World War II, he went to Yale Law School after the war, where he became intrigued by Russian law. There were only two problems: no one on the Yale faculty taught Russian law, and he didn't speak Russian. He conquered both, teaching himself Russian and then Soviet law.

After graduation, Berman spent a year on the Stanford Law School faculty, then moved to Harvard, where he taught for thirty-seven years before moving again, this time to Emory University. His interest in Soviet law persisted, and he frequently visited the Soviet Union, family in tow, as a student, teacher, and lecturer. Rumor has it that the FBI got interested in Berman's travels to Moscow, so much so that J. Edgar Hoover himself once asked "Who is this kook, anyway?"

Berman found his way to the courtroom from time to time. In the 1950s, he represented the Estate of Arthur Conan Doyle in a claim against the Soviet government for unpaid royalties from the Sherlock Holmes books. (He won at trial but lost on appeal.) Many years later, he filed an amicus brief with the United States Supreme Court, on behalf of Pat Robertson and others, defending the State of Texas's right to maintain a "Ten Commandments" monument on the capitol grounds. (He won this time.)

The Texas case highlights another of Berman's lifelong interests: the intersection between law and religion. Berman saw a crisis in our modern legal system, caused by the loss of understanding by lawmakers and citizens of the historic fundamentals of our system: "the structural integrity of law, its ongoingness, its religious roots, its transcendental qualities." As a result, "the law is becoming more fragmented, more subjective, geared more to expediency and less to morality, concerned more with immediate consequences and less with consistency or continuity."[4] Equity's disappearance comes from this loss of belief in law's moral foundation.

Before the end of the eleventh and beginning of the twelfth century, according to Berman, there were no such things as Western legal "systems": that is, "a distinct, integrated body of law, consciously systematized."[5] There were legal "orders," but they were largely customary, or part of political or religious institutions rather than establishments in their own right. The systemization of law was started in large part by the first of what Berman calls six "great revolutions," the Papal Revolution starting in 1075, when Gregory VII declared that the papal court was "the court of the whole of Christendom."[6]

The church's canon law, according to Berman, was the first collection of laws that could properly be called a legal system in the modern sense.[7] The church courts, under canon law, exercised jurisdiction (sometimes exclusively, and sometimes concurrently with secular courts) over family law, marriage, inheritance, contracts, trusts, and much more. This jurisdiction was based on a perceived connection between the subject matter and biblical law, often the Ten Commandments. For instance, church courts claimed jurisdiction over crimes of violence under the Sixth Commandment,[8] family law under the Fifth and Seventh, and contract law under the Eighth and Ninth.

Although the English legal system did not have the same connections to canon law as Continental systems, in medieval ages, all courts, including English, operated under principles that had strong associations with canon law. Three of those principles relevant for our discussion were: (1) the poor and helpless required the law's protection; (2) relationships of trust and confidence were to be legally enforced; and (3) the law's task is to maintain peace and good will, and in the process necessarily takes jurisdiction over and compels compliance from individuals, regardless of status or holdings.[9]

---

4. Berman, *Law and Revolution*, 39.
5. Berman, *Law and Revolution*, 49.
6. Berman, *Law and Revolution*, 18–19, 99.
7. Berman, *Faith and Order*, 43.
8. "Thou shalt not kill"; I use here the numbering shared by the Anglican and Reformed traditions.
9. Berman, *Faith and Order*, 67–68.

CLIENTS VS. COURTS: THE DILEMMA IN HISTORY AND THEOLOGY

Over time, the King's Courts lost touch with these principles in favor of rigid forms of writs and rules of evidence. Therefore, the Chancellor and the Court of Chancery took jurisdiction over these cases, not in order to implement a new or separate law, but to carry out the common law according to the true purposes that had been instilled therein from canon law.

Most relevant to the theme of equity was the second of these "revolutions," the Protestant Reformation. We discussed in chapter 6 how the strong communitarian spirit in Calvinism lies at the heart of the social revolution it engendered. Berman writes:

> Anglo-Calvinist Puritanism was essentially a communitarian religion. It emphasized the existence of a divine covenant, under which the congregation of the faithful was to be "a light to all the nations of the world," "a city on a hill." This in turn, led to an emphasis not only on the virtues of hard work, austerity, frugality, discipline, self-improvement, and other features of what has come to be called the Puritan work ethic, but also on the sanctity of human covenants of public responsibility, community service, corporate enterprise, mutual trust, and other qualities associated with the concept of public spirit.[10]

This commitment to the "common good" lies at the heart of theories of equity. From Aquinas through Perkins, the common good has been equity's goal: "the end of this virtue [equity]," Perkins said, "is to maintain justice and to preserve peace, which two are the very sinews and strength of a Christian kingdom: for where we do not to other men as we would others would do to us, there is no justice."[11] Even after equity began to lose some of its explicitly Christian association, its connection to the common good survived. Henry Home, in his *Principles of Equity*, written in the mid-eighteenth century, said that a court of equity corrects the common law "for the public good."[12]

By contrast, Berman finds a fundamental flaw in Max Weber's "Calvinist" thesis. Weber, a German sociologist and economist, became fascinated with a seeming correlation between Protestant confession and economic success; in plain words, Weber thought that something about Protestantism helped businessmen make money. In *The Protestant Ethic and the Spirit*

---

10. Berman, *Law and Revolution II*, 10.

11. Perkins, "Epieikeia," 483.

12. Home, *Principles of Equity*, 268–69, quoted in Fortier, *Culture of Equity in Restoration*, 18–19.

of Capitalism, which remains a landmark in sociological scholarship to this day, Weber hypothesized a series of links in a chain that connected Protestant confession to economic success. The theory is highly complex, but can (more or less) safely be summarized thus: (1) Protestantism obligated all persons to follow a vocation; (2) for Protestants, vocations were not, as in the Catholic view, limited to the church, but included all trades, professions, or livelihoods; (3) because of Calvinist notions of predestination, Protestants were obsessed with whether they were saved or damned; (4) in the absence of direct proof of salvation, success in a vocation, especially economic success, was the best evidence that one was among the elect; (5) because vocations had religious significance, wasting the money earned in those vocations was a sin; and (6) rather than wasting hard-earned money on luxuries, Protestants chose to invest their money in new enterprises, which led to the rise of capitalism. As Berman puts it, "Calvinism, as found especially among seventeenth-century English Puritans, was congruent with, and supportive of, 'the spirit' . . . of the bourgeois industrial capitalism that later emerged in Europe. . . . [Weber] defined the spirit of capitalism as consisting of an overriding desire on the part of individual capitalist entrepreneurs to acquire great wealth, while at the same time he acknowledged that English Calvinists denounced such a desire as sinful worship of Mammon."[13]

With which Berman vigorously disagrees. According to Berman, Weber's book would have been better titled "*The Decline* of the Protestant Ethic and the Spirit of Capitalism."[14] Commercial activity in Geneva was fueled not by a concern for one's soul, as Weber had it, but by a concern for the welfare of the community. This phenomenon was not limited to Geneva. Berman gives the example of the joint stock company in England, organized to marshal private capital for the common good. Berman writes:

> [W]hen one looks at the lawyers and the institutions they were creating, one does not see ascetic individualists trembling before the prospect of ultimate damnation or salvation. Rather, one sees community-minded men creating communitarian legal institutions such as joint-stock companies, bank credits, and the trust device. They understood that the success of a market economy rests on trust, on credit, on common enterprise, not, as many later came to believe, on personal greed. This communitarianism, involving large-scale cooperation among landed gentry and merchant elites, itself had deep Calvinist roots. The spirit of

13. Berman, *Law and Revolution II*, 24.
14. Berman, *Law and Revolution II*, 25, emphasis in original.

Weber's capitalism in the seventeenth and early eighteenth centuries was the product not, as he thought, of "secular asceticism" but of what was called at the time public spirit, which, in turn, reflected not the individualist doctrines of predestination and calling but the collectivist Calvinist doctrines of covenant and covenanted communities.[15]

Capitalism in Calvin's Geneva was not laissez-faire, every person for himself, self-interested accumulation of wealth.[16] In fact, it was specifically anti-feudal.[17] Capitalism as we know it came about through a dwindling lack of concern for the community.

Until we grasp this communitarian instinct, says Berman, we cannot understand modern legal systems. Berman argues that what we now interpret as a secularization of society, with the transfer of activity and power from the church to the government, was initially a "spiritualization of secular responsibilities and activities."[18] The church did not cease to be a social agent; rather, civil institutions, public and private, took on Christian obligations to society. So, for example, civic efforts to improve the lot of the poor, according to the great seventeenth-century jurist Matthew Hale, were at once acts of piety, humanity, and political prudence.[19] Later, when secular activities became desacralized, law found itself severed from its original roots. According to Berman, the modern misinterpretation of this shift distorts the true relationship between natural law and positive law.[20] To understand better why that happens, let us turn to a specific example, the metamorphosis of contract law.

A Historic Example: Contract Theory

As we did in chapter 2, let us start out our discussion of contract theory with another real-life example.

A semi-regular client comes to see you, outraged. About a year and a half ago, the same client asked you to review a contract for the construction of a large, elegant custom home. The builder, you knew from experience,

---

15. Berman, *Law and Revolution II*, 27.
16. McGrath, *Life of John Calvin*, 234.
17. McGrath, *Life of John Calvin*, 229.
18. Berman, *Law and Revolution II*, 369.
19. Berman, *Law and Revolution II*, 368.
20. Berman, *Law and Revolution II*, 381.

is a decent person and a competent builder, but typically over his head in projects of this size. Undercapitalized and understaffed, he can be relied on to competently get the home to substantial completion, sound and habitable. Then, because of his lack of money and staff, he will turn the keys over to the buyer and move on to the next project, neglecting the "punch list" of small defects that accompany every job. At the time, you told your client this, and his response was "But I'll be OK, don't you think?" You tell him again, and also mention to him that, based on your experience, the price of the home is ten to fifteen dollars per square foot below what would be common in the area. Again, your client says, "But I'll be OK, won't I?" Now, he has moved into the home, but he says it is "scarcely livable." The builder only delivered one garage door opener. The doorbell only works intermittently. Several of the marble tiles in the entryway are a different color from the rest. One of the double pane windows has moisture in between the panes. The sprinkler system is not programmed properly. Not all the fixtures have light bulbs. The pool heater doesn't work. And so forth. Your client needs you to defend him, because he has received a demand letter from the contractor's lawyer. What's the demand for, you ask? The retainage on the contract. The entire retainage, you ask? Yes, he says, ninety thousand dollars (10 percent of the contract price). How much would it cost to fix the punch list items? Seven or eight thousand dollars, you're told. But it's the *principle* of the thing.

This very typical example implicates moral versus economic theories of contract formation and liability going back the better part of a millennium. Early theories of general contract law, based on canon law, had a *moral* basis for enforcing contracts.[21] Failure to keep a promise was a sin, because a contract involved an oath. Breach of the oath resulted in punishment by religious, not legal authorities.[22] (Typically, the oath was accompanied by a pledge, and breach of the oath also resulted in forfeiture of the pledge.)

Starting in the twelfth century, to deal with the expansion of commerce and increasing complexity of commercial agreements, the law progressively allowed *legal* remedies for the enforcement of agreements. Because contracts still were viewed as moral obligations, however, judges examined the morality of an agreement, and only enforced agreements that were morally

---

21. Contracts were enforced before the twelfth century, but it was only then that a general theory of contract developed, specifically the idea that a promise standing alone, without some other basis for enforcement (such as partial performance) emerged. See Berman, *Law and Revolution*, 246.

22. Berman, "Religious Sources," 109.

justified, or in the service of reasonable and equitable transactions.[23] For example, a "just price," weighing the benefits of an agreement for both parties, was a basic condition of enforcement.[24] Therefore, the Courts recognized several defenses to enforcement: fraud, unconscionability, duress, mistake, bad faith. Those defenses survive to this day, although in increasingly rigid ways. Although the quasi-moral names these defenses bear would be a clue, I doubt many lawyers realize that they come from a time when legal liability was explicitly based in moral concepts, starting with the notion that a covenant was a promise to God. These principles found their way into canon law, and Berman refers to them as a "*moral* theory of contract law."[25] They pertained to the enforcement of a contract, rather than the question of whether a contract existed.

Over time, however, the grounds for contractual liability shifted from a moral basis to an economic "benefit of the bargain" view, which combined the question of formation and the question of liability into one. Now the existence of the contract was in and of itself sufficient to create liability.[26] A number of things contributed to this change: the battle between common law and equity courts, the explosion of international trade (bringing with it a desire for greater regularity and predictability in commercial cases), and a diminished view of the power of the monarch, including the power of the Chancery.

In England, the Puritan Reformers did not start this shift, but they enthusiastically followed along. The Puritans, who sought to reform power away from the monarch in many ways, saw the chancellor's discretionary powers of judication as part and parcel of an overweening monarchy. In place of the old moral basis for contract, the Reformers added covenant theology to the new concept of bargained-for consideration. As a reflection of the absolutely binding covenant between God and man, civil contracts were to be strictly enforced, with few if any defenses to a contract outside of its "four corners."[27] Puritan society being communitarian, however, contracts would arise out of a close relationship between the parties, members

---

23. Berman, "Religious Sources," 109–11.
24. Berman, *Law and Revolution*, 248.
25. Berman, "Religious Sources," 111, emphasis in original.
26. Berman, "Religious Sources," 116.
27. A clause stipulating a condition precedent to performance is an example of a defense to a promise inside the agreement.

of a larger but equally close-knit community.²⁸ This would have directly influenced both the parties' willingness to make a bargain and the terms of the bargain made. In other words, the *moral* basis for contractual liability that canon law imposed was substantially fulfilled via Puritan community life.²⁹ Contracts were strictly enforced, but the range of allowable contracts was much narrower, and they were enforced, above all, with a high degree of concern for the poor.³⁰ We have artifacts of this today. For example, most states restrict the ability of a homeowner to mortgage his or her homestead (although reverse mortgages, home equity loans, and the like have liberalized the ability to do so).

We see a similar phenomenon in the early American colonies. "Equity," more in Perkins's sense of fairness, was almost a commonplace in colonial charters and legal documents.³¹ It carried over into their legal systems, including in relation to debt and contract. In some places, arbitration took the place of court action for settling debts. In others, the Deuteronomic seven-year forgiveness of debt rule was implemented.

The secularization of law in the nineteenth and especially the twentieth century virtually eliminated both the canon law principles of morality and the Puritan communitarian outlook. Left in place were strict rules of contract enforcement, including, for instance, the principle that only the presence, not the adequacy, of consideration matters. Justice Holmes would have gone farther than that. On the one hand, he argued in *Common Law* that only bargained-for consideration suffices to support a contract; detrimental reliance is not enough.³² On the other hand, bargained-for consideration is not only necessary, but sufficient. The adequacy of the consideration, the benefit to the promise, the detriment to the promisor, the benefit to the promisor: all are irrelevant to the existence of the contract.³³ (I suppose Holmes would have said that Jacob's bowl of stew was quite enough to sustain his claim to Esau's birthright.) As are moral considerations. Thus, Holmes said in "The Path of the Law," "Nowhere is the confusion between legal and moral ideas more manifest than in the law of

---

28. Berman, "Religious Sources," 112–22.
29. Berman, "Religious Sources," 112–23.
30. Berman, *Faith and Order*, 122.
31. See Hall, *Reforming People*, for a full discussion of equity in early New England.
32. Holmes, *Common Law*, 293–94.
33. Holmes, *Common Law*, 290–291.

contract.... The duty to keep a contract at common law means a prediction that you must pay damages if you do not keep it—and nothing else."[34]

Both in canon law and English common law during and after the Reformation, contract law existed in a larger context of legal theory with moral and theological underpinnings. Now, however, having lost those theological bases, all that remains is the stand-alone premise that "promises must be kept," offset only by watered-down notions of "unconscionability" and "public policy" lacking any common foundation.[35] Contracts retain a quasi-moral veneer of obligation, but without either a moral purpose to the contract or a moral relationship between the parties.

In response, during progressive times legislatures and agencies enact economic legislation (such as consumer protection laws) or regulations, aimed at ameliorating the worst abuses of strict contract law. These laws constitute a sort of "legislated equity," supplementing or even overriding the bargain made by the parties. They are *political* acts, not moral. As such, they often give with one hand and take away with the other. So, for instance, the ironically titled "Employee Retirement Investment Security Act" (ERISA) preempts *all* state consumer-protection laws in the area of employee benefits such as health insurance, life insurance, and retirement plans, *and* limits the employee's recovery to the amounts provided by the contract—thus denying the employee both the judicial protection of equity and the statutory protection of quasi-penal deceptive trade practice laws. Then, when political winds shift, the same legislatures curtail or even repeal them. Consider, for example, the sort of spectacle that has surrounded the Consumer Finance Protection Bureau. Created during the Obama administration, it passes thousands of pages of regulation, only to be entrusted, during the Trump administration, to a former congressman who tried repeatedly to abolish it. As Berman points out, this type of legislation fails to reflect both our legal

---

34. Holmes, "Path of the Law," 462.

35. This manifests something Alister McGrath sees as a larger phenomenon. In writing about Calvin's influence on Western culture, McGrath says, "Atheism arises when the religious core of a movement such as Calvinism evaporates, leaving a distinctive residue. That residue takes the form of a cluster of social, political, moral, and economic attitudes, originally linked with religious faith, but apparently proving to be capable of continuing in its absence." McGrath describes this as "the persistence of a crater in the cultural landscape, when the original force of its explosion has been spent." McGrath, *Life of John Calvin*, 251.

tradition and historic ways of thinking about law, in favor of the mistaken impression that legislatures now constitute the *source* of law.[36]

The fault does not entirely lie with the legislative branch. Our courts have so fully accepted the notion that people have a fundamental right and freedom to contract, and so tenaciously hold onto the premise that "promises must be kept," that honoring even unreasonable contracts turns out to be a quasi- (or pseudo-) moral obligation. So, for example, although a contracting party cannot affirmatively misrepresent a state of affairs ("fraud in the inducement" being a long-standing defense to a contract), courts generally now hold that a contracting party has no obligation to share superior knowledge with the other party. I can't lie about my leaking roof, but I can allow you to rely on your own inspection, even if I know that the inspector missed a big hole next to the chimney.[37]

Not only would this have violated equity as conceived by both Aquinas and Calvin; Cicero declared such behavior immoral 2,100 years ago. In Book III of *De Officiis*, Cicero tells stories about two sellers having special knowledge about the property or the market. The first, a grain dealer, holds a stock of imported grain in Rhodes, in a time of famine. He finds out, before the public knows, that relief approaches, in the form of several grain ships from Alexandria. May the seller hide that knowledge and sell at inflated prices to the desperate citizens of Rhodes? The second, a homeowner, knows that there are rats in all the bedrooms and termites in the timbers. Does he have to disclose these flaws?[38]

Cicero says that he does, finding the failure to disclose just as bad as active concealment, on both moral and *practical* grounds.[39] The moral grounds are obvious; the practical ones subtle. According to Cicero, the artful negotiator will, in the fullness of time, be known not as "candid or sincere or straightforward or upright or honest . . . , but rather one who is

---

36. Berman, *Law and Revolution*, 38.

37. Here is an example of legislated equity. The Texas Deceptive Trade Practices-Consumer Protection Act has a laundry list of deceptive practices. One of them is "failing to disclose information concerning goods or services which was known at the time of the transaction if such failure to disclose such information was intended to induce the consumer into a transaction into which the consumer would not have entered had the information been disclosed." So far so good. Except that the statute has a state-of-mind requirement for both the seller and the consumer; and the statute allows for waivers; and the statute has a number of exemptions.

38. Cicero, *De Officiis*, 319–25.

39. Jonsen and Toulmin, *Abuse of Casuistry*, 81–82.

shifty, sly, artful, shrewd, underhand, cunning, one grown old in fraud and subtlety."[40]

Here we have truthfulness supporting social cooperation—the same loyalty to community, from a Roman philosopher, around which Calvin centered his social theology 1,600 years later. We also detect a combination of idealism and political prudence that, much later, characterized Matthew Hale's view of poor laws in the seventeenth century. Thus, the loss of historical sense that Berman describes pulls us away not just from the Christian roots of our legal system, but its just-as-ancient philosophical underpinnings.

The Theological Roots of the Dilemma: Oliver O'Donovan

Both an Anglican priest and an academic theologian, Oliver O'Donovan has spent a broad and lengthy career writing about moral and practical theology, Christian ethics, bioethics, and the ethics of war, among many other topics. Time and again, however, he has returned to the topic of political theology. In *Resurrection and Moral Order* (1994), he addressed the question of how Christ's resurrection could, indeed must, be the foundation of Christian ethics. Following *Resurrection and Moral Order* were two books, companion volumes of a sort, that narrowed that question to political theology. *The Desire of the Nations*, published in 1996, set out O'Donovan's view of a "political theology," "the purpose of which was to show how the political concepts wrapped up in Jewish and Christian speech about God's redemption of the world still had political force."[41] In *The Ways of Judgment*, published nine years later, O'Donovan wrote, essentially, a mirror image of *Desire of the Nations*, examining modern political concepts—justice, mercy, freedom, judgment among them—from a Christian perspective. O'Donovan begins *The Ways of Judgment* by saying "The authority of secular government resides in the practice of judgment."[42] In the context of O'Donovan's book, that includes all acts of political discretion, not just judicial judgment. But it includes judgments issued by courts, and so *The Ways of Judgment* speaks loudly to the questions raised in this book.

O'Donovan confronts theologically the same paradox that Berman describes historically—the conflict between justice and mercy. What does it

---

40. Cicero, *De Officiis*, 327.
41. O'Donovan, *Ways of Judgment*, ix.
42. O'Donovan, *Ways of Judgment*, 3.

mean for our political and judicial institutions that both justice and mercy are divinely ordained? Just as Kant said that he could conceive of politics based on morality but not vice versa, O'Donovan wants to know how justice can find its roots in gospel, rather than what human concepts of justice may tell us about God.[43]

O'Donovan claims that pronouncing judgment, for him the fundamental activity of civil government, carries a specifically Christian justification; in Romans, Paul says that civil authority "is God's servant for your good," but also "the servant of God to execute wrath on the wrongdoer."[44] Judgment has both a political power, by approving or disapproving an action or state of affairs, and a moral aspect, because the *criteria* for approval or disapproval requires discriminating between good and evil. (O'Donovan finds "strong" legal positivism simply incoherent.) Justice, then, takes on two meanings: the reference to the act of judgment and the moral discrimination that lies behind, supports, and justifies the action.

On the one hand, our political institutions must attempt to mirror the divine balance of justice and mercy; we judge truthfully when, as best we can, "we judge of a thing as God has judged of it."[45] Because, however, humans do not share in God's perfection, human institutions—courts, legislatures, administrative agencies—cannot possibly achieve perfect justice, and it is idolatrous to treat them as if they can. O'Donovan cautions us against treating the justice system or any other human institution as a representation of God. Courts cannot *redeem*,[46] in the sense of making things as they were before. Human agencies such as courts "[do] not have the Holy Spirit at [their] disposal to renew the moral consciences of offenders," nor can they "raise . . . victims from the dead, nor restore moral relations to what they were before they were violated."[47]

The "reserve" (O'Donovan's term) we should use when tempted to anoint any human institution, no matter how admirable, as God's representative is precisely the humility called for in Micah.[48] Humans and hu-

---

43. O'Donovan, *Desire of the Nations*, 6–7.
44. Rom 13:4. The reference in O'Donovan is at page 4 of *The Ways of Judgment*.
45. O'Donovan, *Ways of Judgment*, 16.
46. O'Donovan, *Ways of Judgment*, 87.
47. O'Donovan, *Ways of Judgment*, 99.
48. George Washington invoked Micah's call for humility as a model for the relations between citizen and state, between citizen and citizen, and as the political model for the nation. See "Washington's Circular Letter of Farewell to the Army, June 8, 1783." References like this were common in the early years of the United States. Dreisbach, "Micah

man institutions should walk (humbly) with God, but they are not God, nor do they speak for God. As in the parable of the unjust servant,[49] the prospect of divine judgment requires human judgment to be humble, lest we receive the same strict treatment from God. Being "flesh and blood and full of infirmities" means that our judgments cannot be angelic. In fact, O'Donovan (like Hooker) says that a society's peculiar infirmities explain why laws are different from one culture to another. Not that one society's laws are wrong, better, or worse than another's (although that may also be the case). Perhaps their cultural wrongs are different. Thus, "[W]hen Jesus says, 'Moses for the hardness of your hearts commanded you to give a writ of divorce,' we should not take him to mean that the Mosaic law was, from a moral point of view, a second-best law. This regulative arrangement, rather, was the *right* way to condemn divorce, because it told the truth about the Israelites' hardness of heart."[50] So, a violent people need more laws against violence, a college town better regulation of alcohol and driving, a boom town better control of shoddy building practices.

While our judgment, and our judgment systems, may be flawed, we are not to abandon them entirely. Despite the "judge not" trope so popular today, we are called to exercise judgment. According to O'Donovan, "justice" as used in Scripture predominantly refers to "justice as judgment," rather than "justice as right" or "justice as virtue."[51] In the New Testament, "the sphere of public judgment constitutes a carefully circumscribed and specially privileged exception to a general prohibition of judgment."[52] O'Donovan cautions us both against abandoning our political structures entirely and against treating them as walled off from grace. Courts "must resign their judgment to God's in accepting the limitations that their accomplishments betray; but as they do so they are permitted to mirror the unity of truth and grace which we discern in God's deed of justification."[53]

O'Donovan sees political judgment as an act on behalf of the public, designed to promote the public good. Judgment, he says, establishes a new "public context." In other words, judgment defines the community. Moral judgment enhances the morality of a community. Judgment, even exercised

---

6:8," 91.

49. Matt 18:21–35.
50. O'Donovan, *Ways of Judgment*, 20.
51. O'Donovan, *Ways of Judgment*, 7.
52. O'Donovan, *Ways of Judgment*, 99 (quoting Rom 2:1).
53. O'Donovan, *Ways of Judgment*, 100.

imperfectly and tentatively, is how we express whom we see ourselves to be. Thus, O'Donovan firmly rejects the positivist view of law as divorced from morality. We can conceive of law as distinct from morality only if we have a crabbed view of morality as purely an internal affair.[54] Because Christians view morality as concerning not simply private but also public behavior, any such thin view of morality makes no sense. Morality, in fact, determines the nature of our relations with others.

Our relations with others lie at the heart of our Christian obligation. In *Desire of the Nations*, O'Donovan invokes the Episcopalian baptismal covenant's call to "strive for justice and peace among all people, and respect the dignity of every human being":

> One thing is lacking (from the covenant): there is no recognition that this "striving" and "respecting" must take place within a context of political institutions supposedly serving those very ends, and that our political service of the human community consistently involves us in relation with our institutions. We are offered a vision of political responsibility in a vacuum, wherein in life it is mediated through the exercise of, and through obligation to, structures of political authority: government, elected representation, law, policing, administration, and so on.[55]

"Striving" evokes a variety of Christian pilgrimage, carried out in the legislative chambers and the courtroom; like a pilgrimage, the meaning lies in the attempt as much as in the accomplishment. Often, striving is all we can do. We know these to be hostile places for true justice and mercy: the "Valley of the Dry Bones," we might call them. O'Donovan specifically invokes Perkins's Puritan sense of equity when he describes what would constitute a legitimate public judgment, a "merciful judgment, witnessing to the divine work of reconciliation."[56] The legal system, which has the same flaws as any human institution, remains (we hope) open to the same grace. The clemency that equity calls for "befits those who know their own sinfulness."[57] Therefore, courts "must resign their judgment to God's in accepting the limitations that their accomplishments betray; but as they do so they are permitted to mirror the unity of truth and grace which we discern in God's deed of justification."

---

54. O'Donovan, *Ways of Judgment*, 23.
55. O'Donovan, *Desire of the Nations*, 17.
56. O'Donovan, *Ways of Judgment*, 99 (referencing Perkins).
57. O'Donovan, *Ways of Judgment*, 98.

Think back to Micah. We are called both to action ("do justice") and attitude ("love kindness").[58] Justice here, in O'Donovan's view, means human justice carried out by individuals in human institutions, but illuminated by the gospel and moderated by the obligation to act mercifully. In other words, the conflict between justice and mercy can be resolved occasionally and provisionally, but only by admitting that no human can finally and decisively overcome it. We can neither escape it or finally solve it, but only live into it.

Indeed, the conflict cannot be finally resolved; only a perfect legal system could be perfectly just, and by expecting perfection from human institutions we are guilty of idolatry. Nevertheless, we are to strive for justice in just the same way that anti-poverty programs are morally essential, even if their stated goal to "eliminate poverty" lies beyond human possibility. Justice cannot be replaced by mercy, but it must be shaped by it.[59] As it turns out, O'Donovan finds the best expression of this idea in Puritan philosophy of equity. Men are equally reprovable, he quotes Perkins as saying, if they always insist on "justice, justice" or on "mercy, mercy."[60] "The prince's laws cannot be 'perfect and absolute' as God's laws are; but the prince may practice a merciful judgment, witnessing to the divine work of reconciliation."[61]

If the court practices a "merciful judgment," then the lawyer takes heart in being an officer of the court. He participates in a system that not only passes judgment on the parties, but on itself,[62] reminding itself of the humility required by its inability to match divine judgment.[63] Judgment may not be perfect, but it is essential. The lawyer is not shamed by participating in an imperfect system; he is glorified insofar as he strives to perfect it. A system without equity does not strive for perfection, because it expresses confidence that law and precedent (its own "prior pronouncements") can be perfect—which, of course, they cannot.

Judgment is an act of recognition and declaration. Judgment declares who we are as a society (in the same way that an anti-poverty program declares poverty evil). Our inherent sociality requires that wrongs be declared

---

58. Dempster, *Micah*, 156.
59. O'Donovan, *Desire of the Nations*, 261.
60. O'Donovan, *Desire of the Nations*, 261.
61. O'Donovan, *Ways of Judgment*, 98–99.
62. O'Donovan, *Ways of Judgment*, 93.
63. O'Donovan, *Ways of Judgment*, 86–87.

as such, because wrongs are inherently social.⁶⁴ Yet if our declarations of judgment are limited solely to strict enforcement of the law, without the possibility of forgiveness, mercy, or equity (O'Donovan uses all three terms) we give human law and secular justice a faith and a respect to which only divine judgment is entitled. Equity, then, passes a judgment that positive law itself failed in the case at hand.

The Theology of Contract Disputes

O'Donovan makes a claim about judicial action that is both surprising and troubling to litigators: *all* court actions, criminal or civil, lead to judgment against the person or property of the defendant, and hence are a form of *punishment*, philosophically indistinguishable in impact on the civil defendant from the judgment of a criminal court.⁶⁵ Lawyers are taught that the civil lawyer merely enforces his client's rights, and that such enforcement is not "punishment." "Punitive damages," by definition, go beyond what is needed to compensate an injured party for a wrong. Contractual penalty clauses are invalid; hence the need for the careful drafting to establish that liquidated damages are a reasonable attempt to estimate actual damage, instead of an invalid penalty.

O'Donovan, on the other hand, says that retribution, which clearly is a penal concept, carries with it a sense of "requital" or "return," so that civil damages qualify as punishment just as much as criminal conviction.⁶⁶ I suspect that very few of us think of prison sentences as somehow balancing the scales between the perpetrator and the victim, although that may have been true in ancient theories of punishment. In fact, we tend to think of restitution imposed on convicted criminals as being in addition to, not part of, the court's punishment. Nevertheless, O'Donovan does remind us of something important. If the question is whether an adverse civil action can be "punishing," the answer is a resounding "yes." Losing a job or a home devastates just as much as being convicted of a crime, and all too often leads to a life of crime.

Recall that O'Donovan defines judgment as "an act of moral discrimination that pronounces upon a preceding act or existing state of affairs to

---

64. O'Donovan, *Ways of Judgment*, 92.
65. O'Donovan, *Ways of Judgment*, 108.
66. O'Donovan, *Ways of Judgment*, 101.

establish a new public context."[67] Establishing a "new public context" in contract cases could be declaring a mortgage enforceable or invalid; proclaiming a debt due or forgiven; evicting a homeowner or letting her stay. The "task of a theory of punishment is to make this practice of requiting and returning intelligible."[68] By (O'Donovan's) definition, those judgments must be acts of moral discrimination. If a move away from equity towards strict enforcement prevents moral discrimination, courts do something *other* than pronounce judgment. They act more like an executioner, carrying out a sentence previously pronounced by the legislature. Indeed, according to O'Donovan, "the founding of a judiciary is a judicial act, giving judgment in favor of the oppressed—not one particular oppressed person, but the oppressed as a class."[69] Depriving the judiciary the authority to adjudicate fairly both constitutes an act of oppression generally, and makes the courts instruments of oppression in out-of-the-ordinary cases.

Here lies the heart of O'Donovan's theology of justice. Second in importance only to life and death issues, equality of justice requires us "to give equal treatment to human beings . . . when they lack essential resources to participate in social communications as such."[70] Not that O'Donovan would require the completely equal distribution of wealth. Like Perkins and Calvin said before him, "there is no moral significance in distributing goods equally as such." Rather, "to ask about the justice of possessions is to ask about their human significance, i.e. how they empower the possessor to act, how they work as a resource for the exercise of human freedom."[71] Hooker makes the same point:

> All men desire to lead in this world a happy life. That life is led most happily, wherein all virtue is exercised without impediment or let. The Apostle in exhorting men to contentment, although they have in this world no more than very bare food and raiment, giveth us thereby to understand, that those are even the lowest of things necessary, that if we should be stripped of all those things without which we might possibly be, yet these must be left, that destitution in these is such an impediment, as till it be removed, suffereth not the mind of man to admit any other care.[72]

67. O'Donovan, *Ways of Judgment*, 7.
68. O'Donovan, *Ways of Judgment*, 101.
69. O'Donovan, *Ways of Judgment*, 191.
70. O'Donovan, *Ways of Judgment*, 45.
71. O'Donovan, *Ways of Judgment*, 47.
72. *Laws*, 1:97. The "Apostle" is Paul, and the reference is to 1 Tim 6:8.

This inquiry into the human implications of an economic arrangement is precisely the measure by which early forms of equity would have judged the moral usefulness of a contract.

As O'Donovan sees it, "the punishment of an offender requires the community to devise a truthful response to the offense, which is a purposive action, not a blind consequence or an instinctive reaction."[73] To be a *truthful* response, contract law must have a place for equity—for both justice and mercy. Otherwise, the judgment of the court simply reacts, as O'Donovan puts it, to black letter rules; the damage done to the offending party, relative to the benefit conferred on the aggrieved party, becomes a mere "blind consequence." For Christians, *truth* requires the examination of justice versus mercy.

With these points in mind, let me, then, venture some observations on the theology of contract disputes. Rendering of a civil judgment constitutes a form of punishment; the decision in such matters requires an act of moral discrimination; the judiciary itself is called to express political judgment in favor of the oppressed; and the question in cases involving the poor is how the proposed judicial action threatens to deprive a party of "essential resources to participate in social communications." Framed that way, garden variety civil cases assume theological implications, and measure the moral health of the system and the ethical jeopardy into which it places its officers. "Judgment offers society the truth about itself, just as it offers the offender the truth about himself."[74] In civil cases, it offers the claimant the truth about himself also.

And the hypothetical from earlier in the chapter: does any of this help us sort out what to do with our engaged homeowner? (Other than to say, "I told you so," which is tempting, but not particularly helpful.) One thing we can say is that the case illuminates O'Donovan's point that civil judgment is punishment. Withholding ninety thousand dollars from the builder because of a few defects that don't impair the livability of the home seems punitive by any standard. Unless you believe the builder is a scammer, and we've hypothesized that he is not, there is no theory that makes out a moral breach of contract. Your own experience says that is the kind of thing that happens

---

73. O'Donovan, *Ways of Judgment*, 113.
74. O'Donovan, *Ways of Judgment*, 118.

CLIENTS VS. COURTS: THE DILEMMA IN HISTORY AND THEOLOGY

to this builder over and over. It's also difficult to make out a benefit of the bargain theory.[75] Your client got a good price for the home, which is probably worth more, even with the defects, than the sales price. So, it seems unduly harsh to allow your client to keep all the retainage. "Equity abhors a forfeiture." But, undeniably, he didn't get what he contracted for. Do you take this case? Chapters 10 and 12 will help us answer that question.

---

75. There are, at least, two ways to measure damages in a case such as this one. The first, the "benefit of the bargain" theory, asks how much the value of the home as received falls short of the purchase price. Here, that answer might be zero. The second, cost of completion, asks how much it would take to finish the contract. By hypothesis, that figure here is a few thousand dollars.

9

Humility: Virtue or Vice?

Return of the Prodigal Son

Imagine another Friday morning in your office, with another unscheduled visitor. This time, however, it's an old client (and friend), a wealthy rancher, with two sons. A year ago, the younger of the two asked for his share of his inheritance, so that he could go out and make a name for himself. He certainly made a name for himself. Several names, in fact: drunkard, gambler, tramp . . . *prodigal*. Having blown his fortune, he's returned, contrite. Your client welcomed him with open arms and had a huge party for him. But now, two weeks later, the lad sleeps all day, parties all night, and tonight starts his third weekend-long "I'm home" bash. All of which infuriates the elder son, the ranch foreman. Your client wants to know if his forgiveness has gone too far.

Notice the similarities between this story, which we all know from Luke's gospel, and the history of Jacob and Esau from Genesis. In each, inheritance rules are breached. Jacob gets the double, "birthright" share that should have gone to his brother Esau; the "prodigal son" gets his inheritance before his father even dies. The similarities don't stop there. In each story, the younger son departs, leaving behind an older brother seething with resentment. Each younger son has a spiritual revelation: Jacob when wrestling with God, the prodigal son in the pig trough. Each returns home, even though unresolved conflict awaits.

There are also differences between the stories, starting with genre. Genesis tells Jacob's story as one of real persons that exist in history, with lives that begin before the story and continue afterwards. The story of the prodigal son, on the other hand, is a parable. No one takes it as recounting actual events involving real people. Like all parables, it is lean. There are only three characters. We get no explication of the actors' motivations. The story ends abruptly.[1] We don't know what comes after the climax, or what happened off-stage during the action. We don't know, for instance, what the father went through while the son was away. We don't know anything about the rest of the father's family.

Let's compare the parents in the two stories. Return to the Jacob story for a moment. Isaac, no doubt righteous, nevertheless seems to be someone that things happen *to*: bound by his father, married to someone picked by his servant, deceived by his son.[2] Rebekah, on the other hand, intrigues us. We meet her as a model of kindness, as she welcomes Abraham's servant, who searches for a wife for Isaac, and waters his camel.[3] She is obedient, obeying her father and setting off across the desert to marry a man she's never met.[4] She is romantic; contrary to most translations of Genesis, which tell us that she "alighted" from her camel when first seeing Isaac, the better translation would be that she *fell off* her ride—literally swooning at the sight of her future husband![5] She is faithful, sticking by Isaac even when he tries to pass her off as his sister to the king of the Philistines. Finally, Rebekah proves impressively diligent in adopting as her own project the fulfillment of God's promise that Jacob, the younger son, would father the greater nation.[6]

Too diligent, some might say. It's not in Rebekah's personality to accept God at his word. She seems to think that God's promise depends on her to fulfill. She manipulates Isaac into blessing Jacob by mistake, and then sends him off into hiding from Esau. Would things between Jacob and Esau have been different if Rebekah had trusted God a bit more, walking with God rather than trying to stay two steps in front of him?

There is a lesson about humility for us here. Talmud teaches that Isaac's disinheritance of Esau was providential, because Esau was not equipped to do what Jacob did: become the patriarch of the nation. Others, however, find God's use of ordinarily flawed humans to carry out God's purposes bracing.[7]

---

1. These characteristics come from Rudolph Bultmann's discussion in *The History of the Synoptic Tradition*, 188–92.
2. Gen 22:1–14; 24:62–67; 27:5–40.
3. Gen 24:15–21.
4. Gen 24:52–61.
5. Gen 24:64–65.
6. Gen 27:5–17.
7. Luban, "Rabbi Shaffer and Rabbi Trollope," 904.

Those interpretations do not exclude each other. Jacob's pinching of his brother's birthright and his father's blessing was certainly sinful. Calvin says that Rebekah's behavior, while "vicious and reprehensible, was not devoid of faith." Her story shows "how prone the human mind is to turn aside whenever it gives itself the least indulgence." Nevertheless, "the particular error of Rebekah did not render the blessing of no effect."[8]

Now for the prodigal son and his forgiving father. Contemplate what might have happened after the parable ends. The father asks the elder son, who is not nearly so overjoyed to see his wandering brother, to come back in for the party. Did he? We don't know, but we can safely assume his resentment continued. Likewise, we don't know whether the younger son reformed himself, or repeated the same pattern time and again. It seems likely, however, that the three of them did not immediately become one big happy family.

That, of course, is not the point of the story. The parable teaches a lesson about God's infinite forgiveness. But the parable does not portray, let alone answer, a complex moral problem—the reconciliation of the family. Unlike God's, human redemptive capacity remains persistently limited. Rebekah sees her two sons at dagger points because of her conniving, and Luke's forgiving father must deal not only with the consequences of what the prodigal son did, but also the after-effects of his return on the elder son. It certainly is not the point of the story that humans can be too forgiving; none of us would have counseled the father to offer the son the slave's position he asked for. At the same time, however, as O'Donovan told us about the justice system, no human can redeem, in the sense of wipe the slate clean. What happened, happened. In other words, Rebekah and the forgiving father teach us something about the third leg of Micah's stool. They teach us something about humility.

The History of Humility

Aristotle and Nietzsche

Humility has suffered a checkered career. Neither the list of cardinal (fortitude, prudence, temperance, and justice) nor theological (faith, hope and charity) virtues include it. Some cultures have refused to recognize humility as a virtue at all. The Greeks saw humility as a deficit, interfering with the

---

8. Calvin, *Institutes* III, chapter 2, paragraph 31.

proper goal of *magnanimity*—"greatness of soul." Aristotle, who saw ethics as seeking a golden mean between extremes, thought that each of us should properly assess our own abilities and act accordingly. Humility, an underestimation of one's capacities, prevented one from achieving one's full worth. The corresponding vice, vanity, was an overvaluing of one's capabilities:

> Such, then, is the proud man; the man who falls short of him is unduly humble, and the man who goes beyond him is vain. Now even these are not thought to be bad (for they are not malicious), but only mistaken. For the unduly humble man, being worthy of good things, robs himself of what he deserves, and to have something bad about him from the fact that he does not think himself worthy of good things, and seems also not to know himself; else he would have desired the things he was worthy of, since these were good. Yet such people are not thought to be fools, but rather unduly retiring... Vain people, on the other hand, are fools and ignorant of themselves, and that manifestly; for, not being worthy of them, they attempt honourable undertakings, and then are found out; and they adorn themselves with clothing and outward show and such things and wish their strokes of good fortune to be made public, and speak about them as if they would be honoured for them. But undue humility is more opposed to pride than vanity is; for it is both commoner and worse.[9]

Two millennia later, Nietzsche surpassed Aristotle in his disdain for humility, calling it not merely a deficiency but a vice, the fundamental flaw in traditional morality. Nietzsche portrayed the history of civilization as a struggle between "master morality," grounded in power, and "slave morality" values of kindness and humility. Classical culture embodied master morality. Judeo-Christian culture, on the other hand, promoted slave virtues, because the Jews were repeatedly conquered, enslaved, and exiled, and the early Christians were persecuted and, in some cases, literally enslaved. Christianity, the religion of the powerless, took classical virtues (like pride) and turned them into vices, and classical vices (like humility) into virtues. Nietzsche called the attitude *ressentiment*, which turns frustration into blame, and weakness and insecurity into moral superiority. The classic example, for Nietzsche, was the Sermon on the Mount. But, when

---

9. Aristotle, *Nicomachean Ethics*, 71. Note that in this translation Aristotle refers to the "proud man." Many translations refer to "pride" rather than "magnanimity." We'll see in a minute that Aristotle's use of the word "pride" differs from the Christian use of the word.

Christianity spread throughout the Roman Empire and then, against all odds, became the official religion of the empire, slave morality, paradoxically, came to dominate. Or so Nietzsche has it.

Christians scarcely know where to start disagreeing with Nietzsche. There are plenty of books and articles that set out those disagreements. Undeniably, though, humility is a peculiarly Christian virtue. Christians take Christ himself as our model for humility, in that Christ humbled himself simply by becoming human. He then continued to humble himself throughout his life, declining to exalt himself when facing the cross.

Augustine, Humility's Great Champion

Augustine was perhaps the first great champion of humility as a Christian virtue. He saw humility both as a virtue in itself and as an antidote to pride, which for Augustine was the root of all other sin, elevating love of self over love of God.[10] Augustine would have cheerfully pled guilty as charged of turning vices into virtues, and virtues into vices.[11] He found the paradigm of Roman values of pride and valor to be sinful, not in and of themselves (in fact they served to suppress other vices) but because they were misdirected, aimed at self-glory rather than the glory of God.[12]

Augustine's hostility to pride revealed itself in his vigorous anti-Pelagianism. Pelagius was a British monk who lived from the middle of the fourth century through the early fifth century. He dissented from orthodox views on original sin, claimed that humans were essentially good, and thought that human effort was both central to and capable of moral perfection—all of which Augustine violently disputed. Augustine saw sin as more than specific misbehaviors, of which all humans are repeatedly guilty. Because of the fall, sin infected human nature itself, so that human efforts at perfection are doomed to fail. Individual sins, in other words, are the result of sin. Without humility, we cannot acknowledge our dependence on God's grace, the only hope against human frailty and sinfulness.[13] Therefore, far from being a necessary element to human achievement, pride hinders humans from achieving union with God, the greatest human happiness.

---

10. McInerney, *Greatness of Humility*, 11.

11. Nietzsche wrote at some length about Augustine, and this chapter is not a scholarly analysis of Nietzsche's critique. There are many available.

12. Porter, "Virtue," 209–13.

13. McInerney, *Greatness of Humility*, 11.

The theme of humility pervades Augustine's interpretation of Scripture as well as his theology. Humility gets a few mentions in the New Testament: in Matthew and Luke's gospels,[14] in 2 Corinthians and Philippians among the Pauline epistles,[15] and in James and 1 Peter.[16] As important for Augustine as specific moral teachings are the moral interpretations he puts on Old and New Testament stories. Whether it is David slaying Goliath because of his faith in God rather than his own powers, or Jesus's admonition that the poor in spirit (for Augustine, the humble) gain the kingdom of heaven, Augustine reads Scripture as repeatedly portraying our need to rely on God rather than our own capabilities.[17] Proverbs 3:34, "God resists the proud, but gives aid to the humble," is a verse Augustine comes back to time and again.[18] He even finds John the Baptist and the Apostle Peter (two figures we think of as bold, even confrontational) models of humility, because they each subordinate themselves to Christ.[19]

Finally, humility played an essential role in Augustine's view of justice. Augustine, accepting the Aristotelean notion that justice lies in giving each their due, holds that God, being perfect, deserves greater devotion from humans than any creature. Therefore, the highest justice requires us to give God God's due—our greatest and fullest love. Humility prompts us to give God that devotion, by putting love of God before human concerns. We acknowledge how far short of God's perfection we are, rather than pridefully thinking about how much better we are than others or how worthy we are in our own right.[20]

Aquinas and Calvin on Humility

Aquinas took up the question of whether humility is a virtue. How can humility be a virtue if it is opposed to magnanimity, which is itself a virtue?[21]

14. Matt 11:29; 18:4; 21:5; 23:12; Luke 14:11; 18:14.
15. 2 Cor 10:1; 12:21; Phil 2:8.
16. Jas 4:6, 10; 1 Pet 3:8; 5:5–6.
17. McInerney, *Greatness of Humility*, 44–46.
18. McInerney, *Greatness of Humility*, 48.
19. McInerney, *Greatness of Humility*, 49–50.
20. McInerney, *Greatness of Humility*, 94–95.
21. The format of the *Summa* can be a bit confusing. Aquinas asks a question, sets up "Objections" (anticipated responses), then states his own opinion, then answers the objections. So, Aquinas speaks both for his opponents (in the objections) and for himself.

Humility and magnanimity are both virtues, he answers, but they are not opposed. They balance each other out: humility "restrains the appetite from aiming at great things against right reason"; magnanimity, in contrast, "urges the mind to great things *in accord with right reason*."[22] That is, while Aristotle saw humility and vanity as over- and under-abundance of magnanimity, Aquinas considered humility and magnanimity as both virtues, moderating each other in search of a reasoned appraisal of one's own worth.

Humility, Aquinas says, is not the greatest virtue. Charity wins that honor, because the theological virtues are greater than the earthly. Nor is it the greatest earthly virtue; that place goes to justice. Humility, Aquinas says, comes next because it "makes a man a good subject to ordinance of all kinds and in all matters."[23] Humility is the virtue that allows us to live a charitable, reasonable, and just life. For Calvin, true humility lies in the recognition of one's total dependence on God.[24] Thus, when he quotes Augustine, who said that the first, second, and third precepts of Christianity were humility, humility, and humility,[25] he means our inability to merit our own salvation, not our own worldly abilities. Likewise, in his *Commentary on Ezekiel*, he says that "humility is the beginning of true intelligence."[26] Here, he refers not to intellectual humility, but rather to knowledge of the glory of God. Calvin says that the purpose of God's revelation to Ezekiel was to inspire his prophecy, his public pronouncements, "that he might be useful to the whole people."[27] In his *Commentary on Matthew*, Calvin gives this definition of humility: "That man is truly humble who neither claims any personal merit in the sight of God, nor proudly despises brethren, or aims at being thought superior to them, but reckons it enough that he is one of the members of Christ, and desires nothing more than that the Head alone should be exalted."[28]

---

22. Aquinas, *ST* II-II, question 161, article 1, emphasis added.
23. Aquinas, *ST* II-II, question 161, article 5.
24. Calvin, *Institutes* III, chapter 12.
25. Calvin, *Institutes* II, chapter 2, paragraph 11.
26. Calvin, *Commentary on Ezekiel*, 1:13.
27. Calvin, *Commentary on Ezekiel*, 1:13.
28. Calvin, *Commentary on Matthew*, 18:4.

HUMILITY: VIRTUE OR VICE?

Lawyerly Humility

"Lawyerly humility" sounds a bit of an oxymoron. Few people would think of lawyers as humble—five-hundred-dollar haircuts and bespoke silk suits come more readily to mind. Applying to and getting admitted to law school impairs one's humility. Law schools promote themselves as attracting the best and the brightest, in order to launch them on careers making them the greatest, the most powerful, and the wealthiest. First-year students, asked why they wanted to be lawyers, usually respond either with "to make a lot of money" or "to solve _____." (Fill in here one of the world's intractable problems.) Neither answer sags under the weight of its own humility. Neither does law school training promote humility. We are taught to "think like lawyers," which, more often than not, translates as "think more rigorously," until, when we leave school, we all too often decide that it means "thinking better than anyone else."[29]

Therefore, lawyers could learn a bit from Christian ideas about humility. We have two fundamental rules, justice and mercy. Sometimes they align, but sometimes they come into conflict. How do we find the balance? Perhaps the sin lies not in failing to get the balance right, which we are all doomed to do. Rather, our sin comes from having too much confidence in our own ability to get it right, and in not being sorrowful when we fail.

We can sum up the common thread in all of these in two simple concepts. First, none of us is God. We may be created in the image and likeness of God, but we are also subject to human frailty, and so any advice we give must be tentative and contingent. Second, no one has greater intrinsic value than anyone else, and we all have obligations to each other. We are all children of God: me, you, your client, your client's adversary, your opposing counsel. Therefore, there are moral limitations on the extent to which any lawyer can favor his client's interests.

Notice what these two precepts do not say. They do not contend that humans are worthless, or incapable of reason or moral effort. Saying that we are not God does not a criticism make. Nor do they suppose that humans all have equal abilities. Some people are simply smarter, stronger, faster, wiser, or braver than others. Humility does not require Serena Williams to deny that she plays tennis better than I do.

---

29. It should be said that the first semester of law school can promote a high degree of humility, an effect that wanes each succeeding term.

The lawyer, when advising her client, would do well to bear these two precepts in mind. At the same time, she should also avoid the fake humble "my opinion is no better that anyone else's" attitude. Hooker had no use for this kind of false humility, chastised the Puritans for it, and saw it as an especially pernicious sort of pride.[30]

Pride in being humble, we might call it: the Uriah Heep form of pride. One of the things I promised myself when I began this book was that I would not use Atticus Finch[31] as an example of ethical lawyering. No doubt Finch is a very fine moral exemplar for lawyers. However, there have been quite enough books and articles about him. Instead, I would like to hold up Uriah Heep (from Dickens's *David Copperfield*) for consideration. We might think of Uriah as the anti-Atticus. He manages, in the name of humility, to be both unjust and inequitable. He is not satisfied that he has weaseled himself into partnership with Mr. Wickfield; he wants to appropriate all Mr. Wickfield has for himself—his practice, his home, his daughter. Not in the least inclined to mildness, when he has his chance, he goes for it. None of the higher justice for him: he knows his rights and insists on them.[32]

But we digress. Clients pay lawyers precisely because their opinions should be more perceptive. Nevertheless, a lawyer should be cautious about the value of his own advice, and counsel the client to be chary about her own goals. The practice of law teaches us, if anything, that things rarely turn out the way we expect. Undoubtedly, lawyers have the ability to think through things and evaluate situations and analyze choices. Clients would not trust us with their problems if we did not. Something like Aristotelean magnanimity would be more in order; we should be neither too confident nor too diffident about our abilities.

Lawyers are a bit ahead of the game in this regard. Ask a hundred lawyers about the first thing they learned in law school, and many would say "reasonable minds can differ." The public usually finds it surprising that lawyers, of all people, find it possible to have firm convictions and yet respect

---

30. Stafford, "Richard Hooker and the Later Puritans," 188.

31. From Harper Lee's *To Kill a Mockingbird*, of course.

32. The name "Uriah" appears to be no accident. Recall Uriah the Hittite, King David's truly loyal and humble soldier/servant. Dickens's Uriah comes to us as a counterpart to the Uriah of 2 Samuel. But where Uriah the Hittite is truly modest and loyal (he refuses to sleep with his wife Bathsheba while his troops are in the field), Uriah Heep is self-serving and treacherous (all the while protesting how "'umble" he is), coming ever so close to stealing Agnes Wickfield from her father and from her beloved Copperfield. Uriah the Hittite remains loyal to King David; Uriah Heep stabs his David in the back.

the rights of others to have similarly firm ones—to disagree without being disagreeable, as we way. While we are taught to "think like lawyers," we are also taught that other thinking lawyers can reach different conclusions. This constitutes, in fact, humility in Hooker's sense of the word.

A psychiatrist friend was fond of telling teenagers, when asked who (or what) God is, that God is the small voice in his head that says, when he really gets himself into a fine self-righteous lather, "You know, doctor, you might be wrong about this." We see Jacob wrestle with God, but more often we get something more like a gentle tap on the shoulder. Plans to disinherit a child, to divorce a spouse, to liquidate a retirement account in pursuit of a risky venture (or to buy the sportscar the client always wanted and that assuredly will triple in value, because, after all, it's a classic). These are the kinds of problems that walk into a law office every day. We assume, and the client usually thinks, that the advice sought is about what the client can do.[33] In fact, the advice the client often needs—and more often than we might imagine, wants—concerns what the client *ought* to do. Lawyers hesitate to offer that sort of advice unless put on the spot, lest they be thought intrusive, officious, or intermeddling. Often, however, it is exactly what the situation calls for. Assuming otherwise takes the counseling portion of the vocation out.

Humility, like justice, takes a realistic view of human capacities. Human sinfulness requires justice as a response. Human frailty begs for humility in that response. We all overrate both our individual and our collective capacities to achieve goals. Sometimes reforms simply refuse to come. Sometimes reform comes without our own efforts, as a matter of grace, even when we are convinced that it will not.

Calvin tells us that humility is the beginning of true intelligence. For lawyers, this means that our capacity to reform our client or to persuade a judge, jury, or adversary has limits, as does our discernment when asked to assess a problem. We recall what came out of Jacob's deception and guile: Joseph ended up in Egypt and saved his people, from whence, eventually, came Moses. Without Jacob's conniving (with the help of his mother), without Isaac's honoring the fraudulently obtained blessing, without Jacob's fleecing (literally) Laban—there would have been no Moses, no Exodus, no King David.

What would have happened instead? We don't know. As Christians, we rest assured that Abraham's people would not have starved in the desert. Salvation history has a way of rebooting itself. But God expects us to

---

33. Or, as we recall from J. P. Morgan, how to do it.

assist in that reboot. Perhaps this helps the lawyer confront his dilemmas. We cannot control how things turn out. But we can nudge them along the right path.

To put it another way, humility is an epistemological attitude. We realize that our knowledge, unlike God's, is provisional. We don't know what we don't know, as they say. Walking humbly with God, then, implies walking half a step behind—following, that is—God. Our knowledge of our client, our adversary, the facts: all have limits. We cannot make God-like judgments with human-like knowledge. Nor, as we shall see, can we overrule the conscience of our client.

Humility also opens us to the possibility of hope. If we are utterly confident in our own powers, we have no need for hope. We recall Paul's admonition in chapter 8 of his Letter to the Romans: "Now hope that is seen is not hope. For who hopes for what is seen? But if we hope for what we do not see, we wait for it with patience."[34] Christian humility teaches us that we cannot ultimately rely on our own powers, because we are not God. Hope teaches us that we need not rely on our own powers. What does this have to do with equity? If we are humble about our own ability to assess the just, equity opens the hope that true justice will be done.

---

34. Rom 8:24–25.

10

Jacob's Lawyer (Part Two): Equity in Action

> "Use law as physicians use poisons."
> —William Perkins

A typical lawyer's Friday schedule might look like this:

9:30: Initial consultation with Sonia Ramirez

11:00: Final pre-trial: *Harold v Jack*

1:30: Draft proposed agreement re. Project X

5:30: POETS club

In the United States, lawyers are called upon to do two quite distinct things. They *advise* their clients, and they *do* things for clients. They draft documents, or they represent them in court. The sample schedule above reflects both those activities. The final activity, the POETS club, we'll use to illustrate a point about lawyering as a vocation.

THE LAWYER AS PROPHET

Sonia Ramirez, a middle-age schoolteacher, brings you a property issue with her stepmother, Mrs. Esteves. She and Mrs. Ramirez's father married a year after the death of Mrs. Ramirez's mother, and were married for five years before Sonia's father was disabled in an industrial accident. A year later, he died. They bought a home in Mrs. Esteves's name a few months before Sonia's father died. The stepmother wants to refinance her mortgage but has hit an obstacle. According to Sonia, Mrs. Esteves needs her cooperation, preferably in the form of a quitclaim deed to the home, because the title company says that Sonia inherited a share of it when her father died. You ask Sonia whether her father left a will; she tells you yes, one that predates his marriage to Mrs. Esteves, and it left his residuary estate to Sonia's mother, or to Sonia if her mother died first. However, they never probated it, because her father didn't own anything to speak of. Sonia says that she has two specific questions: (1) Is it true that she owns a share of the home, and (2) if so, does she have to give it to her stepmother? You ask about Mrs. Esteves. Sonia says that they don't have any kind of a relationship, and that she hasn't seen her (or been in the house) since her father's funeral. You push a bit, and Sonia tells you that she knows that her stepmother had cancer several years ago, and thinks she works part-time, up to the Social Security allowable, to help make ends meet. She assumes she gets social security. She asks you what that's got to do with anything.

Whether by will or by inheritance, in many states Sonia inherited a share of the property from her father, with no legal obligation to pay the mortgage or to assist in refinancing. Even though the law gives her stepmother a "homestead" right to occupy the home, and even though her father never paid anything against the mortgage, Sonia has legal title to a half interest in the home. Yet this strikes you as harsh, and perhaps Sonia, at least in part, agrees.

But "legal equity" seems of little help here. Property law, more than any other discipline, values predictability, something that equity is alleged to impair. The other highest value in property law is freedom: we believe that persons have the right to do as they wish with their property. Had you been advising Sonia's father, you would have urged him to leave his share of the house to his new wife, but nothing would have required him to do that. (He may have thought that's what would happen anyway, given that the house was in her name.) All of that is now moot. If Sonia were to sue Mrs. Esteves for her share of the home, she would almost certainly win. Therefore, the question is, can you—should you—try to persuade your client to act against her own interests?

Your meeting with Sonia shows how the advice clients want falls into two categories. The first category, the one Justice Holmes said was the client's sole concern, asks questions about "is." What *is* the law that pertains to my problem? What *will be* the consequences of my doing (or not doing)

JACOB'S LAWYER (PART TWO): EQUITY IN ACTION

something? Sonia tries to limit the discussion to this kind of advice. Do I own part of the home?

But clients also ask "ought" questions, as in "what ought I to do?" There are several types of "ought" questions. Some "ought" questions ask about goals. Questions of strategy, for instance; if I want to win this tennis match, ought I serve harder, or softer but more consistently? Sometimes they are questions of prudence; given that I will need to pay my mortgage at the end of the month, ought I buy five hundred lottery tickets today? Clients routinely have both strategic and prudential questions.

Sometimes, however, strategic and prudential questions have moral implications. After we sort out what the law is and decide the best strategic and prudent actions, we still face the question of what is the right thing to do. The answer to how hard to hit my serve will be different if I am playing my local champion or my nine-year-old daughter. And, sometimes clients ask fundamentally ethical questions, or try to elicit ethical advice without asking for it. You suspect that is what Sonia wants: your opinion about whether morally she owes her stepmother anything.

Thomas Shaffer notes that a lawyer spends 80 percent of her time advising clients in matters that do not lead to litigation.[1] Outside of litigation, and even in the pre-litigation phase, "personal" equity, as Calvin and Perkins conceived of it, ought to guide the lawyer's advice. The business lawyer acts as a prophet, whose job (Shaffer says) is to "remind power brokers of a communal pattern of economic life."[2] The "power brokers" can be on either side of a transaction. (I realize that I slide time and again into the assumption that power distributions are invariably in favor of the seller/employer/landlord side of the agreement. For most lawyers in most cases, that will be true, but not inherently true. Anyone who has leased a building to the General Services Administration can attest to this.) The prophetic voice speaks to both sides of a dispute, the claimant and the respondent, the employer and the employee, the landlord and the tenant.

The Model Rules allow us to operate prophetically: "In rendering advice, a lawyer may refer not only to law but to other considerations such as

---

1. Shaffer, "Legal Ethics of the Two Kingdoms," 36.
2. Shaffer, "Business Lawyers, Baseball Players," 1076. Shaffer, who was a corporate lawyer rather than a litigator, errs here only by limiting the prophetic role to the business lawyer. Whether they do so or not, the litigation defense lawyer, sooner or later, gets the chance to discuss the legitimacy of a personal injury claim, and recommend a settlement. "Valuing a case," it is called, and it is one of the hardest, but also the most important things defense counsel does.

moral, economic, social and political factors, that may be relevant to the client's situation."[3] Dr. Johnson went almost this far; recall that he said that lawyers could give moral advice, but only when asked. "If only when asked." Even Homer nods occasionally. Christian moral theology not only allows but requires us to speak prophetically. "A scheme of ethics which allowed each man to shape his own course irrespective of the will and teaching and requirements of society would be utterly untrue to the spirit of a religion which thinks of us primarily as members of a body, and that body the body of Christ."[4] Lawyers act prophetically when they give voice to the best "will and teaching and requirements of society." This was precisely why YHWH inspired the prophet Ezekiel:

> So you, mortal, I have made a sentinel for the house of Israel; whenever you hear a word from my mouth, you shall give them warning from me. If I say to the wicked, "O wicked ones, you shall surely die," and you do not speak to warn the wicked to turn from their ways, the wicked shall die in their iniquity, but their blood I will require at your hand. But if you warn the wicked to turn from their ways, and they do not turn from their ways, the wicked shall die in their iniquity, but you will have saved your life.[5]

So much for giving a client legal advice and minding your own business about his ethics.

As Calvin saw it, equity transformed the self as much as the system by calling souls to promoting the common good. Opening the client's eyes to this possibility may be, then, perhaps what the client needs, even if not initially what the client wants: this is precisely what YHWH calls Ezekiel to do. Shaffer calls this serving the client without becoming the client's servant.[6] Offering the client the chance to transform lies at the heart of being a Christian and a lawyer, which, Shaffer says, "seems to be a matter of learning about power and conscience, since lawyers wield power, even when they do not have it, and Christians wield conscience."[7]

The lawyer cannot transform the client by brute force. That plays no part in the prophetic role (and doesn't work anyway). Prophets do not compel obedience or conversion. Compulsion requires political power, which

---

3. *MR*, 2.1.
4. Kirk, *Conscience and Its Problems*, 61.
5. Ezek 33:7–9.
6. Shaffer, *Faith and the Professions*, 70.
7. Shaffer, *On Being a Christian*, 192.

prophets do not have. YHWH doesn't give Ezekiel the sword to yield against Israel; he tells Ezekiel to warn the Israelites that the sword approaches.

Is the lawyer's role "prophetic"? Christians believe that the Holy Spirit speaks through the prophets.[8] The tradition of the seven gifts of the Holy Spirit, which finds its roots in Isaiah chapter 11, was adopted by Augustine and Aquinas, and now resides in the *Catechism of the Catholic Church*,[9] includes the gifts of wisdom, counsel, and piety. Those could be the essential skills in a prophet's job description (and a lawyer's). Calvin said that it is the Spirit that both illuminates the law for us and allows us to persist in our understanding. In the Episcopal Church we call on the Spirit when we pray for courts of justice,[10] and for local government,[11] and for social justice.[12] All of these prayers take us directly back to Calvin, who saw the Holy Spirit as the source of equity.[13] Thus, lawyers in a real sense are prophets of the Holy Spirit.

While lawyers may have some interest in natural or divine law theories, clients are first and foremost legal realists. They want to know what their likely outcome is. As Holmes famously said, when a client asks if something is illegal, what he really wants to know is whether he is likely to go to jail if he does it. How do we prophesy to someone determined not to hear?[14] It helps to be able to argue that equity serves his best interests—that things may go badly in court. We still have the tradition, perhaps less honored than it used to be, that litigants must go to court with clean hands. One of the rudimentary principles of equity, the "clean hands" doctrine reflects

---

8. Johnson, *Creed*, 237.

9. Section 1831.

10. "We humbly beseech thee to bless the courts of justice and the magistrates in all this land; and give unto them the spirit of wisdom and understanding, that they may discern the truth, and impartially administer the law in the fear of thee alone." *Book of Common Prayer*, 821.

11. "Send down upon those who hold office in this State . . . the spirit of wisdom, charity, and justice; that with steadfast purpose they may faithfully serve in their office to promote the well being of all people." *Book of Common Prayer*, 822.

12. "[T]hat your holy and life-giving Spirit may so move every human heart, that barriers which divide us may crumble, suspicions disappear, and hatreds cease; that our divisions being healed, we may live in justice and peace." *Book of Common Prayer*, 823.

13. Hass, *Concept of Equity*, 75.

14. We all feel tempted at times to try the method Balaam used on his donkey (Num 22) but I don't recommend it (although that did lead to a valuable lesson in humility for Balaam).

equity's foundation in the Golden Rule.[15] A party requesting extraordinary relief from the court must have conducted itself fairly in the transaction. Moreover, lawyers all know that cases are most likely to settle (or in criminal cases, plead) when the outcome remains uncertain. Yet, critics argue that equity impairs legal certainty. However, if the outcome seems certain, why settle? Perhaps consistency in the law helps citizens to regulate their affairs. But if that consistency becomes so predictable that outcomes are foreordained, no matter their relation to primary justice, then we can also expect more adversarial and less cooperative litigation.

The Lawyer as Priest

You have accepted Jack's case. Isaac died, and Harold filed a petition for declaration of heirship, seeking to invalidate the sale of his birthright. The case is on the trial docket for next week. The lawyers have been called in for a final pre-trial hearing.

A number of things happen at final pre-trial. The lawyers either announce that they are ready for trial, or ask for a continuance and explain why they need it. Often, they exchange exhibits and submit a proposed jury charge. They argue motions *in limine* (attempts to exclude certain bits of evidence). Judges ask questions at pre-trial hearings. How long will the trial take? Can the parties stipulate to any facts? Are there any remaining motions that need to be heard? And, usually off the record, can the case be settled?

Eugene Peterson, writing about the high priest Caiaphas, describes the ideal priest like this:

> A priest stands in the middle between us and God, between God and us. The priest presents God to us: tells us who God is, the way he acts, the truth that he reveals, and invites us to receive this God, believe in him, obey and trust and worship him. And the priest presents us to God: presents our sins and guilt, our work and our thanksgiving, our failures and pretensions, our sickness and our ignorance, and asks God to receive us, forgive us, guide us, save us.[16]

Substitute "lawyer" for "priest" and "law" for "God," and you have a pretty good description of what the legal system expects from lawyers.[17] Law-

---

15. Mark Greenlee argues that, more than we realize, the Golden Rule operates as a legal principle. Greenlee, "Echoes of the Love Command."

16. Peterson, *The Jesus Way*, 222–23.

17. The Episcopal catechism says that the ministry of a priest "is to represent Christ and his church, particularly as pastor to the people." In *Book of Common Prayer*, 845–62.

yers tell clients about the law, invite them to believe in the law and even to revere it. The lawyer presents the client to the legal system, faults and all, and asks the system for relief—sometimes literally, for redemption. The lawyer zealously represents his client, and, as Johnson said, turns the justness of a case over to the judge. Doing that is a priestly act, an act of submission to the system. Just as priests are intermediaries between God and humans, the lawyer, as an officer of the court, must be loyal to and respectful of both the client's cause and the legal system itself—the finder of fact (judge or jury), even opposing counsel, and especially the law itself. The lawyer's duty in court is not to achieve justice as the lawyer conceives it, but neither is it to get the client what the client wants by any means necessary. The lawyer's job is to pursue the client's interests within the limits of the system; to "play by the rules," as it were.[18]

Herein lies the rub. If lawyers are priests, what sort of God do they serve? Utilitarians serve a God that views individual interests as irrelevant in themselves, important only as an element in a larger calculation of good and evil. Deidre's welfare fades into the background if evicting her promotes the welfare of the neighborhood or the public housing agency itself. Law and economics partisans make economic efficiency our highest value, and the interests of the individual borrower get trumped by the need for lower interest rates and increased commercial activity. View the law as a strict constructionist, and you worship the Founding Fathers. (Recall, by contrast, Justice Jackson's admonition that the Constitution is not a suicide pact.) Join the legal positivists, and one does the same of national and state legislatures.

Lawyers harness the power of the state in support of private interests. A lawsuit directly does so by seeking a state mandate—a court order—that someone do something (pay money) or stop doing something. The legal system has certain expectations of lawyers in how we call on state power; judges taking a Chicago-school view want us to promote economic efficiency and interpret the law in such a way that our clients lose if they think otherwise.

Just as importantly, law is inescapably social. It involves our client's relations with other people, either specific individuals or the public at large.[19] Basic to theories of human rights is the "principle of correlatives."

---

18 Richard Mouw maps out comparable duties in framing a priestly approach to medicine. Shaffer, *Faith and the Professions*, 57.

19. Occasionally this social aspect to the law gets overlooked. An environmental lawyer may think he works to protect the ecosystem. He does that, however, by using the law to influence, if not control, what other humans can do in (and to) the natural

Any right carries with it a corresponding duty in someone else, just as all coins have two sides. Legal philosophy considers rights and duties as correlative.[20] Moral philosophy does also.[21] In other words, whenever a lawyer, through the judicial system, gets his client something by enforcing a right for him, he does something to someone else by imposing an obligation on him. This "principle of correlatives" is what creates the Lawyer's Dilemma. Although an attorney only has limited *professional* obligations to the adversary, he clearly has *ethical* duties, as to any human being. Here is where the analogy of lawyer as priest falls apart. Priests acting as intermediaries between God and humans are not involved in a "zero-sum" transaction. God's grace is infinite. Not so for the law.

Richard Hooker argued that society was essential to human existence, and that our common life cannot exist without some rules of relationship and order.[22] Employment contracts, life insurance policies, retirement plans, mortgages, and residential leases all impact directly life's necessaries—gainful employment, housing, reasonable financial security—which Calvin believed to be the central legitimate use of commercial law. Thus, litigation always implicates our ethics, in the choice to encourage a client to bring valid but insignificant claims, in the use of delay tactics (motions for continuance), counterpunching (dubious counterclaims), or rope-a-dope discovery as obstacles to other party's legitimate claims, in the settlement of important claims for less than full value, or in the use of the appellate process to further prolong justice's delay.

So, we force lawyers to make fairness arguments in legal terms. We disingenuously call ambiguous contracts that could not be clearer, when we really mean that enforcing the plain language of the agreement would be unfair. This is not as it should be. If lawyers are priests of the law, equity we must have, because our legal institutions "have a way of acting, an official tendency to turn other people into commodities, and to excuse themselves with grand, official phrases such as health, justice, equality, due process, privacy, democracy, and the rule of law."[23] All lawyers should resist being commodities, and must protect their clients from being treated as such, but

---

world. This, of course, ignores the self-evident (and self-centered) fact that maintaining the environment benefits humans.

20. Corbin, "Rights and Duties," 501.
21. Wolterstorff, *Justice*, 34.
22. *Laws*, 1:10.
23. Shaffer, *Faith and the Professions*, 109.

JACOB'S LAWYER (PART TWO): EQUITY IN ACTION

Christian lawyers, devoted to a faith with human dignity at its center, feel the rub especially hard. O'Donovan writes, "While government (i.e., legislatures) pursue policies of prudence only contingently related to justice, courts pursue justice with no relation to political prudence. Such prudence and such justice are purely formal and of little use. Legal positivism, which lies at the root of both, can only pit arbitrariness against arbitrariness, the ruthless on the one hand against the impractical on the other."[24] Equity is not ruthless, and it is imminently practical.

Let us return to *Harold v. Jack*, the case now ready for trial. These issues come to a head at the pre-trial hearing. When the judge asks whether the case can be settled, she is not simply wanting to know whether she can clear her calendar next week. She wants to know which party is being the more reasonable. She will ask you, as Jack's lawyer, to explain again why the transfer of the birthright ought to be honored. She will ask Harold's lawyer why Jack is so scared of his client. She will want to know how Harold and Jack propose to divide the property up. She will definitely want to know about Uncle Laban. Most importantly, she will want to know how hard Harold and Jack have tried to settle the case. Rest assured that the party being, in the judge's eyes, less reasonable will have a hard time of it at trial.

Notice that all of this happens outside of the strict adjudicative process, in many cases off the record. (Years ago, as a young lawyer I had an in-chambers conversation with a wise trial judge about a discovery dispute. My opposing counsel, not hearing what he liked, told the judge that he was going to have to make his argument on the record in open court. Whereupon the judge looked across his desk and said, without a hint of a smile, "Counselor, you are perfectly free to put your arguments on the record, and then I'll give you my ruling on the record." Whereupon opposing counsel asked for two minutes to speak to his client, and came back and said they would produce the documents we wanted. There but for the grace of God go all young lawyers.) Judges still have tremendous procedural discretion. Allocation of jury strikes, admission of contested documents, disputes over lines of witness questioning, precise wording of the jury charge—all these things, to a large degree, lie within the trial court's discretion. But, because substantive law has so effectively been taken away from the trial judge, they often are the judge's only weapon in the battle for fairness.

This is where equity lives—not so much in the formal proceedings, but in the give-and-take leading up to trial. The pre-trial hearing, we might

---

24. O'Donovan, *The Ways of Judgment*, 197.

say, is when the judge checks to see if our clients have washed their hands and scrubbed under the nails. Refusing to act equitably can have real consequences for the client. Equity allows the lawyer to tell his client that, not only ought he act fairly, but the judge will make him prove he did. Urging equitable conduct is both ethical and legal advice. All too often, clients will tell us that all they want is their legal advice. Well, when equity is afoot, this is legal advice. It's the same advice that the unforgiving servant could have used; he ended up in the dungeon because he forgot it.[25]

The Lawyer as Co-Creator

Throughout this book we've talked about the agency factor in the Lawyer's Dilemma. By agency I've meant acting as an agent: on behalf of another person. Lawyers, we've seen, have agency responsibilities both to the client and to the legal system. But, like equity, agency is one of those words that carries a whole bundle of meanings. Agency as a philosophical term means the capacity to act. It means something similar to, but not precisely the same as, free will. Agency has both philosophical and religious significance because our whole view of moral responsibility depends on the existence of human agency.

The standard definition of agency, in this sense, is the capacity to act "in a given environment." Thus, a lawyer might be an "agent" for a client in the environment of the courtroom, but not in the grocery store or the synagogue. In order to be an "agent" for another, the lawyer must have that particular "agency." What bears remembering is that part of a lawyer's agency for a client is not simply to act in a given environment, but to actually mold that environment. Litigators, for example, don't simply take the facts as they find them. They craft a story out of the facts—frame the case, we sometimes say—and select the version of reality that will get presented in court.

Transactional lawyers have an even higher creative agency. Not only do they interpret contracts for clients and advise them of their rights, but they also participate in establishing the legal context into which the parties enter and in which they will exist in the future. When lawyers draft contracts, they frame a future relation between a client and another person. When they draft wills or trusts, they structure their clients' future financial relations with their family or others. When they draft medical powers of attorney or natural death directives, they hope to smooth the client's path

25. Matt 18:21–35.

through life's health challenges. In other words, they don't simply act as prophets towards their clients, or as priests of the courts. Contract drafting is at heart an act of creation, and hence lawyers, when they draft contracts, exercise the uniquely human power to create.

An ancient tradition holds that humans are coworkers in God's kingdom. Saint Paul says so in 1 Corinthians 3:9: "For we are God's servants, working together; you are God's field, God's building." The Roman Catholic *Catechism* says so:

> To human beings God even gives the power of freely sharing in his providence by entrusting them with the responsibility of "subduing" the earth and having dominion over it. God thus enables men to be intelligent and free causes in order to complete the work of creation, to perfect its harmony for their own good and that of their neighbors. Though often unconscious collaborators with God's will, they can also enter deliberately into the divine plan by their actions, their prayers, and their sufferings. They then fully become "God's fellow workers" and co-workers for his kingdom.[26]

Contracts are ultimately about power. A contract expresses someone's willingness to yield control over his or her own life goods to another, in pursuit of some desired end. If I borrow money, I am surrendering control over my time—either time spent in the past in accumulating wealth, or in the future in earning funds to pay the loan back. If I mortgage my home, I surrender control of it to the mortgagee if I can't pay the loan back. If I sign an employment contract, I agree to surrender my time to my employer, and not to work somewhere else, or to tend to my own needs during work hours. A sick child may not be an excuse under an employer's absence/tardiness policy.[27] When I as a lawyer participate in the contract process, I am wielding power. Not just power from the state, although the state issues my license, and a contract gone wrong will probably end up in the state courts. In fact, it is nothing less than power from God. Why from God? Because (as Shaffer says) "the use of power is a moral problem."[28] Christians (and other theists) believe that all moral

26. *Catechism of the Catholic Church*, paragraph 307.

27. You are probably thinking, "Well, what about the Family Medical Leave Act?" The goals of FMLA are admirable ones. Perhaps, however, the FMLA, twenty-four pages of definitions, inclusions, exclusions, exceptions, and requirements, supported by ninety-two pages of regulations (29 CFR Part 825), is what happens when we try to legislate equity.

28. Shaffer, *On Being a Christian*, 189.

problems ultimately are religious problems, and the services we provide for our clients always have moral repercussions.

Anyone who has negotiated a contract knows that it is ultimately a question of power. If each side has something the other side seriously needs, then the power balance is relatively even, and there will be serious negotiation. Most everyday contracts, however, are not this way. Typically, there is a second candidate for a job, a second tenant waiting for an apartment, or another customer kicking the tires on the same car. In those cases, the dominant party's willingness to negotiate lies primarily in his character.[29] How, then, are lawyers to exercise that power? To put it bluntly, may we use mercy as a bargaining chip? Or is doing so making a bargain with the devil? When it comes time to draft the agreement, I face this dilemma: there may be things that I am willing to concede, in the interest of equity, but am I upfront about that, or do I save them as my last card to play to close the deal? When we negotiate, we deduce what really matters to the other side, and then exact concessions in exchange for satisfying the other party's real interest. If I know that an employee has financial problems, I can infer that she worries mainly about the amount of her paycheck or the stability of her job and will likely not raise questions about working conditions, benefits, and so forth. She will put up with things other employees won't. If an injured mother has a child in college, she may settle a personal injury claim for enough money to pay his tuition, even if the claim is worth far more. Not a pretty picture of humanity, but, sad to say, a truthful one. When I call it a deal with the devil, it truly is Faustian in a way we don't like to think about.

And the decision is not entirely mine to make. Just as a prophet can exhort, but not compel, his followers, an attorney cannot veto a client's decision. A lawyer shall abide by a client's decisions concerning the objectives of representation.[30] That comes from more than the rules of professional responsibility; it comes from basic moral philosophy. "*Conscientia semper sequenda*," Kirk says, stands as the "crowning moral doctrine" of Christianity; conscience must always be obeyed.[31] Correlatively, no one can judge the conscience of another.

Here, as always, a bit of humility works. Our clients are frail, but so are we. Absent direct revelations, like Ezekiel received, our judgments are

---

29. I say solely, bearing in mind Cicero's admonition that lying, in the long run, hurts business. The same would be said about inequity. Word gets around.

30. *MR*, 1.2.

31. Kirk, *Conscience and Its Problems*, 60.

JACOB'S LAWYER (PART TWO): EQUITY IN ACTION

human, not divine. Let's once again put ourselves back in the role of Jacob's lawyer for a moment. If ever a story reminds us that our crystal balls can be cloudy, Jacob's story would be it. It seems that nothing ever turns out the way we expected: Isaac thinks he blesses Esau but finds out it was Jacob. Jacob thinks he goes into Rachel's nuptial bed but discovers Leah. Jacob thinks Esau comes to kill him in the desert, but instead finds himself embraced and reconciled. Jacob's special love for Joseph makes his brothers hate him. The brothers think they are selling Joseph into slavery but, it turns out, they send him to the place where, years later, he will rescue them from famine.

Lawyering as a Vocation

Lawyers pride themselves on being engaged in a profession. When I Google the question "what does it mean to be a professional," I get 915 million hits. The first hit, a *US News and World Report* article, offers such advice as "be pleasant and polite to people, even if you don't like them" and "show up reliably." Good advice, certainly, but one hopes for a bit more.

On the other hand, Oliver O'Donovan claims that the gospel expresses ultimate reality, more real than what we see around us. If so, then both justice and mercy are not simply concepts adopted by democratic consensus, and subject to change or limitation at the will of the majority, but are embedded in the very nature of things. (This is the heart of natural law theory.) And if that be so, how can a lawyer wall off his professional role from his personal morality? When can any legal principle, even one as basic as "promises must be kept" (which, admittedly, has its own theological basis) make the enforcement of a valid contract an excuse to act unmercifully? The short answer, I would submit, is "never."

So, this problem is not one we leave behind when we power down our office computer and turn the lights out. We end our hypothetical Friday with the convening of your Friday afternoon tavern group. We end here, in order to make a point about a lawyer's professional life. Many, indeed most, of the hypotheticals we've looked at through the book involve the kinds of questions that get talked about at a Friday afternoon gathering of friends, or after church on Sunday, or at Rotary Club. They involve life situations as much as they do legal questions. The prodigal son story clearly is one. That sort of situation gets posed to lawyers all the time, and yet it doesn't really involve a legal question at all. There may be legal fixes designed to make the unhappy elder son momentarily happy, but that's not the real issue. Probate lawyers know that often heirs have fights over insignificant items—family heirlooms or photo albums—that have little if any financial worth. Those heirlooms frequently provide the basis for a fight over a more deep-seated resentment. One suspects that is the case with Mrs. Ramirez and Mrs. Esteves, and even between Jacob and Esau.

Commonly, these questions purport to be about law, but are actually about law only in the broadest sense. If, for instance, someone at happy hour asked you about Jack's dispute with Harold, and you launched into a mini-lecture about the alienability of inheritances, or the rule against perpetuities, or the statute of frauds, I can promise you that the next comment would be "How about those Cubs?" What your audience wants to know is whether the law is crass enough to allow such a thing as trading an inheritance for a bowl of soup.

Therefore, once again, we turn to Perkins, this time to his brief essay on vocations. "A vocation," he writes, "is a certain kind of life ordained and imposed on man by God for the common good."[32] The early Protestants viewed all occupations as vocations, not limited, as in the Catholic tradition, to religious ones. A calling is "a certain condition or kind of life: that is a certain manner of leading our lives in this world."[33] Likewise, according to John Calvin, the Christian, who "could be called by God to serve him in every sphere of human existence," would discover "a new dignity and meaning to work."[34] Perkins, in fact, captures our dilemma in defining what it means to have a vocation. On the one hand, he says, "[W]hatsoever any man enterprises or does, either in word or deed, he must do it by virtue of this calling, and he must keep himself within the compass, limits, or precincts thereof."[35] In other words, lawyers have to abide by the rules of lawyering. Nevertheless, a vocation involves what one *is*, not what one *does*.

> Every [person] must join the practice of his personal calling with the practice of the general calling of Christianity, before described. More plainly, every particular calling must be practiced in and with the general calling of a Christian. It is not sufficient for a man in the congregation and in common conversation to be a Christian, but in his very personal calling he must show himself to be so. As for example a magistrate must not only in general be a Christian,

---

32. Perkins, "Treatise on the Vocations," 446–47.
33. Perkins, "Treatise on the Vocations," 447.
34. McGrath, *Life of John Calvin*, 232.
35. Perkins, "Treatise on the Vocations," 449.

JACOB'S LAWYER (PART TWO): EQUITY IN ACTION

as every man is, but he must be a Christian magistrate in executing the office of a magistrate in bearing the sword.[36]

A Christian practicing law is, then, a Christian lawyer. The choices she makes about her practice—to only represent injured parties, or employees, because of natural sympathies, or to practice business law, counseling her clients towards more just behavior—are religious choices. What we pay our staff versus what car we drive, what holidays we observe, when we turn off our email—all these are vocational choices.

Perkins specifies two particular duties in all vocations that apply with special force to lawyering. One is "edification": we must use "all good means whereby we may draw our kindred, friends and neighbors to the love and obedience of true religion (1 Cor 10:33). . . . [T]his thing is done by confirming those who are called by often admonitions, exhortations, consolations and all other like duties that serve to this end."[37] In other words, part of vocational living requires acting prophetically. That duty does not stop at five in the afternoon, or at the front door of our office. Lawyers and doctors share at least one thing: they are the targets of requests for free advice. We can decline those requests. We can give the legal equivalent of "take two aspirin and call my office in the morning." There is a nobler choice, however. And that nobler choice often, as in the happy-hour discussion about Harold and Jack, calls for a short lesson in equity.

We could leave the profession entirely, of course. Perkins, however, tells us that it's not so easy as that. "The time is not left in our choice, for we may not leave our callings when we please, but the prescribing thereof belongs to God. . . . Hence it follows that no man is to lay down the calling wherein he is placed till he can say by some warrant in his conscience that it is the good will and pleasure of God that he shall then resign and cease to do the duties thereof any longer."[38] The second choice we saw was to hang in and act as a reformer from the inside. Once again, Perkins weighs in: he tells us that all our activities within the vocation must be within the bounds of the calling. "[T]he second general rule which must be remembered is this: that every man must do the duties of his calling with diligence (Eccles 9:10; Rom 12:8; Jer 48:10; John 4:33)."[39] Perkins continues: "a particular

---

36. Perkins, "Treatise of the Vocations," 456. "Bearing the sword" is, of course, a reference to Romans 13:4 and the power of civil authority.

37. Perkins, "Treatise of the Vocations," 452–53.

38. Perkins, "Treatise of the Vocations," 472.

39. Perkins, "Treatise of the Vocations," 450.

calling must give place to the general calling of Christian when they cannot both stand together."[40] Performing the duties of the calling with diligence, then, might require elevating the calling to its more noble self. How, Tom Shaffer asks, can a Christian be a lawyer? Here it is: we follow our conscience in working within the system, striving to improve it, and (in the rare case) deciding to leave it.

In other words, we must avoid a "two-kingdoms" view of lawyering, the lawyer's private life being one of personal compassion, his public life on the other hand being acted out in an arena that fails to embody any sense of equity beyond strict law. As Shaffer puts it, lawyers can and should live their lives "as if there is only one kingdom, as there is only one God, and as if there can only be one morality in our lives, a single morality to govern both personal life and professional life."[41] Moreover, if there are two kingdoms (or two cities in the Augustinian sense), the lawyer's vocation requires him to work in both. Shaffer says:

> The City of God does not depend on the earthly city, but the earthly city depends on the City of God. Paul and Augustine and Luther and Barth were all interested in showing that the influence of faith on the earthly city is a necessary influence. Their arguments were arguments to the faithful, about what the faithful imply when they claim the freedom to be faithful—in, say, the practice of journalism or teaching or law or medicine. The Faithful, in being faithful, make a claim on the community.[42]

"The Faithful, in being faithful, make a claim on the community." Jesus says, "let your light shine before others, so that they may see your good works and give glory to your Father in heaven."[43] But how does "letting your light shine" make a "claim on the community"? Recall the context in which Jesus said that: the Sermon on the Mount, the first of Matthew's five discourses.[44] Lawyers always want to know, "what was the context in which the witness said that?"

---

40. Perkins, "Treatise of the Vocations," 457.
41. Shaffer, "Legal Ethics," 27.
42. Shaffer, *Faith and the Professions*, 91.
43. Matt 5:16.
44. Matt 5:1—7:29.

JACOB'S LAWYER (PART TWO): EQUITY IN ACTION

Let's look at that context. The pericope about letting your light shine immediately follows the admonition "you are the salt of the earth; but if salt has lost its taste, how can its saltiness be restored?"[45] And right after, Jesus says "Do not think that I have come to abolish the law or the prophets; I have come not to abolish but to fulfill."[46] And, finally, "For I tell you, unless your righteousness exceeds that of the scribes and Pharisees, you will never enter the kingdom of heaven."[47] Can we put all these together in a way that tells us anything about being a lawyer? I think so. For the law to be fulfilled, it needs "salting." Whether that means "preserved," saved from the degradation of the world,[48] or "seasoned," in the sense of "enhanced," depends on whether equity is part of the law, or an addition to it from outside. Either way, equity is the salt that has been taken out of our law.

Look at what Jesus says next. He moves into the six "antitheses": do not simply avoid murder, but avoid anger; shun lust, not simply adultery; turn the other cheek; love your enemies.[49] The antitheses are, in fact, a prescription for equity. Go beyond what the law requires. Indeed, Jesus says, "Settle matters quickly with your adversary who is taking you to court. Do it while you are still together on the way, or your adversary may hand you over to the judge, and the judge may hand you over to the officer, and you may be thrown into prison. Truly I tell you, you will not get out until you have paid the last penny."[50]

Once again, we can turn to William Perkins.

> Here then we are taught to deal in equity and moderation with all men, in the private affairs of our callings, even as we would have them to deal with us; and then God will cause others to deal well with us; but if we deal ill with others, God will reward us in the same kind. This point all usurers, engrossers, tradesmen etc., should well observe, who think they may do with their own what they will; but we must know that we are but stewards, and our account will be exact.
>
> Secondly, here we see Christ alloweth: 1. Of the magistrate and his judgment seat. 2. Of his proceeding against the guilty in delivering him to the officer. 3. Of the office of the serjeant. 4. Of

---

45. Matt 5:13.
46. Matt 5:17.
47. Matt 5:20.
48. N. T. Wright makes this point in *Matthew for Everyone*, 40.
49. Matt 5:21–48.
50. Matt 5:25–26.

casting guilty persons into prison. 5. Of suing at the law, when right cannot be gotten by any other lawful means. But law must not be the first course we take in seeking our right, we must rather suffer some wrong, and seek to end the matter by friends; and use law as physicians use poisons, when gentle physick will not serve the turn, then in case of extremity they do minister stronger physick; yea, sometimes poison itself; so when we cannot otherwise procure our peace and right, then we may lawfully take the benefit of the law.[51]

"Use law as physicians use poisons." An unlikely candidate for adoption as the motto of many law schools. But remember two things: a contract surrenders control over life goods, and all court actions are punishment. Does a contract justify taking away a life good? Perhaps. The enforcement of a contract, in fact the existence of laws themselves, are life goods. As Shaffer says, "interesting moral choices are not those between good and evil, but those between good and good."[52] The choice between good and evil shouldn't present a dilemma. But the choice between good and good, although it doesn't answer itself, at least makes the question a bit clearer. Acting sparingly may be the best answer we can hope for.

---

51. Perkins, "Godly and Learned Exposition," commentary on Matt 5:25–26.
52. Shaffer, *On Being a Christian*, 174.

11

Orley Farm: Trollope's Case Study in Equity

One thing that trial lawyers and law professors have in common is a love for telling stories. Not just war stories, although there is plenty of that. We referred in the last chapter to trial lawyers "framing" a case—trying to explain the facts in a way that benefits the client. Law professors do the same thing. They torment their students with hypotheticals, seemingly clear at first, but increasingly complex or ambiguous, trying to get the poor student to commit to something that will immediately be pulled out from under him.

Joseph Allegretti suggests that we should look at our careers as narratives. Seeing our lives as a narrative can help us solve our ethical dilemmas, by "invit[ing] us to shift the emphasis away from rules and problems to broader questions of personhood and virtue."[1] In the last chapter, we concerned ourselves with examples of what I called "equity in action." Those examples are taken from my own practice, or from stories known to me out of other lawyers' practices. What Allegretti is suggesting is that we should view those stories not as simply one-offs, fodder for lawyer lunches or seminar papers. They are stories from a narrative, not simply illustrative of proper rule-based behavior, but something closer to the virtue ethic that I mentioned long ago in chapter 3.

If viewing lawyering as a narrative helps us understand the ethics of lawyering, the reverse is also true; looking at narratives can give us insight about the lawyer drama. If equity as a virtue is our topic, then the right narratives should tell us something about equity. Now, Western literature is filled with stories "about" equity. Mark Fortier shows in his two books on the "culture of equity" that equity has pervaded Anglo-American culture in social, political, religious, and literary discussion for centuries. Shakespeare's

---

1. Allegretti, "Can Legal Ethics Be Christian?," 461.

THE LAW OF FREEDOM

Measure for Measure and *The Merchant of Venice* revolve around the conflict between strict application of law and concerns for justice. *The Merchant of Venice* tells the story of the lender Shylock, who obtains a lien on a pound of the merchant Antonio's flesh, as security for a debt to Shylock from Antonio's friend Bassanio. Antonio made the pledge assuming that his prosperous trading business could easily cover Bassanio's debt; alas, his entire merchant fleet disappears in a storm. The heroine Portia rescues the day, when (posing as a legal scholar) she rules that strict enforcement works both ways; in executing on his "collateral" Shylock must avoid spilling one drop of Antonio's blood, as the pledge only encumbers Antonio's flesh. Grotesquely fanciful as this sounds, the play "works" dramatically only on the assumption that the law entitles Shylock to the benefit of his bargain—his "pound of flesh," literally.[2] Charles Dickens's *Bleak House* is about equity of a different sort: the formal equity practice in Chancery Court. In *Bleak House*, finding yourself in Chancery is a curse. Cases never end. Litigants either go mad from justice endlessly delayed or die waiting for a decision; Miss Flite, a long-disappointed equity suitor, seems to equate judgment in Chancery with the final day of judgment, and Mr. Gridley dies after being arrested because he had the temerity to challenge Mr. Tulkinghorn, the grand elder statesman of Chancery lawyers. John Jarndyce, the moral center of the novel, urges his ward Richard Carstone not to put his hopes in his equity suit, advice that Richard ignores to his doom. More than anything, England's equity jurisprudence seems itself a villainous character in the novel.

Those works have one thing in common. They all intentionally make a point about "equity." Shakespeare's is what happens when strict law threatens to trump primary justice. Dickens's agenda is to criticize the institutionalization, and hence the corruption, of English equity. Which raises the question: Can we find a story that mirrors society more than comments on it, and see what lessons we can learn about equity?

Using stories to understand legal principles is, in fact, what law schools do. We call it the case method. Said to have been invented by Christopher Columbus Langdell, dean of Harvard Law School in the last quarter of the nineteenth century, the case method uses appellate court decisions, which typically have some recitation of the underlying facts, to reach legal doctrines. In the next chapter, we will discuss a recent article by law professor

---

2. There have been many articles of legal scholarship explaining why *The Merchant of Venice* is incoherent legally (Shylock would have been obligated to take Bassanio's offer to pay the debt). That of course is not the point, this being a time for a small suspension of disbelief.

ORLEY FARM: TROLLOPE'S CASE STUDY IN EQUITY

Cathleen Kaveny that defends the tradition as a way of bringing both legal principles and community standards into the legal discussion. For now, however, let us note that appellate court opinions are by nature selective. They take the evidence admitted at trial, itself a highly restrictive view of reality, and then pick out the few pieces that support the majority opinion. (One of the most common elements of a dissenting opinion is the pointing out of some fact that the majority opinion omits.) Likewise, works of literature, even Shakespeare's plays in all their richness, are choosy. Shakespeare tells us what he wants us to know to make his point. We know that Lady Macbeth had a child; she reminds Macbeth that she has "given suck, and know / How tender 'tis to love the babe that milks me."[3] But we don't know the child's name, the color of his hair, who the father is, or whatever happened to that child. (Presumably it is dead, because Macbeth, we know, is without an heir.) None of that would have been relevant to the point of Lady Macbeth being a mother: the irony of a woman grieving over a lost child while her husband ends family lines right and left.

Something similar is true of *Bleak House*. Critics have accused Dickens of making Esther Summerson, one of the novel's two narrators, a sort of stock character of virtue and modesty, to make the points he wants to make about the tragedy of her mother Lady Dedlock and the hopelessness of the Court of Chancery. All writers by necessity are selective. A book can only be so long, and there are points to be made. Sometimes, therefore, it bears reading something not to learn about the specific points the author wants to make, but about the society in which he wrote and the assumptions he took for granted. E. D. Hirsch calls this the "significance" of a book rather than its meaning.[4] In this chapter, we'll look at the significance, as opposed to the meaning, of equity for two novels by Dickens's contemporary Anthony Trollope.

Trollope was, if nothing else, prolific; he wrote almost four dozen novels, plus travel pieces, short stories, miscellaneous pieces, and an autobiography.[5] Much like Dickens, Trollope was born to a father with chronic

---

3. Shakespeare, *Macbeth*, I.7.53–54.

4. See generally Hirsch, *Validity in Interpretation*.

5. For much of that time he also held down a regular job in the post office. Trollope treated writing as a job. He maintained a regular early-morning writing schedule before reporting to work at the post office. Perhaps this habit, which hints more at industry

financial problems. He began writing novels in his late twenties, but only at forty, with the publication of *The Warden* (1855), did the public notice him. Critical judgment of Trollope has waxed and waned over the years. Perhaps his reputation as a narrator rather than a social commentator, and his basic acceptance of social conventions, contributes to his (in my opinion undeserved) middlebrow standing.

Trollope's two great topics, each the subject of a series of novels with recurring characters, were politics and the church. Politics dominate the "Palliser novels," sometimes referred to as the "Parliamentary novels." The church and its clergy occupy the "Barsetshire novels," of which *The Warden* is the most famous. Amid those grand themes, the law and lawyers pervade the novels, as they did Trollope's life. Trollope's financially unfortunate father was a barrister, as indeed was the author himself (although he never practiced).

Orley Farm: Rebekah in Yorkshire

Orley Farm, published serially in 1861 and 1862, belongs to neither of the grand series of novels, and (with one exception) does not have the same recurring cast of characters that the Palliser or Barsetshire novels do. Nevertheless, Trollope, in his autobiography, says that "[m]ost of those among my friends who talk to me now about my novels, and are competent to form an opinion on the subject, say that this is the best I have written."[6] At nearly a thousand pages, we can also safely assume that Orley Farm is not a simple morality play, and gives us a fair representation of society in the day.

Set in the Yorkshire countryside, *Orley Farm* consciously draws on the Isaac/Rebekah/Jacob tale. Sir Joseph Mason, a wealthy Yorkshireman, has two sons. The elder, Joseph, from Sir Joseph's first marriage, stands to inherit his fortune. Lucius, much younger, is Sir Joseph's child by his second wife, the central character in the book. Sir Joseph makes no secret that his elder son Joseph is his primary heir, with only a modest settlement on the new Lady Mason and Lucius. After Joseph *père* dies, the family discovers a codicil leaving Orley Farm, the small property where Lord and Lady Mason and Lucius resided, to Lucius. (Groby Park, the estate property, remains

---

than inspiration, and his frank admission that he wrote for money, contributes to his sometimes-mediocre ranking in critical circles.

6. Trollope, *Autobiography*, 104.

devised to Joseph *fils*.) Joseph contests the codicil but loses, and Lady Mason retains possession of Orley Farm for Lucius.

As the novel opens, Lucius, now grown, cancels the Orley Farm crop lease held by Samuel Dockwrath, so that Lucius can try out his own modern farming theories. Enraged, Dockwrath, a lawyer as well as a sometime farmer, sets out to prove that the codicil was forged, easily recruiting the still-bitter Joseph Mason to the cause. Dockwrath finds some previously unknown circumstantial evidence—a deed with the same witnesses and the same date as the codicil—which Joseph uses to prosecute his stepmother for perjuring her testimony in the first trial. (The judgment in the first case barred retrying the will contest.)

Society thinks Lady Mason gravely put upon by Joseph Mason and Dockwrath, and at first the many lawyers in the book generally agree. But Trollope makes a bold plot move. Scarcely halfway into the book, Trollope reveals that Lady Mason indeed forged the codicil. Equal parts charming and conniving, and fearing that her son and she would be left poor, Lady Mason used her husband's will as a template for the codicil, imitating his handwriting so artfully that no one ever detected the fraud. For twenty years or more, Lady Mason kept the secret, never revealing her guilt to anyone. She confesses only on the eve of trial, to her closest friend, the widowed Mrs. Orme, who, in turn, forces Lady Mason to tell Sir Peregrine Orme (Mrs. Orme's father-in-law and, more importantly, Lady Mason's fiancé). The night before the jury verdict, Lady Mason also tells her son Lucius.

While Lady Mason occupies center stage in the novel, once Trollope reveals her guilt, our attention shifts to the other characters and their attitudes towards Lady Mason.[7] The novel changes from a "did she do it?" mystery to a character drama. In *Bleak House*, characters are defined by their attitudes towards Chancery. (John Jarndyce spurns it, Tulkinghorn and many other lawyers profit from it, and Richard Carstone is destroyed by it.) *Orley Farm* operates similarly, except that the center of the novel's interest is not an institution, but a person. How other characters treat Lady Mason—equitably or harshly—shapes our opinions about them. Lord Orme, who loves Lady Mason, nevertheless breaks off the engagement for propriety's sake. Mrs. Orme, on the other hand, stays loyal until the end, determined to follow Lady Mason whatever her fate. Joseph Mason, who has more property than he could ever need, is a perfect model of inequity;

---

7. Trollope came to regard the early revealing of the secret as a mistake. Trollope, *Autobiography*, 104.

he pursues his stepmother more out of spite than because of any real sense of grievance. Lucius Mason primarily wants to be his mother's savior, as concerned that he be her rescuer as that she be rescued.

Orley Farm sets up a clear conflict between law and justice.[8] On the one hand, Trollope reminds us time and again that Lady Mason committed a crime, concealed that crime for twenty years, profited from the crime, and was prepared to take the secret of it to her grave. On the other hand, Trollope never defends Sir Joseph's inequitable treatment of Lucius and Lady Mason. In fact, Trollope notes, without comment, that Sir Joseph regarded Lady Mason as a sort of "prize" that came along with his assumption of her father's collapsed business. Lady Mason herself, who repeatedly compares herself to Rebekah, certainly thinks that Sir Joseph treated her son and herself unfairly, and as a result never fully understands her guilt; even when prosecuted, she continues to maintain (at least to Mrs. Orme) that she was the injured party.

The lawyers (and the book is full of them) scarcely mention equities. Dockwrath pursues Lady Mason to punish her for his loss of the Orley Farm tenancy (and to ingratiate himself to Joseph Mason, whom he expects to be the new owner). Thomas Furnival, who represented Lady Mason in the will contest twenty years before, sticks with her even though he becomes increasingly convinced of her guilt, not so much out of scorn for Sir Joseph's inequity as fascination with her many charms. Felix Graham, the very model of a modern free-thinker, agrees to join Lady Mason's defense team, but then (out of strikingly un-litigious notions of fair play) tanks his cross-examination of the one minor prosecution witness assigned to him, apparently thinking that the gross unfairness of Joseph Mason's pursuit of his client is outweighed by professional courtesy to the witness. Lady Mason's "hired guns," Mr. Chaffenbrass and Solomon Aron, could not be more different from Felix Graham. Their job as advocates is to make the best possible case for their client, leaving questions of justice to the court. (Trollope calls Chaffenbrass "a great guardian of the innocence—or rather not guiltiness of the public."[9]) This in fact, seems to be the public view; Moulder, a traveling salesman that wanders in and out of the novel, says, "If a jury of her countrymen don't make a woman innocent, what does?"[10]

---

8. Tom Shaffer meditates on *Orley Farm* in both *Faith and the Professions* and *On Being a Christian*, but for different purposes from those here. They are worth a look.

9. Trollope, *Orley Farm*, 1:342.

10. Trollope, *Orley Farm*, 2:375.

The gentry, on the other hand, take a decidedly different view. Even Lady Mason's friends look at Chaffenbrass and Aron as, well, tradesmen, traveling salesmen of a different sort, necessary evils called upon to sell Lady Mason's assumed innocence to a jury of her inferiors.

Likewise, the trial has little to do with a moral judgment on Sir Joseph or on Lady Mason. The prosecutor's opening statement casts no moral blame on anyone. He makes out a case of simple induction: if only one document was signed that fateful day, and if a deed was signed, then the codicil must have been forged. Mr. Chaffenbrass and Mr. Aron quite efficiently impeach the key prosecution witnesses, even though they have scarcely any doubt that Lady Mason forged the codicil. Tom Furnival, on the other hand, pulls out every trick in the book *except* logic. He attacks Joseph Mason and Samuel Dockwrath as avaricious and rancorous. He impugns the testimony of the two putative witnesses to the codicil, one for testifying too vaguely and the other for being too definite. He says that he has no character witness for Lady Mason, then proceeds to give what amounts to character testimony on behalf of Mrs. Orme (who was in court but was not called as a witness) and speculates about what Sir Peregrine Orme (who was not even in court) would have said. (Although, if actions speak louder than words, Sir Peregrine said all he needed to say when he stayed away from court.) Furnival even expresses his own opinion about Lady Mason's character, something that today would earn at least a stern admonition from the trial judge. In all of that, however, Furnival never makes the obvious argument that leaving Orley Farm to Lady Mason, which after all was her home, was the *likely* thing for Lord Mason to have done, because it was the fair, the right, the *equitable* thing. Furnival assumes that Lord Mason had the right to do with his property as he pleased, even if that means dispossessing his widow and son. We know that Lord Mason's original, genuine will made only a modest settlement on his second family—more modest, in fact, than his bequests to his married daughters. Isn't it odd that, in trying to convince the jury that Lord Mason wrote the codicil, Furnival found no benefit in pointing out that he ought to have done it?

Trollope doesn't preach about the treatment of widows. (Sir Peregrine Orme's treatment of his widowed daughter-in-law, contrasted with Lord Mason's failure to provide for his second wife, would have been instructive on this theme.) In fact, Trollope, essentially conservative, was generally in favor of the custom of primogeniture and entailing estates.[11] Although

---

11. Primogeniture was the custom of passing all the real property in an estate to the

Orley Farm is not entailed to Joseph Mason, Trollope treats it as if it were. Nevertheless, a century-and-a-half removed, we cannot but feel that the equity of Lady Mason's treatment hangs over the entire novel. The theme, if we can call it that, of equitable relations runs straight through the novel, in both main and subplots. Lord Mason's refusal to provide adequately for Lucius and his mother sets up the plot. The catalyst is Lucius's thoughtless, self-centered cancelation of Dockwrath's farm lease, thereby earning Lucius an enemy equally energetic and aggrieved. Dockwrath and Joseph Mason the younger treat a band of traveling salesmen shabbily throughout the novel. Furnival gives his much-abused clerk Crabwitz a generous Christmas bonus and a week off, with a catch: he must spend his "holiday" in Yorkshire, trying to buy off Dockwrath.

It may be anachronistic modern sensibility, but one of the reasons the novel seems to us to be "about" equity is that Trollope, the novelist of Victorian convention, has populated it with characters that become admirable as they step out of their conventional roles. Most notably, Mrs. Orme defies social conventions to stand by Lady Mason, even after she learns her friend's secret.[12] Felix Graham, the free-thinking lawyer, refuses to do certain things even to serve his client, thereby earning the respect of Judge Staveley. The judge's daughter Madeline, in turn, defies her mother by choosing Graham over the wealthier, more respectable Peregrine Orme, and ends up perhaps the happiest character in the novel. Lucius Mason, on the other hand, seems to jump from role to role—future gentleman, modern farmer, avenging son—never perfecting any of them and never finding his own identity. When he learns of his mother's guilt and the loss of Orley Farm, he drifts out of his mother's life, leaving her on the continent for a new life in Australia.

---

eldest son. Entailing an estate was a method of insuring that it passed according to rules of primogeniture. McMaster discusses the practice and Trollope's view of it in chapter 1 of *Trollope and the Law*.

12. A cynic might say that Mrs. Orme serves her own financial interests when she talks Lady Mason into confessing her crime and breaking off the engagement, since Lady Mason would be the potential source of a rival heir to her son Peregrine. If that is part of Mrs. Orme's motivation, however, Trollope leaves it up to the reader to deduce; he nowhere hints of it.

Then there are those who appear conflicted by their roles. Mr. Round, Joseph Mason's long-time solicitor, cannot find it in himself to either prosecute or abandon the case against Lady Mason. Felix Graham knows what he needs to do to defend Lady Mason but can't do it. And Sir Peregrine Orme, so noble for so much of the novel, cannot escape conventions and marry the woman he still loves. (When his daughter-in-law proposes to go to the trial with Lady Mason, exclaiming "think of her misery," Sir Peregrine responds, "think of her guilt.") Sir Peregrine goes far, but only so far, out of loyalty to Lady Mason. He allows her to remain his houseguest even after he knows of her guilt, although he releases her from the engagement, but he refuses to go to court with her. He would prefer to renew the engagement after her acquittal, but, the novel suggests, is talked out of it by Mrs. Orme.

Finally, there are the lawyers, who play out their assigned roles. Samuel Dockwrath epitomizes justice without mercy. No doubt Lucius treated him unjustly, and without question the law is on his side in the will case. On the other hand, he violates one of the fundamental principles of equity, the "clean hands" doctrine—one must do equity to have equity. That plot twist happens thus: Lady Mason, in a bit of inspired cunning, includes in the forged codicil a two-thousand-pound bequest to Miriam Usbech, the daughter of Lord Mason's attorney and the purported drafter of the codicil. Dockwrath ends up marrying Miriam and gets control both of her father's files (where he discovers the crucial piece of evidence) and Miriam's bequest. Absent the forged codicil, that money would have gone to Joseph Mason. In other words, Dockwrath benefited from the codicil he now attacks. In the end, Joseph and Mason end up in a lawsuit over Dockwrath's fee, and, Trollope tells us, Dockwrath is denied his fee and is, in fact, "ruined," and the lawsuit costs Joseph more than paying the fee would have. As Einstein said of God, justice can be subtle.[13]

On the other hand, we feel we ought to admire Tom Furnival.[14] A successful, self-made barrister, Furnival is physically impressive, intelligent,

13. Samuel Dockwrath, intriguingly, seems to have more than a bit of Trollope's father in him. Trollope *père* was known for his violent temper, which ultimately ran off enough clients to ruin his once-thriving practice. His second profession, after his law practice closed? Farming. In fact, the Orley Farm home was modeled on a home in Harrow that the Trollope family leased, and then lost.

14. The names in the book are deliciously appropriate. No one ends up happier than Felix Graham, made happy by his loyalty to his own principles. Thomas Furnival is the great doubter in the novel; he, among all those associated with Lady Graham, first suspects her guilt, but then forces himself to be loyal to her. The implications of "Dockwrath" are obvious. Perhaps less so are those coming out of his client's name. "Joseph"

and loyal to his client. He skillfully assembles the defense team—Chaffenbrass, Aron, and Graham—that gains Lady Mason's acquittal. He immediately grasps the ethical complexities of Lady Mason's situation (and his own as her lawyer.) Nevertheless, he spends much of the novel, it seems to me, as a bit clownish, vacillating between his crush on Lady Mason and his concern for his own respectability, which he suspects will be compromised by defending someone he suspects is guilty. (He also makes life miserable for his wife, who picks up on the emotional attachment to Lady Mason and concludes they are having an intimate affair.)[15] In the trial's closing, however, Furnival steps back into his role as the loyal barrister for Lady Mason and achieves a measure of (ironic) grandeur.

Chaffenbrass and Aron, the hired guns, ultimately come off (at least to me and I suspect to most trial lawyers reading the novel) as the most admirable of all the lawyers in the book. They see their roles in a distinctly modern light: making the prosecution prove its case. Although it may not be recognized by everyone as a benefit to society, even today, lawyers know that holding law enforcement to account, even in the clearest case of guilt, benefits everyone, by leading to more professionalism. Certainly, Chaffenbrass and Aron play their roles to the hilt, and whatever the Masons and Ormes may think, today we recognize that as a good thing.

In *On Being a Christian and a Lawyer*, Tom Shaffer meditated at some length on Orley Farm. Loyalty was the theme he came back to, time and again. How does a lawyer serve a guilty client (like Lady Mason)? By being loyal to her. How does a lawyer remain loyal to a bad client? By "remain[ing], as Mrs. Orme did, in the presence of an evil design, if the lawyer is willing, as she was, to exercise moral influence against the design."[16] By acting *prophetically*, in other words. That is certainly part of the Lawyer's Dilemma

---

Mason is clearly his father's favorite son, but, unlike the Joseph in Genesis, this one never matures into the savior of his family. And was there ever a more upper-crust British name than "Peregrine"? This novel has two: the elder, who loses his last great love because he cannot step out of his nobility, and his grandson, who gets reprimanded for not behaving enough like a nobleman, but nevertheless hopes to enjoy the fruits of nobility by a sort of entitlement to Madeline Stavely's hand.

15. In fact, his meeting with Lady Mason at all breaches legal ethics. Furnival being a barrister, he should have heard her story only through a solicitor. Meeting with her directly (which of course has everything to do with her charms) incites his ethical dilemma. Solicitors meet with clients, and then brief the barrister in advance of trial, to shield the barrister from having doubts about his client's innocence. I owe this insight to McMaster, from chapter 2 of *Trollope and the Law*.

16. Shaffer, *On Being a Christian*, 85.

we're concerned with here. How does a lawyer remain loyal to a bad client? But our concern goes beyond that. How, in a world of law without equity, do we tell who a bad client is? Was Lady Mason a bad client? Trollope seems to think so. So does Tom Shaffer; he says she becomes "repulsive to everyone in the story."[17] And Tom Furnival wrestles with that question throughout the book. But for all her guile, her perpetual eye on the main chance, it is difficult to dislike Lady Mason, and impossible not to admire her. We have none of those emotions towards Dockwrath, or Joseph Mason. Does Trollope see Dockwrath as a bit of an *arriviste*? Perhaps. Is Dockwrath Trollope's revenge on his father? Impossible to say. Nevertheless, it seems to me that the problem with Mason and Dockwrath for modern readers is precisely the equity deficit. They treat everyone, including each other, as tools for advancement—as *instruments*. Joseph or his stepmother: Who is really the bad client?

Cousin Henry: The Comedy of Equity

Cousin Henry, a late, shorter novel, has the same themes as *Orley Farm*, rendered in a comic key. Henry Jones, the title character, does not forge a will, but he does conceal one. The probated will of Indifer Jones, Henry's childless uncle, leaves Henry his uncle's estate in Carmarthen, Wales. Henry discovers, but does not produce, a later will that disinherits him in favor of his cousin Isabel Broderick. She, in every way the daughter her uncle never had, is handsome, charming, intelligent, and devoted to her uncle. Henry is none of those things. Indifer wants to leave the property to Isabel. The only thing stopping him is his belief in the English heritage of primogeniture; because Indifer has no son, Henry is the nearest male heir.[18]

Henry doesn't particularly want the estate, although he would enjoy the life of leisure that would accompany it. He discovers the new will by accident, stuffed in a book in his uncle's library, and places it back where he found it. Everyone acknowledges that Uncle Indifer wrote a new will; the two witnesses are quite firm about that. The question is whether the old man destroyed it. Indeed, he might have; Uncle Indifer rewrote his will several times.

17. Shaffer, *On Being a Christian*, 49.
18. For complicated reasons having to do with English entailment law, the property does not automatically pass to Henry. Indifer, apparently, feels obligated to observe the tradition, although not bound by the rule.

Henry spends much of the novel in constant, internal "special pleading" of the type that gave casuistry a bad name. He reasons that if he doesn't hide the will, but only leaves it where he found it, he's innocent of any crime. He vacillates between surrendering the new will (if he can figure out a way to do so without heaping further scorn on himself) and destroying it as a manner of revenge on his tormentors. And tormented he certainly is. Uncle Indifer tells Henry he doesn't like him. Isabel, in perhaps her one un-charming moment, tells Henry that she loathes him and wouldn't take the property from him if he offered it. The estate's servants begin deserting Henry as soon as the will in favor of Henry is probated.

Into this breach comes Nicholas Apjohn, who had been Indifer Jones's lawyer and now is nominally Henry's. Apjohn seems what a twenty-year-older Felix Graham might be; skillful and shrewd, he wants to know what the truth is, client obligations be damned. (Indeed, while Apjohn technically represents Henry, it is the deceased Indifer, and even the property itself, that seem to be Apjohn's real clients.) Apjohn deduces from Henry's demeanor that Henry knows of a subsequent will. Apjohn gradually reasons out that Henry must have concealed, but not destroyed, the new will. Apjohn cajoles, encourages, and bullies Henry into bringing a criminal libel action against the local newspaper who has been reporting on the matter, knowing that, if Henry conceals the will, the trial will unravel him. Even though he represents Henry, Apjohn agrees to pay, and perhaps even selects, the barrister to represent the newspaper—Mr. John Cheekey, "Supercilious Jack," the most feared cross-examiner in all the land, who could intimidate a witness simply by raising his eyebrows.

In other words, Apjohn sets up his own client. He talks Henry into bringing a charge he doesn't want to bring (because he knows it's a false one), so that he can be subjected to cross-examination by Cheeky, the human lie detector. Such things would get a lawyer disbarred today. The trial never happens, however, because Apjohn catches Henry preparing to destroy the will. (A plot turn readers, at least the trial lawyers among them, regret, having been deprived of Supercilious Jack's cross-examination of the sniveling Henry.) Once the will is found, Apjohn shifts from treating Henry as a client (and a difficult one at that) to a friend, by fighting off the worst rumors about Henry and allowing the world to believe that the new will was late discovered. In so doing, Apjohn even absorbs the costs of the abortive libel suit himself, and, in the end, professes that he had all along "pitied (Henry) from the bottom of my heart."[19]

We admire Apjohn, I think, unreservedly, even as he betrays his "client." How can that be? Two reasons, I think. First, Apjohn remains loyal: first to Indifer, seeing that his will gets carried out, and then to Henry, steering him through the shoals of public scorn. Second, Apjohn has a sense of equity more finely tuned than anyone in *Orley Farm*. Near the end of *Cousin Henry*, Apjohn makes a speech to Isabel that amounts to a virtual *précis* of equity. In discussing whether Uncle Indifer's belief in primogeniture justified his mistake, Apjohn says (in response to Isabel's comment that Uncle Indifer "meant to do his duty"):

> Certainly, but he mistook it. He did not understand the root of that idea of a male heir. The object has been to keep the old family, and the old adherences, and the old acres together. England owes much to the manner in which this has been done, and the custom as to a male heir has availed much in the doing of it. But in this case, *in sticking to the custom, he would have lost the spirit*, and, as far as he was concerned, would have gone against the practice which he wished to perpetuate. [20]

Unlike the array of lawyers in *Orley Farm*, Apjohn manages to see that both legal and higher justice are done. Yet his own treatment of his client leads to the mess as much as anything. Apjohn prepares for Uncle Indifer the will that disinherits Isabel, but so frankly disapproves of the action that when Uncle Indifer changes his mind at the last he writes out the will in his own hand, rather than asking Apjohn to prepare it. Apjohn indeed acts prophetically when he takes Indifer to task, but it's decidedly in the Jeremiad vein. Perhaps a bit of humility might have allowed Indifer a path to return to Apjohn to correct his mistake.

We have, then, two novels, two estates, two claimants in each to the estate, and two sets of lawyers. In the first, *Orley Farm*, all the lawyers act out stock character roles, and none seem attuned to the equities in the case. In the second, *Cousin Henry*, one lawyer breaks all the rules of lawyer decorum, but in the end comes off as more equitable than any of his colleagues from the earlier novel, or anyone else in the second one. Can we defend Henry Apjohn? Can we excuse Samuel Dockwrath?

---

19. Trollope, *Cousin Henry*, 177.
20. Trollope, *Cousin Henry*, 273, emphasis added.

12

Conclusion: The Decadence of Equity?

Back to the city attorney's office, where we left Ms. Morales in chapter 2. As Monday morning quarterbacks, what sort of advice can we give her?

First, what should we tell the HR director about Brennan, the substance-impaired, ready-to-retire maintenance man? Ms. Morales's conversation with the HR director gives her the chance to act "prophetically." Granted, there are good—very good—reasons why maintenance men (whose job involves ladders, trucks, and power tools) shouldn't use cocaine. None of those reasons, however, justifies denying Brennan his retirement. The specter of losing his retirement makes it less likely, not more, that a middle-aged laborer will come out of the shadows and get treatment for an addiction. So, strict application of this rule flunks the equity test from both perspectives. It is both a harsh misapplication of a general rule, and it deprives Brennan of the necessities to survive. Firing Brennan in the name of workplace safety would be, to invoke Hooker's analogy, the medicine that kills the patient. It is "extremity," not equity.

Our second case, Deidre, the single mother on the eviction list, is the type that keeps lawyers awake at night. On the one hand, just as with Brennan's case, Deidre's situation threatens life's necessaries—here, a safe place to live. Moreover, this case extends beyond Deidre herself. Deidre's children will suffer as least as much as their mother. The sins of the parents, it seems, are sometimes visited on the children. Other rights, however, are at issue also. We have the rights of other residents to a safe living environment; the rights of the persons on the waiting list, ready and willing to pay the rent, to decent housing; and society's rights to have its laws obeyed

CONCLUSION: THE DECADENCE OF EQUITY?

and its obligations met. Not all those rights can be met. Deidre's case is complex, but what case isn't?

Deidre's case is deeply troubling. Lawyers think of themselves as fixers, but this case cannot be easily fixed. In any just society, everyone should have decent housing.[1] Does Deidre, however, have a moral claim to *this* house? Clearly not: except that, in many communities, for some people, public housing is the only realistic option.

There are certainly plenty of philosophical tools that we can try to help her with. There is the concept of casuistry: ethical reasoning on a case-by-case basis. There is a close relationship between equity and casuistry.[2] Like equity, casuistry attempts to apply a rule in a logical way, according to its best use, given all the circumstances. For example, casuistry recognizes the "principle of double effect," which, like so many things we've talked about, originated with Aquinas. Sometimes we are torn between competing moral principles, and, the theory goes, our intent to achieve a moral good allows us to cause harm as a byproduct.[3] The principle, which Aquinas used to justify self-defense, arises today in discussions of medical ethics. May we give a dying patient enough morphine to relieve her pain, knowing that the dose may kill her? The principle of double effect suggests that we may. The doctor doesn't intend to kill the patient; she hopes to relieve the pain.

Ms. Morales could invoke the principle of double effect to justify evicting Deidre and her children. After all, the city doesn't *intend* to harm Deidre or her children. It wants to achieve the goals of the housing system—to make safe and affordable housing available to as many people as possible in a fair and efficient manner.[4] Any harm to Deidre and family is an unavoidable, but

---

1. I intentionally avoid saying that everyone has a "right" to decent housing, because many philosophers, for technical reasons, would avoid characterizing the concept as a "right" held by individuals, even as they concede that society ought to provide everyone decent housing. The issues in this book do not require us to enter that debate.

2. E.g., Brown, *Donne and the Politics of Conscience*, 21.

3. There are generally said to be four requirements for the principle of double effect: (i) The act *itself* must be morally good or at least indifferent. (ii) The agent may not positively will the bad effect but may permit it. If he could attain the good effect without the bad effect, he should do so. The bad effect is sometimes said to be indirectly voluntary. (iii) The good effect must flow from the action at least as immediately (in the order of causality, though not necessarily in the order of time) as the bad effect. In other words, the good effect must come directly from the action, not by the bad effect. Otherwise the agent would be using a bad means to a good end, which is never allowed. (iv) The good effect must be sufficiently desirable to compensate for the allowing of the bad effect.

4. The HUD mission statement includes as goals "create strong, sustainable, inclusive

acceptable, byproduct of achieving that goal. But is it? Aquinas said that the action must be proportional to the end. Is the harm done to Deidre proportional to the end of a safe neighborhood? Or are there other things that can be done (such as running Deidre's brother off)?

Casuistry also shows a preference for a higher over a lower principle. For instance, avoiding a "wrong" does not justify committing a "sin." Recall that personal equity, according to Calvin, is based on the Golden Rule. There could certainly be no higher rule than that: love your neighbor as yourself. But the question Ms. Morales faces is, who counts as the "other"? Deidre? Her children? The neighbors? The people on the waiting list? All have claims on the housing authority. Casuistry does allow us to make distinctions between those that are close to us and strangers, so that, within reason, we may prefer our families over strangers when we share our wealth or make moral choices.[5] However, when the lawyer's client is the public, which is the case for government lawyers, our prima facie obligation is to treat all persons equally. Who, then, is Ms. Morales's neighbor? Another swing and a miss, it appears.

Casuistry also recognizes the principle of compromise, deferring a decision in hopes that it will resolve itself. However, decisions must be made. We cannot defer decision forever. Kirk says that failure to decide eventually hardens into a decision, usually in favor of the status quo ante.[6] Allowing Deidre to stay eventually means acquiescing in her behavior. We need a reasoned decision, not a backdoor one. Strike three for casuistry, I'm afraid.

How about a utilitarian answer? After all, we live in a utilitarian world, and Ms. Morales works for an agency that by its very nature seeks to be useful to the public. Unfortunately, Deidre's case illustrates how utilitarianism, in practical ethics, proves to be, well, useless. A utilitarian might say that the scales tip towards eviction, because the good done to the next family in line equals the harm that eviction would do to Deidre and her family, and the neighborhood will also benefit from seeing Deidre's brother go, so that the scales tip towards eviction. Even if we could make such a calculation (and to do so would require a crystal ball much clearer than most of us enjoy) when we think that way, we turn persons into factors. (As an aside: if I

---

communities and quality affordable homes for all," "meet the need for quality affordable rental homes," "utilize housing as a platform for improving quality of life," and "build inclusive and sustainable communities free from discrimination."

5. Kirk, *Conscience and Its Problems*, 139, regarding Stoicism in relation to family ties.

6. Kirk, *Conscience and Its Problems*, 366.

were king, I would banish the term "human resources" in favor of the older "personnel." Thinking of our co-workers as persons rather than resources would be a small blow against utilitarianism.)

In other words, we cannot quantify the relative requirements of justice and mercy. They are each first-order demands. Choosing mercy over justice as a higher-order duty seems fundamentally incompatible with the lawyer's professional duty to the law. Refusing to enforce Deidre's lease ignores a basic premise about life in society: keeping promises. Still, it seems difficult to come up with a non-utilitarian argument for preferring justice over mercy, and the utilitarian arguments fall apart.

There is only one thing we can tell Ms. Morales. The real problem—the shortage of decent affordable housing—is one that Ms. Morales can't solve. Nothing Ms. Morales decides with Deidre will bring about global housing equity. What Ms. Morales can do is make society confront itself.

A hundred years ago, as we saw, Dean Roscoe Pound warned of the "decadence of equity," expressing the fear that equity was becoming neutralized through absorption into the rule-driven legal system.[7] Kaveny's article, mentioned in the last chapter, asks the question of whether that is so.[8] Kaveny sees contract law as a tradition rather than a body of rules, and contract cases as individual narratives within that tradition. She concludes that contract law at its best illustrates how law can be an expression of "common morality." Judges at their best achieve "a rich and subtle sensibility . . . which take [sic] account of not only the relevant rules and principles, but also the relevant virtues and vices, and the relevant strengths and vulnerabilities, of the contested parties."[9] This sensibility harmonizes with religious belief, but does not depend on it.[10] If a case ever called for a "rich and subtle sensibility," Deidre's eviction is it.

Kaveny's article reads as a stirring call for equity, accompanied by a sophisticated practice of casuistry. Except for one thing: she never mentions "equity" or "equitable."[11] She writes: "specific facts always exert moral pressure on abstract rules and categories in the context of practical, legal-moral

---

7. Pound, "Decadence of Equity," 20, 25–27.
8. Kaveny, "Between Example and Doctrine."
9. Kaveny, "Between Example and Doctrine," 694.
10. Kaveny, "Between Example and Doctrine," 672.
11. Nor does it mention Pound's article. I bring this up not to criticize Kaveny's very fine article, but as an indication of how equity has slipped out of legal consciousness.

decision making."[12] That, in a nutshell, is what Aquinas meant by "equity" (and what causes the Lawyer's Dilemma). Her description of "common morality" in court decisions reminds us of Hooker's belief in communal rather than individual reason. Kaveny even talks about several doctrines, notably promissory estoppel, that come straight from equity.[13] But she talks of them as doctrines that are part of the common law, proving how the terms of our discussion have changed in just the way that Berman describes, and how Pound's diagnosis of equity's decay into just another doctrine of law, rather than its highest use as both a part of law—the best part—and a moral chorus commenting from outside the law, seems upon us.

Therefore, let me propose my own view, what I might call a twenty-first-century version of equity. First, the effort to separate the law from non-legal moral standards has failed. We should just admit that. In the same way that scientific materialism requires just as much faith as religion, albeit faith in something different (human rationality), current theories of legal scholarship include value judgments as much as do legal systems based in morality. They simply substitute non-ethical criteria, such as efficiency or cost-benefit analysis. We would like to persuade ourselves that these are more objective. They are not. Calculations of efficiency and cost-benefit are highly abstract. True justice, however, decides particular cases involving real people. Moreover, in deeming efficiency the highest value promoted by our laws, we determine that efficiency outweighs some other value (compassion, for instance). That is itself a moral judgment.

Second, to reinsert a moral sensibility into the legal system, we need to reimagine the roles of client, lawyer, adversary, and court. This is more than a legal question; it goes to fundamental questions of who we are and how we exist together. How we resolve problems reveals just as much about us as what behaviors and conditions we call problems. Once we conceive of the law as a moral endeavor, we liberate ourselves from the restrictive way in which we think about legal problems and find all sorts of nonlegal resources available to guide us.

Such as philosophy. I suggest we consider the recent work of political and moral philosopher Henry Richardson—specifically, his concept of

---

12. Kaveny, "Between Example and Doctrine," 692–93.

13. "Promissory estoppel," which in the name of justice gives effect to certain promises that fail to rise to contractual status for technical reasons, is an archetypal doctrine of equity. As noted in chapter 8, doctrines such as promissory estoppel (in this case, in the form assumpsit) were originally embedded in the common law because of its relations to canon law. That day passed, however, many centuries ago.

the "moral community" engaged in "joint moral reasoning." Richardson describes a process of "joint, socially embodied reasoning" as an alternative to individual concrete moral analysis.[14] Richardson says that "in an articulated moral community . . . we begin more fully to determine the extent of morality by sincerely and conscientiously attempting to work out moral difficulties together."[15] He describes three stages of moral discourse: (i) "authorized input"—the "give-and-take of working things out," during which "the parties . . . communicate with one another explicitly asking for and offering considerations in favor of one approach over another";[16] (ii) "convergence"—the parties' chance to sort out the various proposals, counter-proposals, objections, and concerns raised during the input phase, with the goal of reaching a moral consensus about the particular problem at hand—one that presumably has one or more universal moral rules embedded with it, but that does not itself reflect a universal moral norm;[17] and (iii) "ratification"—a broader process with a larger community, addressing the question of whether the particular moral innovation reached by the parties should give rise to a new, more general moral norm.[18]

In a legal context, where are we to find such a community? Perhaps in the judicial process itself. Richardson disclaims any intent to describe anything more than a hypothetical way of looking at moral discourse. Nor does he propose a structure for dispute resolution in any formal sense. Nevertheless, Richardson's model parallels the legal-dispute-resolution process. Richardson's initial "input" stage sounds very much like both the negotiation stage of a contract and the pre-trial phase of litigation. Although there is much to object to in Holmes's "bad man" theory, it is true that, whether in litigation or contract negotiation, parties are less concerned with abstract propositions of law than with meeting their needs and avoiding adverse consequences. (One hopes that they are also concerned with what is right in a moral sense, a possibility Holmes excludes as irrelevant to legal discussion.) Inputs at this stage should range widely. According to Richardson, it should include a discussion from both sides, the rights holder and the duty-bound counterpart, to discuss what the nature and extent of the duty is.

14. Richardson, *Articulating the Moral Community*, 155–75.
15. Richardson, *Articulating the Moral Community*, 154.
16. Richardson, *Articulating the Moral Community*, 155.
17. Richardson, *Articulating the Moral Community*, 136–42.
18. Richardson, *Articulating the Moral Community*, 176–92.

If the parties can reach agreement, then they enter the convergence stage, when they take their agreement on relevant considerations and construct a new status quo—one that exists within a legal framework but effects a new social or economic reality. This might be a new contract under which the parties move forward with a matter of joint interest, or it might be a settlement of a dispute over a previous arrangement or relationship. Either way, the parties have "converged." That is exactly what happened in the real-life case on which the hypothetical "Brennan" is based. He filed an age-discrimination complaint with the Equal Employment Opportunity commission. EEOC rules allow the parties to opt for an early mediation. It quickly emerged that "Brennan's" real concern was preserving his retirement. The employer (my client) conceded that impairing Brennan's pension benefits was the last thing it wanted. The parties entered into a consent decree, under which Brennan's discharge was set aside, he was suspended without pay until his fifty-fifth birthday, upon which he agreed to retire. This result could not have been reached outside of the dispute-resolution process.

Sometimes, the parties cannot converge. When that happens in a contract discussion, the status quo remains. (A difficult part of contract negotiation is always weighing the prospect of a mediocre deal with no deal at all; it's essential, however, that the other party believe that you are willing to walk away with no deal at all.) When the discussion centers around a dispute concerning an existing relation, however, the status quo typically cannot remain, and the parties invoke the power of the state for help in resolving the dispute.

Lawyers always tell their clients, and mediators always tell both sides to a dispute, that a judicial resolution will come from a stranger (or, in a jury trial, strangers) and will be a zero-sum, binary decision. Perhaps a better way to look at it, indeed a better goal for judges, might be trial as an "imposed convergence." As contradictory as that might sound, it is a broader, more sophisticated, indeed a nobler, view of what courts do. The court makes a decision in the context of all the relevant considerations, including moral ones, that concerned the parties as they traveled to this place, unable to converge themselves.

But all this works only if at the end of the day the court has the authority to reach a result both legally sustainable and morally defensible. This does not mean that legal requirements such as standing, or rules of evidence, are out the window. It does mean, however, that such rules are viewed in a moral context. Victim's rights and grandparent rights are two

CONCLUSION: THE DECADENCE OF EQUITY?

areas of recent concern. In our hypothetical of Deidre, the neighbor's complaints and perhaps even the brother's perspective would be also. A morally defensible decision must hear all relevant voices, even if we treat them as friends of the court, rather than parties with standing.

In other words, we make our courts a reflection of a "common but complex" morality. (Kaveny speaks of a common morality, and I think the complexity is implicit.) Common because it is a joint morality, held by virtually all people. Complex because it is multifarious, attempting to balance competing, even incommensurable, values. This common but complex morality does not depend on a particular confession of faith; nor does it ask us to give up our own faith claims. In nations with a Western European heritage, it has its roots in Christian morality, even if it has gradually been divorced from it.

Common morality shares certain values—justice and mercy would be two—although those truths inevitably come into conflict. It places great faith in community wisdom, while at the same time realizing the limitations on even the community's abilities to balance the conflicting truth claims. Respect for basic legal premises (such as the obligation of contracts) plays a part in common morality, but only a part. Mercy, in the form of regard for the poor, unfortunate, needy, and disadvantaged, most definitely plays a part. Far from being divorced from questions of morality, our legal system, in this view, attempts to implement the hopes that the community has to see its common morality realized.

These elements are key to understanding the Lawyer's Dilemma, and how the concept of equity helps relieve that dilemma. Morality must be both held in common by most people and be complex enough to go beyond strict rules of conduct. No one, I presume, would want justice devoid of mercy. The difficult task is balancing the demands of mercy compared with those of justice, efficiency, predictability, social utility, and personal benefit. Because morality is complex, none of us has perfect solutions to all problems.

Richardson suggests that no single individual can resolve such conflicts. They can only be answered through joint moral reasoning. In that sense, Deidre's case may be not only disturbing but potentially liberating. If we could turn Deidre's case over to the judicial process, it would be both deeply liberating and, in fact, an act of faith. But is that faith justified? For the judicial process to have moral authority, and not simply legal, over the problem, the judge must have the ability to express moral, and not simply legal, considerations.

This is why turning Deidre's case over to the eviction court is an act of faith. (In Texas and many other states, eviction suits come before a justice of the peace, nomenclature we should take seriously.) But it can be so only if the courts to which Ms. Morales entrusts Deidre's case have the capacity to explore the interstices of this common morality. The attitude that the court would take towards the legislature is one of respect. Courts cannot simply ignore plain statutory language, but neither are they obligated to impose unjust results because of a fictional legislative intent.

There are several implications in this. I will deal only with a few.

First, it reorients the relation between lawyer and client. It makes the lawyer's prophetic advice to his client, at the beginning of the representation, crucial. Thomas Shaffer portrays law practice as a ministry independent of results. In fact, according to Shaffer, the ministry is enhanced when the probable result is adverse to the client. I submit, though, that the Christian act of ministry involves more than standing by a client on the way to the cross. The lawyer's prophetic ministry to his client may be just as great when law entitles the client to a favorable but unjust result. Allegretti writes: "Lawyers and clients are called to form a moral community—a kind of covenant—in which each respects and honors the other as made in the image and likeness of God. My task as a lawyer is not only to give competent legal advice, though that is always required, but to serve as the moral companion of my client, encouraging my client to be the kind of person she can be at her best rather than helping her do what she can get away with at her worst."[19] Standing by someone being persecuted may be professionally hard but can be personally rewarding. But what about standing by the persecutor? What if your client is Javert, rather than Jean Valjean?

Let me put it another way. This model allows the lawyer to ask a client that most crucial of questions, one that rarely gets asked and probably even less often answered: How will we know when we've *won*? That is a different question from "what do you want," although the client's desires certainly form part of the answer. In a contract negotiation, a win may be getting a deal, or getting the best deal. In litigation, a jury verdict is not necessarily a win, and certainly not a final win, given the uncertainties of appeals, collection, bankruptcy, and so on. In a harassment case, it may be an apology, a firing, medical bills paid, or a change in company policy. A win involves not

---

19. Allegretti, "Can Legal Ethics Be Christian?," 460.

CONCLUSION: THE DECADENCE OF EQUITY?

only getting the client what she wants but getting her what can be gotten. And at some point, the moral implications of a "win" hit home. How much will the head on a pike (if that's what the client thinks he wants) really satisfy, in the fullness of time? Javert comes to see, in his final moments, how apprehending Valjean is not the win he hoped for, but is in fact complete failure.[20] Did Jacob ever feel as if he had "won" against Esau?

Second, it means that we must reinvigorate the jury. If the lawyer is to make the "best" argument for his client, he needs to be judged by both legal and community standards, for "best" arguments necessarily appeal to a "higher" standard. The jury represents the community; the judge represents the law, including basic rights embedded in the law. Juries have long had the acknowledged right of "nullification" in criminal cases. Perhaps it is time to think about that right in civil cases. Kaveny's article concerns itself almost entirely with the behavior of appellate judges. It talks about juries only in the context of a single case out of Iowa, involving gross imposition by a dance instructor on an elderly spinster.[21] Kaveny takes a dubious view of the jury verdict (which awarded both actual and punitive damages), but then praises the Iowa Supreme Court for finding a legally plausible way to sustain it. Having spent years in trial courts, I have a different reaction: thank God for the jury, which expressed the community's outrage at the defendant's behavior. Without the jury, justice would have failed, because the appellate court could not have imposed on its own initiative what the jury found.

Third, Richardson's model has real implications for the role of a judge. The judge becomes an active participant in the parties' attempts to resolve the case. As we saw when we followed Jack's lawyer to the final pre-trial hearing, good judges do this now, and more should. A good judge will regularly call parties in for informal status conferences, to find out what the status of settlement negotiations are, pose areas of concern for the court, and play devil's advocate about crucial facts or law for each side of the case. A good judge will also be quite forthright about sharing the judge's view

---

20. The corollary of this, with which trial lawyers are all too aware, is persuading the adversary that he has lost. A loss can come long before the jury comes in. Cases can be essentially "over" once a party admits something in a deposition, or a court admits a key piece of evidence, or an appellate court issues an opinion in an unrelated case that clarifies a disputed point of law. Just as it's time to stop fighting when a case is won, so it is when a case is lost. Many cases fail to settle because one side wants to win something it will never get or the other side doesn't know or won't admit that it's lost.

21. *Syester v. Banta*, 133 N. W. 2d 666 (Iowa 1965).

of the matter, as well as predicting what a jury might think about a case. Admittedly, such expressions are often as much strategic as candid, but in fact they renew the "input stage" of the moral discourse. The parties don't have to participate in such discussions, but they are well advised to. Nearly every trial lawyer alive has failed to settle a case because he misread the judge's thoughts about it. That should never happen.

This, in fact, means a different way of thinking about legal problems. It recasts many legal questions from a "what" to a "why" question. Asking why we should allow Deidre to stay in public housing (or why she should be forced to move) gets to the heart of the matter in a way that "does Deidre have to go?" fails to. "Why" questions lead to dialogue; "what" questions call for answers. The answer to "why" implicates legal propositions, but those propositions don't necessarily determine the answer. Thus, "promises must be kept" becomes more of a legal presumption than a determinative answer.

The shift from proposition to presumption, from pronouncement to question, is what I mean by equity. This is how our system, at its best, operates now. Lawyers know that they had best convince the trial judge of more than who the law says should win: the real question is why, according to higher justice, the client ought to win.[22] This view of equity merely acknowledges that view as legitimate, indeed superior.

Even more radically, it asks us all to answer this question: What does it mean to win? The Lawyer's Dilemma is the Legal Dilemma, too often simply shoved off on the lawyer. What would this mean for Ms. Morales? It means that, under this model, Ms. Morales's best choice is to turn Deidre's eviction over to the judicial process, rather than exercise self-help lockout rights. It should be a trial, with a jury, and the opportunity to be heard, and the opportunity to appeal. No theory of morality requires either Ms. Morales or the city to simply ignore the law. Likewise, no employment law theory obligates the city to retain an attorney who refuses to enforce the city's contracts. This is how Ms. Morales makes society confront itself. As O'Donovan reminds us:

> The trouble is not that law hopes to express some moral truth, for law must express moral truth if it is to command authority; the trouble is that it underestimates the complexity of the moral truth it must express. The truth of a law must also be the truth about

---

22. I owe this insight, and many others, to my late contracts and choice of law professor, the great Russell Weintraub.

CONCLUSION: THE DECADENCE OF EQUITY?

the society in which the law will function. An over-demanding or over-restrictive law bears false witness to the totality, while intending to bear true witness to the part.[23]

Augustine thought that the Roman virtues of pride and valor were not so much sinful as misdirected—to lower rather than higher righteousness. So it is for over-restrictive law, which is not so much positively evil as it is mistaken about the true goal of law.

Strict law without equity, even so fundamental a proposition as "promises must be kept," bears false witness to the totality of the true relation between a specific creditor and a particular debtor, *this* landlord and *this* tenant, while intending to bear true witness to one part, the importance of promises. It also bears false witness to the relation between that proposition and all the other propositions of law or morality that we consider equally fundamental. For lawyering to be vocational, it must (again quoting O'Donovan) "take us beyond identity, to a fulfillment in service that is extended to us personally by God."[24] Freedom is "the individual's discovery and pursuit of his or her vocation from God."[25] The same God that extends that vocation sets the model for perfection that the law seeks. For the lawyer, equity, the "law of freedom," truly is the source.

---

23. O'Donovan, *Ways of Judgment*, 19.
24. O'Donovan, *Ways of Judgment*, 72.
25. O'Donovan, *Ways of Judgment*, 72.

AFTERWORD

Equality versus Equity

Before we finish, we should talk about the connections, and distinctions, between equity and another fundamental moral concept, "equality." It seems that the importance of equality as a social value has escalated at the same time, and even at the same pace, as equity has diminished. Admittedly, one of the principles of equity is that "equality equals equity." In the absence of some compelling reason, people should be treated the same, and social benefits should be divided proportionally. On the other hand, equity also reminds us that there are often good reasons to treat people differently or distribute benefits disproportionately. Hence, we have another paradox. *Equal* treatment can be *inequitable*. Recall Perkins's case of the boy stealing a loaf of bread to avoid starvation. Treating him equally with other thieves (in the Elizabethan era) would have meant hanging him. We don't execute thieves today, but we still treat persons harshly in the name of fairness or equality. Mandatory sentencing rules treat all offenders equally, but they can be profoundly inequitable, because they don't—can't—give case-specific particulars the relevance they may deserve.

By contrast, affirmative action programs, which attempt to correct past injustices, by their very nature treat people unequally. Hence, they are under constant attack because they allegedly violate felt norms of legal equality. Those attacks ignore the way in which entire groups of persons are disadvantaged by what are facially neutral laws. Moreover, those in power, even those of good will, don't correct the problem, not out of malice but myopia. Positive law becomes a blinder, justifying the inability to see from another's perspective. Job qualifications (such as requirements for advanced degrees or certification) unrelated to capacity to do the work, credit scores that fail to take past circumstances into account, physical fitness tests for desk jobs, even SAT scores, all apply equally to, but impact unequally, different groups of citizens.[1]

Thus, equity, which historically has been focused on individual hardships, finds itself called upon to address a broader, communal problem. All too often, society treats us the same when it should treat us as different, because of truly significant differences. We are all human, yet sometimes we need differential treatment to realize our true humanity. This recasts the Golden Rule question. When we say that equity requires doing unto others as we would have them do unto us, what we really mean is that we should treat others as we would have them treat us *if we were them*. It's one thing for the privileged to say that we only owe the unprivileged an equal chance, because that's all we expect. Would they say the same if they were poor and uneducated?

This "collective" equity would differ from individual equity because it would apply at a policy rather than an adjudication level and would apply to groups of persons rather than individuals. It would bear, however, the same two hallmarks of legal equity. It would recognize that exceptions must be made to strict law because of the circumstances of (here) a disadvantaged group. And it would call on dominant social groups to yield a bit of their advantages in the interest of the common good.

In the United States, this has a particular moral urgency, because the disadvantages arise especially from our sorry racial past—and only somewhat less-sorry present. We enslave a people for two hundred years, then declare those people free, promise them forty acres and a mule, and profess them equal in the eyes of the law. At the same time, we structure our economies, our social relations, our politics, and more than anything our attitudes to defeat their efforts to realize true equality. The word "disingenuous" comes from the Latin word *ingenuus,* meaning "freeborn" as in "native citizen." So, our country's treatment of African Americans, especially, is quite literally "disingenuous": not native or freeborn, or fully citizen.

And, what is most insidious, our sincere belief in society's commitment to racial equality blinds us to this reality. "Critical race theory," which examines the complex relationship between all law (not just racially motivated discriminatory statutes) and racial equality, makes the fundamental

---

1. To be sure, specific areas of law look at the discriminatory impact, as opposed to the discriminatory intent, of practices or policies. The "disparate impact" cases are limited in scope, highly contested, and concerned as much with burdens of proof as they are with essential justice. And they miss the point that a more just society, not an unjust society with ameliorative policies, is the real goal.

assertion that members of one racial group literally cannot see the law from the perspective of another group. Not only is the law (as applied) not color blind, but those in the majority are blind to its bias, making the absence of racial justice as much a matter of blind neglect as of gross discrimination. W. B. Carter, writing about the absence of legal scholarship from an African-American perspective, writes:

> Perhaps the benefits of racism for the white majority made the pain it brought to victims' lives difficult to see or easy to rationalize; perhaps the widespread acceptance of dominant modes of scholarly discourse among whites rendered challenging those modes too lonely a course. Thus, the fact of those white writers' whiteness determined what subjects did and did not receive the benefits of their efforts and, moreover, what approaches they would take in their work. This principle seems to hold true whether or not these writers ever actually consciously thought a single racist thought—in other words, the principle is true irrespective of whether they individually harbored any specific racist intent.[2]

I would like to disbelieve Professor Carter, and the whole premise of critical race theory. I find I cannot, because it captures something about the fallenness of the world. In fact, we cannot take Professor Carter's admonition seriously enough. Racism, America's original sin, makes us literally blind to our own prejudices.

Blindness pervades the Bible. Jesus time and again heals the blind. Paul is struck blind on the road to Damascus, there to have his site restored. He then uses the metaphor of seeing and blindness over and over in his letters.[3] The book of the prophet Isaiah likewise is shot through with references to sight and blindness.[4] And where do we find the first instance of blindness in the entire Bible? In the story with which we began this book: Isaac, "whose eyes were dim," blesses Jacob rather than Esau.

Carter suggests a remedy for this blindness, one Calvin would be proud of: reinvigoration of the Golden Rule. Why, Carter asks, don't we act more like the Good Samaritan? Because, she says, we are blinded by group prejudice. "Those who want a better world must accept that it takes

---

2. Carter, "What's *Love* Got to Do with It?," 143.
3. Rom 2:18–20; 11:8–10; 1 Cor 13:12; 2 Cor 3:18; 4:4; Eph 3:9 are a few.
4. Isa 29:9, 18; 35:5; 42:7, 16–19; 43:8; 56:10; 59:10.

AFTERWORD: EQUALITY VERSUS EQUITY

a special consciousness to be fair to groups to which we do not belong, particularly when the other group is in some way subordinated."[5]

We need, that is, a new way of seeing. Once again, let's think like lawyers and return to the context of the story. Jesus sets up the parable of the Good Samaritan by greeting his returning disciples like this:

> At that same hour Jesus rejoiced in the Holy Spirit and said, "I thank you, Father, Lord of heaven and earth, because you have *hidden* these things from the wise and the intelligent and have *revealed* them to infants; yes, Father, for such was your gracious will. All things have been handed over to me by my Father; and no one knows who the Son is except the Father, or who the Father is except the Son and anyone to whom the Son chooses to *reveal* him."
>
> Then turning to the disciples, Jesus said to them privately, "*Blessed are the eyes that see what you see! For I tell you that many prophets and kings desired to see what you see, but did not see it,* and to hear what you hear, but did not hear it."[6]

Immediately following is Jesus's colloquy with a lawyer about eternal life, ending with a very lawyerly question ("Rabbi, define 'neighbor,' please" is how it would be said by a law school professor today). Jesus answers him not with a lawyerly response, but (in case his audience missed the point about things seen and not seen) with a parable about seeing. The priest and the Levite "saw" the injured man lying by the side of the road and crossed over to the other side, either out of fear that the bandits still lurked about, or to avoid ritual impurity, or for some other reason. (Again, parables don't reveal character motivations.) When the Samaritan, however, sees him, he is "moved with pity," washes and bandages the man's wounds, and takes him to an inn, breaking all sorts of laws and customs in the process. Jesus is very careful to say that all three "saw" the man. But whereas the priest and the Levite (the "wise and intelligent") saw the man, but did not really see, the Samaritan sees him for what he is, and cares for him. And when Jesus asks the lawyer "who was the man's neighbor?" we can almost hear him reply, "I see your point, Rabbi."

Just as the Holy Spirit enabled the early, pentecostal church to understand each other in a multitude of languages, we need a new way of seeing each other. The parable is in fact all about seeing. Professor Carter suggests that we need a new way of looking at things, what philosophers call a new

---

5. Carter, "What's *Love* Got to Do with It?," 147.
6. Luke 10:21–24, emphasis added.

hermeneutic. Hermeneutics (named after Hermes, the messenger of the gods in Greek mythology) is the study of interpretation: How do we interpret a statement or an action? Various hermeneutical models have been suggested: a hermeneutic of charity (giving the speaker the benefit of the doubt) or of suspicion (taking nothing at face value) are two often suggested. I suggest that the principle of equity meets Carter's demand for a new hermeneutic. Equity can be not only a legal and a religious principle, but a way of understanding law and a way of conveying and interpreting that understanding. So, when we say that equity, in Aquinas's sense, involves determining what the legislator would have done if faced with the particular facts, we ask a hermeneutical question. How do we read the law in question? What message does the legislator want to convey? We hear all the time about a judge's obligation to adhere to the "original intent" of the legislature. I contend that "original intent" is no more than a lens, a hermeneutical presupposition that is yet another way of reading the law. Equity is another and a better one. Likewise, when the practicing lawyer urges clients to take a more equitable view of their rights and remedies, we point them to a new hermeneutical practice. We ask them to interpret the world in an equitable light. Lady Justice is blindfolded. Aequitas Augusti is not.

Michelle Alexander makes a similar point in *The New Jim Crow*. Colorblindness is, in the end, another form of blindness—blindness to the profound inequities caused by supposedly race-neutral laws. (Alexander's book is primarily concerned with the criminal justice system.) She looks back, in fact, to Martin Luther King Jr., who warned us about the blindness of colorblindness.

> More than forty-five years ago, Martin Luther King Jr. warned of this danger. He insisted that blindness and indifference to racial groups is actually more important than racial hostility to the creation and maintenance of racialized systems of control. Those who supported slavery and Jim Crow, he argued, typically were not bad or evil people; they were just blind. Even the Justices who decided the infamous Dred Scott case, which ruled "that the Negro has no rights which the white man is bound to respect," were not wicked men, he said. On the contrary, they were decent and dedicated men. But, he hastened to add, "They were victims of a spiritual and intellectual blindness. They knew not what they did. The whole system of slavery was largely perpetuated through spiritually ignorant persons." He continued: "This tragic blindness is also found in racial segregation, the not-too-distant cousin of slavery. Some

AFTERWORD: EQUALITY VERSUS EQUITY

of the most vigorous defenders of segregation are sincere in their beliefs and earnest in their motives. Although some men are segregationists merely for reasons of political expediency and political gain, not all of the resistance to integration is the rear-guard of professional bigots. Some people feel that their attempt to preserve segregation is best for themselves, their children, and their nation. Many are good church people, anchored in the religious faith of their mothers and fathers.... What a tragedy! Millions of Negroes have been crucified by conscientious blindness.... Jesus was right about those men who crucified him. They knew not what they did. They were inflicted by a terrible blindness."[7]

Calvin and Perkins found equity in the willingness to forego one's selfish interests. We need the same ethos when we think about how laws impact larger groups that have been historically oppressed. But blind people cannot see the continuing effects of that oppression. We must consider the collective life history when we make larger policy decisions. Should we be surprised, then, that a revival of equity requires us to forego some of our current social values—efficiency and utility, and (dare I say) a bit of personal freedom? It may very well be that equity undermines the overall sum of benefits over costs that utilitarianism professes to promote. If we make it easier to foreclose on a home, that may very well hold interest rates down, which theoretically benefits everyone. My point is that the utilitarian calculus makes us blind to the damage done to *this* family, and the color-blindness argument for equality makes us blind to the damage done to the poor or underprivileged.

Likewise, equity perhaps makes our legal process less efficient, the *sine qua non* of the law and economics scholars. If we allow failing businesses to fail, or large conglomerates to crowd out small shops, perhaps the economy becomes more efficient, and prices go down overall. But at what cost? And perhaps equity makes law less predictable, the highest value for the legal positivists. If we know the results of a lawsuit in advance, there may be fewer fully litigated disputes, which saves costs. But what kind of people have we become in the process?

Perhaps—and here is where it really hits home—equity even causes us to worry a bit less about individual rights, and a bit more about mutual responsibilities. Hooker reminds us: "every Christian man know[s] that in Christian equity he stands bound so to think and speak of his brethren as of men that have a measure in the fruit of holiness and a right unto the

---

7. Alexander, *New Jim Crow*, 240–42, quoting King, *Strength to Love*.

titles wherewith God, in token of special favor and mercy, vouchsafes to honor his chosen servants."[8]

The standard theological defense of "prescriptive equality"—the idea that all persons should be treated equally—is that humans are created in the image of God. Wolterstorff, troubled by the obvious differences among humans in talents, capacities, and endowments, takes a slightly different view. He says that equality lies in all humans being equally *beloved* by God.[9] Wolterstorff captures precisely why Christians should find equity to be both consistent with equality and essential to a truly just society. Both the Hebrew Bible and the Christian New Testament abound with the idea that certain individuals or classes of individuals should be singled out for special treatment: widows, orphans, the poor, aliens. Just as justice and mercy are neither identical or opposite, equity and equality complement each other. We would do well to remember that.

---

8. Quoted in Fortier, *Culture of Equity in Early Modern England*, 36.
9. Wolterstorff, *Justice*, 357–61.

Further Reading

As far as I can tell, few books have been written by private practice lawyers about the issues raised in this book. I've tried to be diligent in sticking to the theme of how those issues impact practicing lawyers. Therefore, there is quite a lot of material available that I have not mentioned, or mentioned in passing, in these pages. I offer the following as suggested reading for anyone interested in the broader topic.

There are accessible biographies of all four of the major theologians discussed in chapters 6 and 7. G. K. Chesterton's *Saint Thomas Aquinas: The Dumb Ox* is more of a sketch than a biography, has almost as much of Chesterton as of Aquinas in it, and focuses substantially on theist versus atheist battles of a century ago. Having said all that, it is sheer brilliance, and worth a read. Denys Turner's *Thomas Aquinas: A Portrait*, is a very fine, somewhat more conventional introduction to Aquinas. Anything by the British philosopher Brian Davies on Aquinas will be first rate.

Alister McGrath's *A Life of John Calvin* is, not surprisingly, a very readable account of Calvin's life, his theology, and his significance both for European history of Calvin's day and since.

There has been much scholarly attention paid to Richard Hooker in the past half century, some of which is cited in this book. I am aware, however, of only one nonspecialist biography of Hooker: Philip Secor's *Richard Hooker: Prophet of Anglicanism*. (That does not include Izaak Walton's *The Life of Mr. Richard Hooker*, one of Walton's *Lives* published in the second half of the seventeenth century.) Perhaps that is because Hooker, despite living in turbulent times, had a fairly tranquil life. Likewise, I am aware of only one contemporary biography of William Perkins: W. B. Patterson's *William Perkins and the Making of a Protestant England*. It, also, is worth a look.

In the interests of full disclosure, I should reveal that I have not read either the *Summa Theologiae* or Calvin's *Institutes* front to back as one would read a novel or biography. There are websites that outline programs for reading each in a year, like the popular "Bible in Ninety Days" schedules. I do not know anyone that has attempted that, but I do know that both the *Summa* and the *Institutes* are not like encyclopedias in having discrete articles on individual topics. They are theological expositions, building from one premise to the next, and would certainly warrant a close cover-to-cover reading.

Brett Scharffs, as of this writing professor of law at Brigham Young University, has a very fine article with much the same themes as this book: drawing on the book of Micah, how humility can be seen as a form of *phronesis* (practical wisdom) to balance the inevitable conflicts between justice and mercy.[1] I have intentionally avoided drawing on Scharffs's article for two reasons. First, it focuses primarily on judging rather than lawyering. The moral issues are similar, but not identical, in that lawyers have the additional complication of client loyalty. Second, Scharffs takes a decidedly Aristotelean view that justice and mercy are a continuum, rather than separate values to be balanced. That discussion, intriguing though it might be, would go beyond the self-imposed limits of this book.

William Chriss's *The Noble Lawyer* takes up the premise of my last chapter, that the jury system is democracy's essential way to resolve disputes, and that the lawyer's participation in that system is service to democracy itself. Any lawyer tired of lawyer jokes should read *The Noble Lawyer*. It will give you plenty of ammunition with which to respond.

Harold Berman's two volumes *Law and Revolution* and *Law and Revolution II* are majestic. Both are still in print. Berman wrote voluminously, and his many law journal articles are readily available on the internet. The same can be said of Thomas Shaffer and Joseph Allegretti. This book does not even scratch the surface of what could be learned from them. Sadly, Professor Shaffer died on February 6, 2019, just days before I sent the final manuscript to the publisher. May flights of angels sing thee to thy rest.

---

1. Scharffs, "Role of Humility."

Bibliography

Alexander, Michelle. *The New Jim Crow: Mass Incarceration in the Age of Colorblindness.* New York: New Press, 2010.
Allegretti, Joseph. "Can Legal Ethics Be Christian?" In *Christian Perspectives on Legal Thought*, edited by Michael W. McConnell et al., 453–69. New Haven: Yale University Press, 2001.
Alschuler, Albert W. *Law Without Values: The Life, Work and Legacy of Justice Holmes.* Chicago: University of Chicago Press, 2000.
American Bar Association. *Model Rules of Professional Conduct.* December 4, 2018. https://www.americanbar.org/groups/professional_responsibility/publications/model_rules_of_professional_conduct/model_rules_of_professional_conduct_table_of_contents/.
Andrews, Carol Rice. "The Lawyer's Oath: Both Ancient and Modern." *Georgetown Journal of Legal Ethics* 22 (2009): 3–62.
Aquinas, Thomas. *Summa Theologiae.* http://www.newadvent.org/summa/.
Aristotle. *The Nicomachean Ethics.* Translated by David Ross. Edited by Lesley Brown. Oxford World's Classics. Oxford: Oxford University Press, 2009.
Austin, John. *Lectures on Jurisprudence.* London: Murray, 1875.
———. *The Province of Jurisprudence Determined.* London: Murray, 1832.
Barton, John, and John Muddiman. *The Oxford Bible Commentary.* Oxford: Oxford University Press, 2001.
Ben Zvi, Ehud. "Micah." In *The Jewish Study Bible*, edited by Adele Berlin and Marc Zvi Brettler, 1194–1206. Oxford: Oxford University Press, 2014.
Berman, Harold. *Faith and Order: The Reconciliation of Law and Religion.* Grand Rapids: Eerdmans, 2000.
———. *Law and Revolution.* Cambridge: Belknap, 1983.
———. *Law and Revolution II.* Cambridge: Belknap, 2003.
———. "The Religious Sources of General Contract Law: An Historical Perspective." *Journal of Law and Religion* 4 (1986): 103–24.
Blackstone, William. *Commentaries on the Laws of England, Vol. 1.* Oxford: Clarendon, 1765.
The Book of Common Prayer. New York: Seabury, 1979.
Booty, John E. "Hooker and Anglicanism." In *Studies in Richard Hooker: Essays Preliminary to an Edition of His Works*, edited by W. Speed Hill, 207–39. Cleveland: Case Western University Press, 1972.

BIBLIOGRAPHY

Boswell, James. *The Journal of a Tour to the Hebrides with Samuel Johnson*. London: Everyman, 1958.

———. *Life of Johnson*. Oxford: Oxford University Press, 1970.

Breward, Ian. "Introduction." In *The Work of William Perkins*, edited by Ian Breward, 1–131. Courtenay Library of Reformation Classics 3. Appleford: Sutton Courtenay, 1970.

———. "The Significance of William Perkins." *Journal of Religious History* 4 (1966): 113–28.

Breward, Ian, ed. *The Work of William Perkins*. Courtenay Library of Reformation Classics 3. Appleford: Sutton Courtenay, 1970.

Brown, Meg Lota. *Donne and the Politics of Conscience in Early Modern England*. Leiden: Brill, 1995.

Budziszewski, J. *What We Can't Not Know*. San Francisco: Ignatius, 2003.

———. *Written on the Heart: The Case for Natural Law*. Downers Grove: InterVarsity, 1997.

Bultmann, Rudolf. *The History of the Synoptic Tradition*. New York: Harper & Row, 1968.

Calvin, John. *Commentaries on the Epistle of Paul the Apostle to the Corinthians, Vol. 1*. Translated by John Pringle. Christian Classics Ethereal Library. http://www.ccel.org/ccel/calvin/calcom39.xiii.i.html.

———. *Commentaries on the First Twenty Chapters of the Book of the Prophet Ezekiel*. Translated by Thomas Meyers. Christian Classics Ethereal Library. https://www.ccel.org/ccel/calvin/calcom22.i.html.

———. *Commentary on a Harmony of the Evangelists, Matthew, Mark and Luke*. Translated by William Pringle. Christian Classics Ethereal Library. http://www.ccel.org/ccel/calvin/calcom31.ix.xlv.html.

———. *Commentary on Isaiah, Vol. 4*. Christian Classics Ethereal Library. https://www.ccel.org/ccel/calvin/calcom16.

———. *Commentary on Philippians, Colossians, and Thessalonians*. Christian Classics Ethereal Library. https://www.ccel.org/ccel/calvin/calcom42.

———. *Commentary on Psalms, Vol. 3*. http://www.documenta-catholica.eu/d_1509-1564-%20Calvin,%20John%20-%20Commentary%20on%20Psalms%20-%20Vol%2003-%20EN.pdf.

———. *Commentary on Seneca's De Clementia*. http://media.sabda.org/alkitab-7/LIBRARY/CALVIN/CAL_SENE.PDF.

———. *Institutes of the Christian Religion*. Translated by Henry Beveridge. Peabody: Hendrickson, 2008.

Carnes, John. "Christian Ethics and Natural Law." *Religious Studies* 3 (1967): 301–11.

Carpi, Daniela. "Law, Discretion, Equity in *The Merchant of Venice* and *Measure for Measure*." *Cardozo Law Review* 26 (2005): 2317–30.

Carter, W. Burdette. "What's *Love* Got to Do with It? Race Relations and the Second Great Commandment." In *Christian Perspectives on Legal Thought*, edited by Michael W. McConnell et al., 133–48. New Haven: Yale University Press, 2001.

Cary, George. *Reports, or Causes in Chancery*. London: Stevens, 1872.

Catechism of the Catholic Church. New York: Doubleday, 2003.

Chriss, William. *The Noble Lawyer*. Austin: State Bar of Texas, 2011.

Chroust, Anton Hermann. "Common Good and the Problem of Equity in the Philosophy of Law of St. Thomas Aquinas." *Notre Dame Law Review* 18 (1942): 114–18.

Cicero. *De Officiis*. Translated by Walter Miller. Cambridge: Loeb Classical Library, 1913.

BIBLIOGRAPHY

Corbin, Arthur. "Rights and Duties." *Yale Law Journal* 33 (1924): 501–27.
Cramton, Roger. "The Ordinary Religion of the Law School Classroom." *Journal of Legal Education* 29 (1978): 247–63.
Dackson, Wendy. "Anglicanism and Social Theology." *Anglican Theological Review* 94 (2012): 615–37.
Davies, Brian. *Thomas Aquinas's Summa Theologiae: A Guide and Commentary*. Oxford: Oxford University Press, 2014.
Dempster, Stephen. *Micah*. Grand Rapids: Eerdmans, 2017.
Diamond, James A. "Talmudic Jurisprudence, Equity, and the Concept of *Lifnim Meshurat Hadin*." *Osgoode Hall Law Journal* 17 (1979): 616–31.
Dickinson, John W. "Renaissance Equity and *Measure for Measure*." *Shakespeare Quarterly* 13 (1962): 287–97.
Dreisbach, David. "Micah 6:8 in the Literature of the American Founding Era: A Note on Religion and Rhetoric." *Rhetoric and Public Affairs* 12 (2009): 91–105.
Dunkel, Wilbur. "Law and Equity in *Measure for Measure*." *Shakespeare Quarterly* 13 (1962): 275–85.
Dworkin, Ronald. *Justice for Hedgehogs*. Cambridge: Belknap, 2011.
———. *Law's Empire*. Cambridge: Belknap, 1986.
Eliot, T. S. "The Metaphysical Poets." In *The Perfect Critic: 1919–1926*, 375–85. Vol. 2, *The Complete Prose of T. S. Eliot: The Critical Edition*. Baltimore: Johns Hopkins University Press, 2014.
Finnis, John. *Natural Law and Natural Rights*. Oxford: Oxford University Press, 2011.
Floyd, Timothy W. "The Practice of Law as a Vocation or Calling." *Fordham Law Review* 66 (1996): 1405–24.
Fortier, Mark. *The Culture of Equity in Early Modern England*. Farnham: Ashgate, 2005.
———. *The Culture of Equity in Restoration and Eighteenth Century Britain and America*. Farnham: Ashgate, 2015.
Francis, Richard. *Maxims of Equity*. Richmond: Shepard & Pollard, 1823.
Gillis, Trent T. "Martin Luther King's Last Christmas Sermon." *On Being* (blog), December 25, 2015. https://onbeing.org/blog/martin-luther-kings-last-christmas-sermon/.
Green, Allison. "What Does It Mean to Be Professional at Work." *U.S. News and World Report*. July 22, 2013. https://money.usnews.com/money/blogs/outside-voices-careers/2013/07/22/what-does-it-mean-to-be-professional-at-work.
Greenlee, Mark B. "Echoes of the Love Command in the Halls of Justice." *Journal of Law and Religion* 12 (1995): 255–70.
Grislis, Egil. "The Hermeneutical Problem in Richard Hooker." In *Studies in Richard Hooker: Essays Preliminary to an Edition of His Works*, edited by W. Speed Hill, 159–206. Cleveland: Case Western University Press, 1972.
Haas, Guenther H. *The Concept of Equity in Calvin's Ethics*. Waterloo: Wilfred Laurier University Press, 1997.
Hall, David D. *A Reforming People: Puritanism and the Transformation of Public Life in New England*. New York: Knopf, 2011.
Hill, W. Speed. *Studies in Richard Hooker: Essays Preliminary to an Edition of His Works*. Cleveland: Case Western University Press, 1972.
Hirsch, E. D. *Validity in Interpretation*. New Haven: Yale University Press, 1967.
Holmes, Oliver Wendell, Jr. *The Common Law*. London: Macmillan, 1882.
———. "The Path of the Law." *Harvard Law Review* 10 (1897): 457–78.

BIBLIOGRAPHY

Hooker, Richard. *Books I–IV.* Edited by Georges Edelen. Vol. 1, *The Laws of Ecclesiastical Polity.* Cambridge: Belknap, 1977.

———. *Book V.* Edited by W. Speed Hill. Vol. 2, *The Laws of Ecclesiastical Polity.* Cambridge: Belknap, 1977.

———. *The Sermons of Richard Hooker.* Edited and with an introduction by Philip Secor. London: SPCK, 2001.

Johnson, Luke Timothy. *The Creed: What Christians Believe and Why It Matters.* New York: Doubleday, 2004.

Jonsen, Albert R., and Stephen Toulmin. *The Abuse of Casuistry: A History of Moral Reasoning.* Berkley: University of California Press, 1988.

Joyce, A. J. *Richard Hooker and Anglican Moral Theology.* Oxford: Oxford University Press, 2012.

Kaveny, M. Cathleen. "Between Example and Doctrine: Contract Law and Common Morality." *Journal of Religious Ethics* 33 (2005): 669–95.

King, Martin Luther, Jr. *Strength to Love.* Minneapolis: Fortress, 2010.

Kirk, Kenneth. *Conscience and Its Problems: An Introduction to Casuistry.* London: Longmans, Green, 1927.

Klinck, Dennis. *Conscience, Equity, and the Court of Chancery in Early Modern England.* Farnham: Ashgate, 2010.

Koch, Klaus. *The Prophets, Volume One: The Assyrian Period.* Translated by Margaret Kohl. Philadelphia: Fortress, 1983.

Laycock, Douglas. "The Triumph of Equity." *Law and Contemporary Problems* 56 (1993): 53–82.

Lewis, Anthony. *Gideon's Trumpet.* New York: Random House, 1964.

Littlejohn, W. Bradford. *Richard Hooker: A Companion to his Life and Work.* Eugene, OR: Wipf & Stock, 2015.

Littlejohn, W. Bradford, and Scott N. Kindred-Barnes. *Richard Hooker and Reformed Orthodoxy.* Gottingen: Vandenhoeck & Ruprecht, 2017.

Luban, David. "A Midrash on Rabbi Shaffer and Rabbi Trollope." *Notre Dame Law Review* 77 (2002): 889–903.

Mays, James Luther. *Micah.* Philadelphia: Westminster, 1976.

McConnell, Michael W., et al., eds. *Christian Perspectives on Legal Thought.* New Haven: Yale University Press, 2001.

McGrath, Alister E. *A Life of John Calvin.* Malden: Blackwell, 1990.

McInerney, Joseph J. *The Greatness of Humility. St. Augustine on Moral Excellence.* Eugene, OR: Pickwick, 2016.

McMaster, R. D. *Trollope and the Law.* New York: St. Martin's, 1986.

Mencken, H. L. "Mr. Justice Holmes." *The American Mercury* (May 1930): 121–23.

Mill, John Stuart. *On Liberty.* 1859. Reprint, Indianapolis: Hackett, 1978.

Milton, John. *Areopagitica, A Speech of Mr. John Milton for the Liberty of Unlicenc'd Printing to the Parliament of England.* 1644. Reprint, Cambridge: Cambridge University Press, 1918.

Moliterno, James L. "Lawyer Creeds and Moral Seismography." *Wake Forest Law Review* 32 (1997): 781–818.

Neff, Stephen C., ed. *Hugo Grotius on the Law of War and Peace.* Cambridge: Cambridge University Press, 2012.

O'Donovan, Oliver. *The Desire of the Nations.* Cambridge: Cambridge University Press, 1996.

———. *The Ways of Judgment*. Grand Rapids: Eerdmans, 2005.

Patterson, W. B. "Richard Hooker and William Perkins: Adversaries or Allies?" In *Richard Hooker and Reformed Orthodoxy*, edited by W. Bradford Littlejohn and Scott N. Kindred-Barnes. Gottingen: Vandenhoeck & Ruprecht, 2017.

———. *William Perkins and the Making of a Protestant England*. Oxford: Oxford University Press, 2014.

Perkins, William. "Epieikeia." In *The Work of William Perkins*, edited and with an introduction by Ian Breward, 3:477–510. Courtenay Library of Reformation Classics 3. Appleford: Sutton Courtney, 1970.

———. "A Godly and Learned Exposition of Christ's Sermon in the Mount." https://quod.lib.umich.edu/cgi/t/text/text-idx?c=eebo;idno=A09432.0001.001.

———. "A Treatise on the Vocations or Callings of Men." In *The Work of William Perkins*, edited and with an introduction by Ian Breward, 3:441–76. Courtenay Library of Reformation Classics 3. Appleford: Sutton Courtney, 1970.

Peterson, Eugene H. *The Jesus Way: A Conversation on the Way that Jesus is the Way*. Grand Rapids: Eerdmans, 2007.

Porter, H. C. "Hooker, The Tudor Constitution, and the *Via Media*." In *Studies in Richard Hooker: Essays Preliminary to an Edition of His Works*, edited by W. Speed Hill, 77–116. Cleveland: Case Western University Press, 1972.

Porter, Jean. *Ministers of the Law: A Natural Law Theory of Legal Authority*. Grand Rapids: Eerdmans, 2010.

———. "Virtue." In *The Oxford Handbook of Theological Ethics*, edited by Gilbert Meilaender and William Werpehowski, 205–19. Oxford: Oxford University Press, 2007.

Posner, Richard. "Euthanasia and Health Care." The Tanner Lectures on Human Values, Yale University, October 10–11, 1994. https://tannerlectures.utah.edu/_documents/a-to-z/p/Posner96.pdf.

Pound, Roscoe. "The Decadence of Equity." *Columbia Law Review* 5 (1905): 20–35.

Re, Edward D. "The Roman Contribution to the Common Law." *Fordham Law Review* 29 (1961): 447–94.

Richardson, Henry. *Articulating the Moral Community: Towards a Constructive Ethical Pragmatism*. Oxford: Oxford University Press, 2018.

Riley, Chris. "Jeremy Bentham and Equity: The Court of Chancery, Lord Eldon, and the Dispatch Court Plan." *The Journal of Legal History* 39 (2018): 29–57.

Scharffs, Brett. "The Role of Humility in Exercising Practical Wisdom." *University of California Davis Law Review* 32 (1998): 127–98.

Secor, Philip. *Richard Hooker: Prophet of Anglicanism*. Toronto: Anglican Book Centre, 1999.

Selden, John. *Table Talk*. London: Smith, 1856.

Shaffer, Thomas. "Business Lawyers, Baseball Players, and the Hebrew Prophets." *Valparaiso University Law Review* 42 (2008): 1063–80.

———. *Faith and the Professions*. Provo, UT: Brigham Young University Press, 1987.

———. "The Legal Ethics of the Two Kingdoms." *Valparaiso University Law Review* 17 (1983): 1–39.

———. *On Being a Christian and a Lawyer*. Provo, UT: Brigham Young University Press, 1981.

Shakespeare, William. *Hamlet*. Edited by Robert S. Miola. New York: W. W. Norton & Company, 2010.

BIBLIOGRAPHY

———. *Macbeth*. Edited by Robert S. Miola. New York: W. W. Norton & Company, 2013.
Snell, Edmund T. T. *The Principles of Equity*. London: Stevens & Haynes, 1880.
St. Germain, Christopher. *The Doctor and Student, or Dialogues Between a Doctor of Divinity and a Student in the Laws of England*. Cincinnati: Clarke, 1886.
Stafford, John K. "Richard Hooker and the Later Puritans." *Perichoresis* 11 (2013): 187–98.
Stevenson, William R., Jr. "Calvin and Political Issues." In *The Cambridge Companion to John Calvin*, edited by Donald K. McKim, 173–87. Cambridge: Cambridge University Press, 2004.
Stückelberger, Christoph. "No Interest from the Poor: Calvin's Economic and Banking Ethics." In *Calvin Global: How Faith Influences Societies*, edited by Christoph Stückelberger and Reinhold Bernhardt, 53–70. Globethics.net Series 3. Geneva: Globethics.net, 2009.
Taylor, Edward Robeson. "The Fusion of Law and Equity." *University of Pennsylvania Law Review* 66 (1917): 17–27.
Thompson, W. D. J. Cargill. "The Philosopher of the Politic Society." In *Studies in Richard Hooker: Essays Preliminary to an Edition of His Works*, edited by W. Speed Hill. Cleveland: Case Western University Press, 1972.
Trollope, Anthony. *An Autobiography*. Introduction by John Sutherland. London: Trollope Society, 1999.
———. *Cousin Henry*. Introduction, note on the text, and explanatory notes by Julian Thompson. Oxford: Oxford University Press 1987.
———. *Orley Farm*. Edited with an introduction and notes by David Skilton. Oxford: Oxford University Press, 1985.
Tuininga, Matthew J. "Good News for the Poor: An Analysis of Calvin's Concept of Poor Relief and the Diaconate in Light of His Two Kingdoms Paradigm." *Calvin Theological Journal* 49 (2014): 221–47.
Washington, George. "Washington's Circular Letter of Farewell to the Army, June 8, 1783." http://www.loc.gov/teachers/classroommaterials/presentationsandactivities/presentations/timeline/amrev/peace/circular.html.
Weber, Max. *The Protestant Ethic and the Spirit of Capitalism*. Translation and introduction by Peter Baehr and Gordon C. Wells. New York: Penguin 2002.
Williams, Raymond. *Keywords*. London: Fontana, 1983.
Williamson, H. G. M. "Micah." In *The Oxford Bible Commentary*, edited by John Barton and John Muddiman, 595–98. Oxford: Oxford University Press, 2001.
Witte, John, Jr. *Law and Protestantism: The Legal Teachings of the Lutheran Reformation*. Cambridge: Cambridge University Press, 2002.
Wolterstorff, Nicholas. *Justice: Rights and Wrongs*. Princeton: Princeton University Press, 2008.
———. *Justice in Love*. Grand Rapids: Eerdmans, 2015.
Wright, Louis B. "William Perkins: Elizabethan Apostle of 'Practical Divinity.'" *Huntington Library Quarterly* 3 (1940): 171–96.
Wright, N. T. *Matthew For Everyone: Part One*. Louisville: Westminster John Knox, 2004.
———. "The Royal Law." http://ntwrightpage.com/2017/01/30/the-royal-law/.
Zaretsky, Robert. *Boswell's Enlightenment*. Cambridge: Belknap, 2015.

Index of Persons

Abraham, 7, 95, 103
Ahaz, 33–34
Alexander, Michelle, 152–53
Allegretti, Joseph, 29–30, 123, 144, 156
Alschuler, Albert W., 23n9
Amos, 33
Andrews, Carol Rice, 48n27
Aquinas, Thomas. *See* Thomas Aquinas
Aristotle, xi, 41, 49, 51, 54, 57, 61, 96–97, 100
Augustine, Saint, 98–100, 109, 120, 147
Austin, John, 21, 56

Bentham, Jeremy, 20, 45, 56
Berman, Harold, 16–17, 28, 37, 40, 42, 43, 59, 61, 65, 67, 72–73, 75–85, 140, 156
Blackstone, William, 16
Booty, John E., 65
Boswell, James, 10–14
Breward, Ian, 62–63, 67–68
Brown, Meg Lota, 137n2
Budziszewski, J., 15, 53
Bultmann, Rudolf, 95

Caiaphas, 110
Calvin, John, xi, 16–17, 51, 57–61, 63–64, 66–70, 72, 74, 77–79, 83–85, 91, 96, 99–100, 103, 107–9, 112, 118, 138, 150, 153, 155–56
Carnes, John, 14–15
Carpi, Daniela, 10n2
Carter, W. Burdette, 150–51

Cary, George, 45n17
Chapman, Steven Curtis, 35
Chroust, Anton Hermann, 54n16
Cicero, 39, 48, 84–85, 116n29
Corbin, Arthur, 112
Cramton, Roger, 25–26

Dackson, Wendy, 18
David, King, 99, 102–3
Davies, Brian, 52, 155
Dempster, Stephen, 33n3, 34n8, 36, 89n58
Diamond, James A., 40–41
Dickens, Charles, 45, 124–25
Dickinson, John W., 10
Dreisbach, David, 86
Dunkel, Wilbur, 10
Dworkin, Ronald, 24, 30

Esau, 5–6, 8, 94–95, 117–18, 145, 150
Ezekiel, 32, 100, 108–9, 116

Finnis, John, 15
Floyd, Timothy, 48
Fortas, Abe, 26
Fortier, Mark, 18, 39–40, 45–46, 49, 66, 77, 123, 154
Francis, Richard, 45

Greenlee, Mark, 110
Gideon, Clarence, 25–26
Grisez, Germaine, 15
Grislis, Egil, 63–64

INDEX OF PERSONS

Grotius, Hugo, 15–16

Haas, Guenther H., 48n29, 57–58, 60–61, 69
Hale, Matthew, 79, 85
Hall, David D., 82
Hezekiah, 33
Hirsch, E. D., 125
Holmes, Oliver Wendell, 22–23, 82–83, 106, 109, 141
Home, Henry, 77
Hooker, Richard, 16, 51, 61–70, 72, 74, 87, 91, 102, 112, 153, 155

Isaac, 1–3, 6–7, 95, 110, 117, 126, 150

Jackson, Robert, 111
Jacob, 5–8, 94–95, 103, 117–18, 126, 145, 150
James IV and I, 44, 46
Javert, 144–45
Jesus Christ, xii, 5, 7, 14, 18, 37, 52, 59–60, 87, 98–100, 108, 110, 120–21, 150–51, 153
John the Baptist, 99
Johnson, Lyndon, 26
Johnson, Luke Timothy, 109
Johnson, Samuel, 10–14, 16, 18, 24, 108, 111
Jonsen, Albert R., 84
Joseph, 7, 103, 117, 131n14
Jotham, 33
Joyce, A. J., 62–63, 65, 67

Kaveny, Cathleen, 125, 139–40, 143, 145
King, Martin Luther, Jr., 35, 152–53
Kirk, Kenneth, 108, 116, 138
Klinck, Dennis, 65
Koch, Klaus, 34

Laban, 2, 6, 103, 113
Langton, Stephen, 17
Laycock, Douglas, 46–47
Leah, 2, 117
Lee, Harper, 102
Lewis, Anthony, 26
Littlejohn, W. Bradford, 62–63

Luban, David, 95
Luther, Martin, 57, 120

Mays, James Luther, 38
McGrath, Alister, 79, 83, 118
McMaster, R. D., 130, 132
Melancthon, Philip, 42
Mencken, H. L., 23
Mill, John Stuart, 28n26
Milton, John, 28, 39
Moliterno, James L., 48
Morgan, J. P. 16, 103
Moses, 7, 35, 37, 87, 103

Neff, Stephen, 15
Nietzsche, Friedrich, 96–98

O'Donovan, Oliver, 16, 36n14, 55n18, 60n45, 69n33, 72–73, 75, 85–92, 96, 113, 117, 146–47
Oldendorp, Johann, 16–17, 42

Patterson, W. B., 68–69
Paul (apostle), 60, 86, 91, 99, 104, 115, 120, 150
Pelagius, 98
Perkins, William, xv, 16, 51, 61–62, 67–72, 77, 88–89, 91, 105, 107, 118–22, 153, 155
Peter (apostle), 99
Peterson, Eugene, 110
Porter, H. C., 66
Porter, Jean, 15, 55, 98
Posner, Richard, 25
Pound, Roscoe, 46–47, 139

Re, Edward D., 42
Rebekah, 6–7, 95–96, 126, 128
Richardson, Henry, 140–41, 143
Riley, Chris, 45

Scharffs, Brett, 20, 156
Secor, Philip, 63
Selden, John, 39, 43
Shaffer, Thomas, 107–8, 111n18, 112, 115, 120, 122n52, 128n8, 132–33, 144

INDEX OF PERSONS

Shakespeare, William, 10, 58, 123–25
Snell, Edmund T. T., 51
St. Germain, Christopher, 43
Stafford, John K., 102
Stevenson, William R., Jr., 61
Stückelberger, Cristoph, 59

Taylor, Edward Robeson, 42
Thomas á Becket, 17
Thomas Aquinas, xi, 15–17, 2, 51–57, 61, 63–66, 69, 72, 74, 77, 84, 99–100, 109, 137–38, 140, 152, 155
Thompson, W.D.J. Cargill, 63, 65
Toulmin, Stephen, 84
Travers, Walter, 63
Trollope, Anthony, 18, 123, 125–35
Tuininga, Matthew, 60

Uriah, 102

Valjean, Jean, 144–45

Washington, George, 86
Weber, Max, 77–79
Weintraub, Russell, 146
Williams, Raymond, 49
Williams, Rowan, 17
Williams, Serena, 101
Williamson, H. G. M, 33
Witte, John Jr., 17, 42
Wolterstorff, Nicholas, 17, 36n14, 112n21, 154
Wright, Louis, 68
Wright, N. T., xii, 121

YHWH, 4, 7n6, 34, 37–38, 41, 108–9

Zaretsky, Robert, 13

Index of Words, Phrases, and Titles

Abuse of Casuistry (Jonsen and Toulmin), 84
advocates and advocacy, 11–12, 27–28, 73
Aeropagetica (Milton), 28
agents and agency, 5–6, 28, 29, 71, 79, 111, 114, 138
Anglican and Anglicanism, 13, 17–18, 62–65, 67, 76, 85
Articulating the Moral Community (Richardson), 140–43
Autobiography (Trollope), 125–27

Bleak House (Dickens), 45, 124–25, 127
Book of Common Prayer (Episcopal Church USA), 109–10

Calvinism, 51, 59, 63, 66, 68, 70, 77–79, 83
canon law, 42, 67, 76–77, 80–83, 140
casuistry, 68, 84, 134, 137–39
Catechism of the Catholic Church, 109, 115
Catechism of the Episcopal Church USA, 35, 110
Chancery, xi, 17, 42–45, 47, 65, 67, 77, 81, 124–25, 127
Christianity, 5, 13–15, 18, 29, 37, 50, 71, 97–98, 100, 116, 118
Church of England, 17, 63, 67–68
clients: see lawyer-client relationship
Commentaries (Calvin)
    The Epistle to the Corinthians, 59

Ezekiel, 100
Isaiah, 60
Matthew, 60, 100
Second Thessalonians, 61
Commentaries on the Laws of England (Blackstone), 16
Commentary on Seneca's De Clementia (Calvin), 57
common good, 30, 39, 43, 45, 54–56, 59–60, 67, 74, 77–78, 108, 118, 149
common law, xii, 17, 24–25, 39, 42–47, 56, 62, 77, 81–83, 140
The Common Law (Holmes), 22–23, 82
communitarianism, 59–60, 77–79, 81–82
compassion, xi, 4, 10, 13, 18, 37, 120, 140,
conscience, 7, 12, 29, 39, 42, 44–45, 54, 65, 67–68, 104, 108, 116, 119–20, 137–38
Consumer Finance Protection Bureau, 83
contracts, 42, 66, 112, 114–17, 141–42, 144
contract law, 6, 10, 12, 16, 23, 28–29, 76, 79–84, 90–93, 122, 139, 143, 146
    moral basis of contract law, 80–83
correlatives, principle of, 112
Cousin Henry (Trollope), 133–35

David Copperfield (Dickens), 102
Desire of the Nations (O'Donovan), 36, 85–86, 88–89, 91
divine command theology, 14, 37
divine imitation theology, 14, 37, 72

INDEX OF WORDS, PHRASES, AND TITLES

The Doctor and Student (St. Germain), 43

Earl of Oxford's Case, 44–45
Eikonoclastes (Milton), 39
Elizabethan settlement, 17, 62, 64
Employee Retirement Income Security Act of 1974 ("ERISA"), 9, 83
epieikeia
    As Aristotelean concept, 51, 68
    Work by William Perkins, 68–72, 77
equity, ix–xii, 5–7, 8, 10, 16–26, 32, 34, 38–51, 55–63, 65–72, 74–77, 81–84, 88–93, 104, 106–16, 119–21, 123–25, 130–31, 133–35, 136–41, 143, 146–47, 148–49, 152–54
    and the common good, 76–77
    as legal concept, xii, 8, 10, 16–17, 39–44, 83–84, 88–93
    as theological concept, xi, 16–18, 32, 34, 48, 49–72, 146–47
    equality, compared with, 148–54
    harshness, contrasted with, 4, 12, 20, 74, 93, 106, 127, 136, 148
    in law practice, 105–22, 131, 134–35, 136–37
    merger of law and equity, 45–46
    two types of equity, 6, 74, 107–9

fair/fairness, xi, 4, 14, 24–25, 40–42, 44, 47, 49, 57–58, 82, 112–13, 128–29, 137, 148, 151
Faith and the Professions (Shaffer), 108, 111–12, 120, 128
fiduciaries and fiduciary duty, 26–27, 31, 48, 73

Gideon v. Wainwright, 25–26
The Greatness of Humility (McInerney), 98–99

Hamlet (Shakespeare), 58
Hebrew Bible (Old Testament), xi, 4–5, 7, 32, 33, 35–36, 154
humility, 7–8, 20n2, 61, 65, 72, 74, 86, 89, 94–104, 109n14, 116, 135, 156

Institutes of the Christian Religion (Calvin), 57–58, 61, 64, 96, 100, 156
intent, legislative, 41, 43, 55, 71, 144, 152

Journal of a Tour to the Hebrides with Samuel Johnson (Boswell), 10–12
judges and judging, ix–x, xii, 11, 18, 22, 42, 46–47, 54, 80, 83, 85–86, 90–92, 110–13, 139, 141–43, 145–46
judgment, xii–xiii, 7–8, 13, 36, 42–43, 48, 55, 85–92, 124, 140
judicial discretion, 10, 13, 24, 46–47, 56, 113
jurisprudence, xii, 13, 18, 21, 40–41, 45, 48, 124
juries and jury system: 26, 34, 36, 74, 110–11, 113, 128–29, 142, 144–46, 156
justice, ix–x, xii, 3, 11–12, 16–18, 21–23, 26, 28, 30, 34–38, 41–42, 44–46, 48–51, 55–60, 65–66, 69–70, 73–75, 77, 82, 85–92, 96, 99–104, 106, 109–13, 117, 124, 128, 131, 135, 139–40, 143–46, 149–50, 152, 154, 156
Justice in Love (Wolterstorff), 74n3
Justice: Rights and Wrongs (Wolterstorff), 36, 112, 154

law and economics model, 15, 24–25, 111, 153
Law and Revolution (Berman), 28, 37, 40, 67, 73, 76, 80–81, 84, 156
Law and Revolution II (Berman), 16n18, 59nn40 and 41, 65, 77–79, 156
law school and legal education, 12, 18, 25, 101–2, 122, 124, 151
Laws of Ecclesiastical Polity (Hooker), xv, 51, 62–67, 91, 112
lawyers
    lawyer-client relationship, xii, 25, 7, 11–12, 21, 26–31, 47, 70, 72–74, 79, 101–9, 111–16, 119, 131–36, 140, 142, 144–46, 152
    Lawyer's Dilemma, 3–5, 8–18, 19–31, 38, 55, 71–72, 74–75, 112, 114, 116, 118, 132, 140, 143, 146

INDEX OF WORDS, PHRASES, AND TITLES

profession of law, 4, 15, 26–27, 38, 47 70, 112, 117, 120, 139
Life of Johnson (Boswell), 10–11, 14
Lochner v. New York, 23

Macbeth (Shakespeare), 125
magnanimity, 97, 99–100, 102
Maxims of Equity (Francis), 45
Measure for Measure (Shakespeare), 10, 124
The Merchant of Venice (Shakespeare), 10, 124
mercy, xii–xiii, 18, 35–37, 41, 43–44, 47–48, 50, 57–58, 66, 74–75, 85–86, 88–90, 92, 101, 116–17, 131, 139, 143, 154, 156
Micah, Book of (generally), 13, 32–38, 86, 89, 156
mispat, 34
Model Rules of Professional Conduct (American Bar Association), 3, 28–29, 107–8, 116,

natural law, 14–15, 20, 37–38, 42, 53–54, 58, 60, 64–65, 79, 109, 117
negotiation, 116, 141–46
The New Jim Crow (Alexander), 102–3
New Testament, xii, 87, 99, 154
Nicomachean Ethics (Aristotle), 49, 97

On Being a Christian and a Lawyer (Shaffer), 108, 115, 122, 128, 132–33
On Liberty (Mill), 28n26
Orley Farm (Trollope), 18, 123, 126–32

parables
Good Samaritan, 150–51
Prodigal Son, 94–96, 117
Unforgiving Servant, 50, 87, 114
phronesis, 20, 156
positivism (legal), 13, 15, 17–19, 21–25, 28, 30, 45, 86, 113
primogeniture, 3, 129–30, 133, 135
Principles of Equity (Home), 77
Principles of Equity (Snell), 51
prophets, lawyer as, 12, 105–110, 116, 144

The Protestant Ethic and the Spirit of Capitalism (Weber), 77–79
punishment, 14, 18, 37, 58, 69, 80, 90–92, 122
Puritans and Puritanism, xv, 62–64, 77–78, 81–82, 88–89, 102

reason
divine, 5, 15, 53, 58, 65
human, 15, 16, 21, 44, 51, 54, 56, 58, 64–65, 74, 100, 140
law of, 15, 43, 45, 64–66, 74
Reformation, Protestant, 5, 17, 42, 60n45, 61–62
Reformed tradition, 51, 57, 62–63, 67–68, 76
Resurrection and Moral Order (O'Donovan), 85
Richard Hooker: A Companion to his Life and Work (Littlejohn), 62–63
Richard Hooker and Anglican Moral Theology (Joyce), 62–63, 65, 67
Riv, 32–33, 37
Roman Catholic church, 42, 57, 62, 67–68, 78, 109, 115
Roman law, 41–42, 48
Rummel v. Estelle, 24

"salus populi suprema lex", 39
secularization of law, xii, 42, 48, 79, 82
strict enforcement, 7, 10, 13, 18, 37, 40–42, 46–47, 50, 55–59, 61, 66, 70, 74, 82–83, 90–91, 111, 120, 124, 136, 147, 149
Summa Theologiae (Aquinas), xi, 52–57, 66, 99–100

Table Talk (Selden), 39, 43
Temple Church, London, 63–64, 67
Ten Commandments, 76
Torah, 4, 40, 59
To Kill a Mockingbird (Lee), 102
"A Treatise on the Vocations or Callings of Men" (Perkins), 68, 118–20

vassal treaty tradition, 32–33

INDEX OF WORDS, PHRASES, AND TITLES

virtues, 20, 50, 55–56, 58, 60–61, 77, 87, 91, 123
   virtue ethics, 20
   see also fairness, humility, magnanimity, mercy
vocation (and vocations), 18n20, 48n28, 52, 68, 71, 78, 103, 105, 117–20, 147

The Warden (Trollope), 126
The Ways of Judgment (O'Donovan), 60n45, 69n33, 72, 85–92, 113, 147

utilitarianism, 13, 19–21, 24–25, 138–39, 153

Index of Scriptural References

Genesis

Generally	94, 132
22:1–21	95
24:52–67	95
27:5–40	95
32:1–21	6
33:9	6

Exodus

23:7	21–22

Deuteronomy

Generally	4, 5, 32, 37, 82
6:18	40
25:13–16	34
28:30	44

2 Samuel

Generally	32, 102

2 Kings

Generally	33

2 Chronicles

Generally	32–33
27:2	33

Proverbs

3:34	99

Ecclesiastes

9:10	119

Isaiah

Generally	32–33
11:1ff.	109
29:9ff.	150
35:5ff.	150
42:5ff.	150
42:6	7
43:8	150
56:10	150
59:10	150

Jeremiah

Generally	32
48:10	119

Ezekiel

Generally	32, 100, 109, 116
33:7–9	108

Hosea

Generally	32

INDEX OF SCRIPTURAL REFERENCES

Amos

Chapter 5	33

Micah

Generally	32–38
2:2	34, 36
6:1–7	35
6:8	35–36, 69, 72, 86, 89, 96
6:9	36
6:11	36
6:12	36
6:14–15	38
6:16	36
7:3	36
7:18–19	37

Matthew

5:1—7:29	120
5:13	121
5:16	120
5:17	121
5:20	121
5:21–48	121
6:24	5
7:12	xi, 58
11:29	99
18:4	99
18:21–35	50, 87, 114
21:5	99
23:12	99

Luke

10:21–24	151
14:11	99
16:13	5
18:14	99

John

4:33	119

Romans

2:18–20	150
8:24–25	104
11:8–10	150
12:8	119
13:4	86, 119

1 Corinthians

3:9	115
10:33	119
12:27	4, 29
13:12	55, 150

2 Corinthians

3:18	150
4:4	150
10:1	99
12:21	99

Ephesians

3:9	150

Philippians

2:8	99
4:5	72

2 Thessalonians

3:10–12	60

1 Timothy

6:8	91

INDEX OF SCRIPTURAL REFERENCES

James

Generally	xii
2:13	xiii
4:6–10	99

1 Peter

3:8	99
5:5–6	99

www.ingramcontent.com/pod-product-compliance
Lightning Source LLC
Chambersburg PA
CBHW020849160426
43192CB00007B/850